SUICIDE:
THE PHILOSOPHICAL ISSUES

SUICIDE:
THE PHILOSOPHICAL ISSUES

Edited by
M. PABST BATTIN
and
DAVID J. MAYO

St. Martin's Press
New York

Library of Congress Cataloging in Publication Data
Main entry under title:

Suicide, the philosophical issues.

1. Suicide—Addresses, essays, lectures.
I. Battin, M. Pabst. II. Mayo, David J.
BD445.S93   179′.7   79-27372
ISBN 0-312-77531-8

TB   4/6/81

Acknowledgments

A. Alvarez, "The Background," from *The Savage God. A Study of Suicide*. New York: Random House, Bantam edition June 1973. Reprinted by permission of Random House, Inc. British Commonwealth rights by permission of Weidenfeld and Nicolson.

R. G. Frey, "Did Socrates Commit Suicide?", adapted from *Philosophy* 53 (1978). Reprinted by permission of Cambridge University Press.

P. R. Baelz, "Suicide: Some Theological Reflections," adapted from "Voluntary Euthanasia: Some Theological Reflections," *Theology* 75 (May 1972). Reprinted by permission of The Society for Promoting Christian Knowledge.

Karen Lebacqz and H. Tristram Engelhardt, Jr., "Suicide and Covenant," adapted from "Suicide," in *Death, Dying and Euthanasia*, ed. Dennis J. Horan and David Mall. Washington, D. C.: University Publications of America, 1977. Reprinted by permission of University Publications of America, Inc.

Mary Rose Barrington, "Apologia for Suicide," abridged from *Euthanasia and the Right to Death*, ed. A. B. Downing. London: Peter Owen, 1969. Reprinted by permission of Peter Owen, Ltd.

Richard B. Brandt, "The Rationality of Suicide," from "The Morality and Rationality of Suicide," in *A Handbook for the Study of Suicide*, ed. Seymour Perlin. Copyright © 1975 by Oxford University Press, Inc. Reprinted by permission of Oxford University Press.

Philip E. Devine, "On Choosing Death," adapted from *The Ethics of Homicide*, by Philip E. Devine. Copyright © 1978 by Cornell University. Used by permission of the publisher, Cornell University Press.

Joyce Carol Oates, "The Art of Suicide," adapted from *The Reevaluation of Existing Values and the Search for Absolute Values*, Proceedings of the Seventh International Conference on the Unity of the Sciences (Boston, 1978). Copyright © 1979 by the International Cultural Foundation, Inc. Used by permission of the International Cultural Foundation Press.

Thomas S. Szasz, "The Ethics of Suicide," first published in *The Antioch Review*, Vol. XXXI, No. 1 (1971). Reprinted by permission of Thomas S. Szasz.

Eliot Slater, "Choosing the Time to Die," from *Proceedings of the Fifth International Conference for Suicide Prevention* (London, 1969), ed. Richard Fox. Vienna: The International Association for Suicide Prevention, April, 1970. Reprinted by permission of Eliot Slater.

Jerome A. Motto, "The Right to Suicide: A Psychiatrist's View," from *Life-Threatening Behavior*, Vol. 2, No. 3 (Fall, 1972). Reprinted by permission of Human Sciences Press.

Joel Feinberg, "Suicide and the Inalienable Right to Life," abridged and revised from "Voluntary Euthanasia and the Inalienable Right to Life," the 1977 Tanner Lecture on Human Values at the University of Michigan and Stanford University. From *The Tanner Lectures on Human Values*, Vol. 1. Copyright © 1979 by the University of Utah Press. Reprinted by permission. Also published in *Philosophy and Public Affairs*, Vol 7, No. 2, Winter 1978.

All other papers are original in this volume. M. Pabst Battin, "Manipulated Suicide," will also appear in *Bioethics Quarterly*, Vol. 2, No. 2 (Summer 1980).

Table of Contents

SUICIDE:

THE PHILOSOPHICAL ISSUES

INTRODUCTION

It may at first appear that there are no *philosophical* issues in suicide, but only that suicide is a tragic, often preventable phenomenon, one which calls for skilled attention by those who practice medicine, psychotherapy, first aid, rescue work, or pastoral care. No doubt there is indeed something tragic in any situation that would lead a human being to end his or her life, and no doubt these tragic situations ought as much as possible to be prevented. It is here, though, that the philosophical problems begin, not end.

Suicide has not always been assumed to be tragic or a phenomenon that is always to be prevented. In both early Greek and Hebrew culture, suicide was apparently recognized as a reasonable choice in certain kinds of situations; some Greek and Roman Stoics considered suicide noble and heroic, the kind of thing the truly wise man ought to do. For early North African Christians, suicide—like martyrdom—was a mark of religious devotion, practiced as a way of insuring the attainment of immediate salvation. In response to St. Augustine's repudiation of early Christian enthusiasm for voluntary death, however, the medieval Church began to develop strict suicide prohibitions and taboos; by the height of the Middle Ages, suicide had become not only a mortal sin, but a felony at law. Eighteenth-century rationalists and nineteenth-century romantics reopened the philosophical discussion of suicide, but these issues were eclipsed at the close of the nineteenth century, as sociological studies of suicide by Morselli and by Durkheim launched a new field of scientific study, correlating suicide mortality rates with a variety of social and environmental variables. At about the same time medically oriented thinkers began to view suicide as the product of illness, and

1

inaugurated contemporary interest in depression and other types of mental disorder associated with suicide. But as suicide came to be seen as a symptom—both of individual psychopathology and of social disorganization—it came to be viewed less and less as an appropriate topic for philosophic discourse. Until quite recently almost nothing had been written in the twentieth century by philosophers or other thinkers about *philosophical* issues concerning suicide—despite increasingly active scientific work on suicide, despite European philosophy's overriding concern with death, despite remarkable variations in the legal status of suicide, and even despite Camus's celebrated dictum: "There is but one truly serious philosophical problem, and that is suicide."

However, the philosophical issues in suicide are now rapidly resurfacing. This has been due very largely to the development of sophisticated medical techniques, which make it possible to extend human life to lengths which are sometimes not desired, and the recognition that voluntary euthanasia, over which there has been so much recent controversy, is, at root, a kind of suicide. But what began as a topic within the specialized field of medical ethics is now being seen as part of a much broader issue. The questions of what counts as suicide, whether suicide is ever moral, whether it can be rationally chosen, and whether one has a right to end one's life are seen to be crucial in a number of additional medical and nonmedical areas: patients' refusal of lifesaving medical treatment, voluntary but fatal organ donation, elective capital punishment, consent to potentially lethal experimental studies, self-sacrificial social protest, high-risk exploration and sports, chronic self-destructive behavior such as alcoholism, and planned death in preference to old age. Central to all these is the issue of control over the circumstances and character of one's own death—that is, the issue of suicide.

Questions surrounding the issue of suicide are not simply abstract intellectual puzzles; they are concrete human problems, encountered in many areas of human experience, rooted in human despair, delusion, and pain. But if we sometimes err in failing to see that suicide involves real people in real distress, we may also fail to see that it involves difficult and disputed theoretical issues, upon which depend the resolution of serious practical concerns. Is suicide a right? Then some—or all—forms of suicide prevention may be wrong. Can suicide be rational?

Then we must reexamine our psychiatric treatment policies and the role of physicians in treating those who contemplate suicide. Can suicide be morally correct, or perhaps even obligatory? Then we must look again at our policies and practices with regard to heroism, self-sacrifice, self-senicide or killing oneself in old age, voluntary capital punishment, and even fundamental distaste for life. *

The papers in this volume represent the full range of contemporary discussion of these theoretical issues. Some of these discussions involve primarily conceptual issues. Others probe the moral issues. And others speak directly to professionals in areas such as psychiatry, counseling, nursing, general medicine, religious practice, and law—to individuals who must deal directly with suicidal persons on a practical basis. All action, in all these areas, involves an antecedent philosophic stance, and it is the purpose of this volume to clarify what these stances may be.

One practical issue stands by itself: this is the matter of law. Although England's Suicide Act of 1961 decriminalized suicide, there is little consensus on whether rights to suicide in this jurisdiction are now protected by law. In the United States there is presently no U.S. court decision which rules directly on the right of a competent individual to terminate his or her life. These legal facts have considerable bearing on almost all the practical areas, particularly suicide prevention, mentioned above. Some observers believe that a major U.S. court decision on the fundamental issue of suicide is not far away.

In assembling this anthology we have focused on contemporary discussions and on philosophical issues in suicide as such. Thus we have excluded many now-classic discussions from the vast historical literature: those of Plato, Seneca, Augustine, Thomas Aquinas, John Donne, Hume, and Kant, to name but a celebrated few. We have also omitted papers or parts of previously published papers which focus primarily on voluntary euthanasia and deal only indirectly with the broader issues in suicide.

In reopening the issues involved in suicide against the background of a long taboo, many of the present authors call for radically changed attitudes toward suicide and only a few argue for retention of the traditional prohibition and taboo. In this respect the collection may seem to be "pro-suicide"; indeed, only very few of the authors writing today—in this volume and outside it—take fully conservative views. But the volume is, we think, as a whole not so much "pro-suicide" as it is "anti-taboo"; to assume otherwise is to confuse advocacy with argument and analysis, and that is something this volume is not intended to do.

M.P.B.

D.J.M.

The
Historical
Background

THE BACKGROUND

A. Alvarez

Alvarez surveys the history of attitudes toward suicide, from the nonpunitive outlook of many primitive groups and the strongly prosuicide view of Stoic Greece and Rome, through the Middle Ages' categorical repudiation of suicide, to the eighteenth century's defense and the Romantic era's glorification of it. Alvarez traces the origins of the Christian antisuicide position to Augustine's reaction to the "suicide-mania" of the early Christian martyrs, in the fourth and fifth centuries A.D.

Alfred Alvarez—poet, literary critic, fiction, nonfiction, and screenplay writer—has been poetry editor of The Observer *and is widely known for his study of suicide* The Savage God, *from which this selection is taken.*

A man was hanged who had cut his throat, but who had been brought back to life. They hanged him for suicide. The doctor had warned them that it was impossible to hang him as the throat would burst open and he would breathe through the aperture. They did not listen to his advice and hanged their man. The wound in the neck immediately opened and the man came back to life again although he was hanged. It took time to convoke the aldermen to decide the question of what was to be done. At length the aldermen

7

assembled and bound up the neck below the wound *until he died*. Oh my Mary, what a crazy society and what a stupid civilization.[1]

Thus Nicholas Ogarev writing to his mistress Mary Sutherland around 1860, with news from the London papers. Ogarev was an alcoholic Russian exile of mildly revolutionary politics, the son of a wealthy landowner and close friend of Alexander Herzen's; his mistress was a good-natured prostitute whom he had reformed and was slowly educating. I suspect that it took two complete outsiders, one of them an enlightened and political foreigner, to notice the barbarity of a situation which the newspaper had reported simply as an unexpected twist to a public execution, odd enough to be newsworthy but not otherwise sufficiently shocking or remarkable to require comment.

Yet by pursuing their poor suicide with such weird vindictiveness—condemning a man to death for the crime of having condemned himself to death—the London aldermen were acting according to a venerable tradition sanctified by both church and state. The history of suicide in Christian Europe is the history of official outrage and unofficial despair. Both can be measured by the dry, matter-of-fact tone in which the accepted enormities were described. Writing in 1601, the Elizabethan lawyer Fulbecke says that the suicide "is drawn by a horse to the place of punishment and shame, where he is hanged on a gibbet, and none may take the body down but by the authority of a magistrate." In other words, the suicide was as low as the lowest criminal. Later another great legal authority, Blackstone, wrote that the burial was "in the highway, with a stake driven through the body,"[2] as though there were no difference between a suicide and a vampire. The chosen site was usually a crossroads, which was also the place of public execution, and a stone was placed over the dead man's face; like the stake, it would prevent him from rising as a ghost to haunt the living. Apparently the terror of suicides lasted longer than the fear of vampires and witches: the last recorded degradation of the corpse of a suicide in England took place in 1823, when a man called Griffiths was buried at the intersection of Grosvenor Place and King's Road, Chelsea. But even then self-murderers were not left in peace: for the next fifty years the bodies of unclaimed and destitute suicides went to the schools of anatomy for dissection.

With variations, similar degradations were used all through

Europe. In France, varying with local ground rules, the corpse was hanged by the feet, dragged through the streets on a hurdle, burned, thrown on the public garbage heap. At Metz, each suicide was put in a barrel and floated down the Moselle away from the places he might wish to haunt. In Danzig, the corpse was not allowed to leave by the door; instead it was lowered by pulleys from the window; the window frame was subsequently burned. Even in the civilized Athens of Plato, the suicide was buried outside the city and away from other graves; his self-murdering hand was cut off and buried apart. So, too, with minor variations in Thebes and Cyprus. Sparta, true to form, was so severe in its ruling that Aristodemus was punished posthumously for deliberately seeking death in the battle of Plataea.[3]

In Europe these primitive revenges were duly dignified and made economically profitable to the state by law. As late as 1670 *Le Roi-Soleil* himself incorporated into the official legal code all the most brutal practices concerning the degradation of the corpse of a suicide, adding that his name was to be defamed *ad perpetuam rei memoriam;* nobles lost their nobility and were declared commoners; their escutcheons were broken, their woods cut, their castles demolished. In England a suicide was declared a felon *(felo de se).* In both countries his property reverted to the crown. In practice, Voltaire sourly noted, this meant: *"On donne son bien au Roi qui en accorde presque toujours la moitié à la première fille de l'opéra qui le fait demander par un de ses amants; l'autre moitié appartient de droit à Messieurs les Fermiers généraux."**[4]

In France, despite the derision of Voltaire and Montesquieu, these laws lasted at least until 1770, and, indeed, were twice reinforced in the eighteenth century. The confiscation of the suicide's property and defamation of his memory finally disappeared with the Revolution; suicide is not mentioned in the new penal code of 1791.[5] Not so in England, where the laws concerning the confiscation of property were not changed until 1870, and an unsuccessful suicide could still be sent to prison as late as 1961.** Thus the phrase "suicide while the balance of his mind

---

*"His goods are given to the King, who almost always grants half of them to the leading lady of the Opera, who prevails upon one of her lovers to ask for it; the other half belongs by law to the Inland Revenue."

**Plus ça change . . . In 1969 an Isle of Man court ordered a teen-ager to be birched for attempting suicide.

was disturbed" was evolved by lawyers as a protection against the inanities of the law, since a verdict of *felo de se* would deprive the dead man of a religious burial and his inheritors of his estate. An eighteenth-century satirist put it this way:

> From reading the public prints a foreigner might naturally be led to imagine that we are the most lunatic people in the world. Almost every day informs us that the coroner's inquest has sate on the body of some miserable suicide and brought in their verdict lunacy. But it is very well known, that the inquiry has not been made into the state of mind of the deceased, but into his fortune and family. The law has indeed provided, that the deliberate self-murderer should be treated like a brute and denied the rites of burial. But of hundreds of lunatics by purchase, I never knew this sentence executed but on one poor cobler, who hanged himself in his own stall. A penniless poor dog, who has not left enough money to defray the funeral charges, may perhaps be excluded the churchyard; but self-murder by pistol genteelly mounted, or the Paris-hilted sword, qualifies the polite owner for a sudden death, and entitles him to the pompous burial and a monument setting forth his virtues in Westminster-Abbey.[6]

Whence Professor Joad's aphorism that in England you must not commit suicide, on pain of being regarded as a criminal if you fail and a lunatic if you succeed.

These official, legal idiocies were, mercifully, the last pale flourishing of prejudices which had once been infinitely more virulent and profound. Since the savagery of any punishment is proportional to the fear of the act, why should a gesture so essentially private inspire such primitive terror and superstition? Fedden produces evidence to suggest that Christian revenges repeat, with suitable modifications, the taboos and purification rituals of the most primitive tribes. The learned jurists who decreed that a suicide should be buried at a crossroads had at least that prejudice in common with the witch doctors of Baganda.[7] They were also harking back to a pre-Christian Europe where victims were sacrificed on altars at these same crossroads. Like the stake and the stone, the site had been chosen in the hope that the constant traffic above would prevent the restless spirit from rising; should that fail, the number of roads would, hopefully, confuse the ghost and so hinder his return home. After the introduction of Christianity, the cross formed by the roads became a symbol which would disperse the evil energy concentrated in the dead body.[8] It was a question, in short, of an archaic fear of blood wrongly spilled crying out for revenge. That is, it was a question of that peculiarly baffled terror which is produced by guilt. Freud's early theory that suicide is transposed murder, an act of hostility turned away from the object back onto the self, seems to be borne out by Christian superstition and law.

In primitive societies, the mechanics of revenge are simple: either the suicide's ghost will destroy his persecutor for him, or his act will force his relatives to carry out the task, or the iron laws of the tribe will compel the suicide's enemy to kill himself in the same manner. It depends on the customs of the country. In any case, suicide under these conditions is curiously unreal; it is as though it were committed in the certain belief that the suicide himself would not really die. Instead, he is performing a magical act which will initiate a complex but equally magic ritual ending in the death of his enemy.*

So, the primitive horror of suicide, which survived so long in Europe, was of blood evilly spilled and unappeased. In practice, this meant that suicide was equated with murder. Hence, presum-

---

*The same magical thinking still prevails in some modern political suicides. In January 1969, Jan Palach burned himself to death in the desperate belief that nothing less than his own self-immolation could effectively protest against the Russian invasion of Czechoslovakia. About a year later, when the first anniversary of Palach's death coincided with the end of the Biafran affair, seven people took their own lives in France in the space of ten days, mostly in the same terrible way. The second victim, a nineteen-year-old student from Lille, left a message saying he was "against war, violence, and the destructive folly of men . . . If I die, do not weep. I have done it because I could not adapt myself to this world. I did it as a protest against violence and to draw the attention of the world of which a very small part is dealt with here. Death is a form of protest on condition that it is desired by a human being for himself. One can very well refuse it."[9] Behind these horrors, and behind the boy's confusion of altruism and egoism, is a certain residue of primitive magic: it is as though the suicide believes, despite all evidence to the contrary, that he will finally have his posthumous way, provided his death is sufficiently terrible. There seems to me to be nothing to justify such optimism.

ably, the custom of punishing the body of a suicide as though he were guilty of a capital crime, by hanging it from a gibbet. Hence, too, the terminology of the act. "Suicide," which is a Latinate and relatively abstract word, appeared late. The *Oxford English Dictionary* dates the first use as 1651; I found the word a little earlier in Sir Thomas Browne's *Religio Medici,* written in 1635, published in 1642.* But it was still sufficiently rare not to appear in the 1755 edition of Dr. Samuel Johnson's *Dictionary.* Instead, the phrases used were "self-murder," "self-destruction," "self-killer," "self-homicide," "self-slaughter"—all expressions reflecting the associations with murder.

They also reflect the difficulty the Church had in rationalizing its ban on suicide, since neither the old nor the New Testament directly prohibits it. There are four suicides recorded in the Old Testament—Samson, Saul, Abimelech and Achitophel—and none of them earns adverse comment. In fact, they are scarcely commented on at all. In the New Testament, the suicide of even the greatest criminal, Judas Iscariot, is recorded as perfunctorily; instead of being added to his crimes, it seems a measure of his repentance. Only much later did the theologians reverse the implicit judgment of St. Matthew and suggest that Judas was more damned by his suicide than by his betrayal of Christ. In the first years of the Church, suicide was such a neutral subject that even the death of Jesus was regarded by Tertullian, one of the most fiery of the early Fathers, as a kind of suicide. He pointed out, and Origen agreed, that He voluntarily gave up the ghost, since it was unthinkable that the Godhead should be at the mercy of the flesh. Whence John Donne's comment in *Biathanatos,* the first formal defense of suicide in English: "Our blessed Savior . . . chose that way for our Redemption to sacrifice his life, and profuse his blood." [10]

The idea of suicide as a crime comes late in Christian doctrine, and as an afterthought. It was not until the sixth century that the Church finally legislated against it, and then the only Biblical authority was a special interpretation of the Sixth Commandment: "Thou shalt not kill." The bishops were urged into action by St. Augustine; but he, as Rousseau remarked, took his

---

*"Herein are they in extremes, that can allow a man to be his own assassin, and so highly extol the end and suicide of Cato." *Religio Medici,* Sect. XLIV.

arguments from Plato's *Phaedo*, not from the Bible. Augustine's arguments were sharpened by the suicide mania which was, above all, the distinguishing mark of the early Christians, but ultimately his reasons were impeccably moral. Christianity was founded on the belief that each human body is the vehicle of an immortal soul which will be judged not in this world but in the next. And because each soul is immortal, every life is equally valuable. Since life itself is the gift of God, to reject it is to reject Him and to frustrate His will; to kill His image is to kill Him—which means a one-way ticket to eternal damnation.

The Christian ban on suicide, like its ban on infanticide and abortion, was, then, founded on a respect for life utterly foreign to the indifference and casual murderousness of the Romans. But there is a paradox: as David Hume pointed out, monotheism is the only form of religion that can be taken seriously, because only monotheism treats the universe as a single, systematic, intelligible whole; yet its consequences are dogmatism, fanaticism and persecution; whereas polytheism, which is intellectually absurd and a positive obstacle to scientific understanding, produces tolerance, a respect for individual freedom, a civilized breathing space. So with suicide: when the bishops decided it was a crime, they were in some way emphasizing the moral distance traveled from pagan Rome, where the act was habitual and even honored. Yet what began as moral tenderness and enlightenment finished as the legalized and sanctified atrocities by which the body of the suicide was degraded, his memory defamed, his family persecuted. So although the idea of suicide as a crime was a late, relatively sophisticated invention of Christianity, more or less foreign to the Judeo-Hellenic tradition, it spread like a fog across Europe because its strength came from primitive fears, prejudices and superstitions which had survived despite Christianity, Judaism and Hellenism. Given the barbarity of the Dark and early Middle Ages, it was no doubt inevitable that the savage mind should once again have its day. The process was much the same as that by which the Christian calendar took over the pagan festivals, and the first Spanish missionaries in Mexico invented saints to whom they could dedicate the churches they built on the altar of each Aztec and Mayan god. In the modern business world this process is called "buying the good will" of a defunct firm. As far as suicide is concerned, Christianity bought up the pagan bad will.

Yet there is evidence that even to the savage mind, the horror

of suicide did not always come naturally. The primitive fear of the
dead may have been overpowering, particularly the terror of the
spirits of those who had died unnaturally and willfully, murdered
or by their own hand. It was largely as a protection against these
restless and unappeased ghosts that the whole ornate complex of
taboos was elaborated.[11] But to be afraid of the vengeful dead is
something rather different from being afraid of death itself.*
Thus in some warrior societies whose gods were those of violence
whose ideal was bravery, suicide was often looked on as a great

---

*We should be aware of projecting our own anxieties onto other
periods. The idea of death as an unmentionable, almost unnatural, subject
is a peculiarly twentieth-century invention. What was once public, simple
and commonplace has now become private, abstract and shocking, a fact
almost as furtive and secret as sex once was to the Victorians. Yet we are
constantly told that the violence of our societies is preternatural and is
augmented by the violence served up, continually and inescapably, to
entertain our leisure on film, television, in pulp fiction, even on the news.
Perhaps. But I wonder if all this is not now remote and antiseptic
compared with habits not long passed. A Roman holiday involved the
slaughter of, literally, thousands in gladiatorial shows. After Spartacus'
uprising, the crucified bodies of six thousand slaves lined the road from
Rome to Capua like lampposts. In Christian Europe, executions replaced
the Roman circuses. Criminals were beheaded publicly; they were hanged,
their intestines drawn out and their bodies quartered; they were
guillotined and elaborately tortured in front of festive crowds; their
severed heads were exposed on pikes, their bodies hung in chains from
gibbets. The public was amused, excited, more delighted than shocked.
An execution was like a fun fair, and for the more spectacular occasions
even apprentices got the day off. This casual bloodthirstiness continued
long after the last suicide had been buried at a crossroads. Executions
were public in England until 1868. In Paris, the Morgue was a tourist
attraction, where the corpses were displayed like the waxworks at
Madame Tussaud's; it was even rebuilt to improve the facilities in 1865
and was not closed to the public until the 1920s. In wars, hand-to-hand
fighting with swords, daggers, axes and primitive guns left battlefields
looking like butcher shops. Our own massacres may be infinitely greater,
but they take place by remote control and at a distance; in comparison
with the great pitched battles of the past, they seem almost abstract. Of
course, there is a difference. Unlike our ancestors, who, at best, read
about them later, we actually see the results. But in the eye of television, as
in the eye of God, all things are equal; a real atrocity on the screen in our
own home seems neither more nor less genuine than some fantasy acted
out in a studio for our amusement. In these circumstances, death is a kind
of pornography, at once exciting and unreal: "Death is something that we
fear/But it titillates the ear."

good. For example, the paradise of the Vikings was Valhalla, "the Hall of those who died by violence," where the Feast of Heroes was presided over by the god Odin. Only those who had died violently could enter and partake of the banquet. The greatest honor and the greatest qualification was death in battle; next best was suicide. Those who died peacefully in their beds, of old age or disease, were excluded from Valhalla through all eternity. Odin himself was the supreme God of War, but according to Frazer, he was also called the Lord of the Gallows or the God of the Hanged, and men and animals were hanged in his honor from the sacred trees of the holy grove at Upsala. The weird, beautiful lines of the *Havamal* suggest that the god also died in the same ritual, as a sacrifice to himself:

> I know that I hung in the windy tree
> For nine whole nights,
> Wounded with the spear, dedicated to Odin,
> Myself to myself.[12]

According to another tradition, Odin wounded himself with his sword before being ritually burned.[13] Either way, he was a suicide and his worshipers acted according to his divine example. Similarly, there was a Druid maxim promoting suicide as a religious principle: "There is another world, and they who kill themselves to accompany their friends thither, will live with them there."[14] That, in turn, links with the custom once common among African tribes: that the warriors and slaves put themselves to death when their king dies, in order to live with him in paradise. Whence, with more sophistication, Hindu *suttee,* the ritual in which the wife burned herself to death on the funeral pyre of her husband.

Elsewhere, tribes as far apart as the Iglulik Eskimos and the inhabitants of the Marquesas Islands believed that a violent death was a passport to paradise, which the Iglulik called the Land of Day. In contrast, those who died peacefully from natural causes were consigned to eternal claustrophobia in the Narrow Land. In the Marquesas they went to the lower depths of Hawaiki.[15] Even the victims of the terrible Aztec rites, the youths who became gods for a period on the understanding that they would eventually have their living hearts cut out, went to the altar with a kind of perverse optimism.

Obviously, to promote the idea of violent death as glorious

was an efficient way of preserving a properly warlike spirit; the Pentagon might have been spared some of its present embarrassment in Vietnam had it been able to instill its conscripts with the same primitive virtues. Thus the ancient Scythians regarded it as the greatest honor to take their own lives when they became too old for their nomadic way of life; thereby saving the younger members of the tribe both the trouble and the guilt of killing them. Quintus Curtius described them graphically:

> Among them exists a sort of wild and bestial men to whom they give the name of sages. The anticipation of the time of death is a glory in their eyes, and they have themselves burned alive as soon as age or sickness begins to trouble them. According to them, death, passively awaited, is a dishonor to life; thus no honors are rendered those bodies which old age has destroyed. Fire would be contaminated if it did not receive the human sacrifice still breathing.[16]

Durkheim called this style of suicide "altruistic"; one of the supreme examples is Captain Oates, who walked out to his death in the Antarctic snow in order to help Scott and his other doomed companions. But where the whole of a tribe's morality and mythology made it seem that suicide was a way to a better life, the motives of those who took their own lives were evidently not altogether pure and self-sacrificing. They were, instead, intensely narcissistic: ". . . dedicated to Odin,/Myself to myself." "Through the primitive act of suicide," writes Gregory Zilboorg, "man achieved a *fantasied* immortality, *i.e.,* uninterrupted fulfilment of the hedonistic ideal through mere fantasy and not through actual living."[17] Since death was both inevitable and relatively unimportant, suicide ultimately became more a matter of pleasure than of principle: one sacrificed a few days or years on this earth in order to feast with the gods eternally in the next. It was, essentially, a frivolous act.

In contrast, a serious suicide is an act of choice, the terms of which are entirely those of this world; a man dies by his own hand because he thinks the life he has not worth living. Suicides of this kind are usually thought to be an index of high civilization, for the simple reason that the act goes against the most basic of instincts, that of self-preservation. But it is not necessarily so. For example, the Tasmanian aborigines died out not just because they were hunted like kangaroos for an afternoon's sport, but also because a world in which this could happen was intolerable to them; so they committed suicide as a race by refusing to breed. Ironically, perhaps, and as though to confirm the aborigines' judgment, the mummified remains of the old lady who was the last to survive have been preserved by the Australian government as a museum curiosity. Similarly, hundreds of Jews put themselves to death at Masada rather than submit to the Roman legions. More extreme still, the history of the Spanish conquest of the New World is one of deliberate genocide in which the native inhabitants themselves cooperated. Their treatment at the hands of the Spaniards was so cruel that the Indians killed themselves by the thousands rather than endure it. Of forty natives from the Gulf of Mexico who were brought to work in the mine of the Emperor Charles V, thirty-nine starved themselves to death. A whole cargo of slaves contrived to strangle themselves in the hold of a Spanish galleon, although the headroom was so limited by the heavy ballast of stones that they were forced to hang themselves in a squatting or kneeling position. In the West Indies, according to the Spanish historian Girolamo Benzoni, four thousand men and countless women and children died by jumping from cliffs or by killing each other. He adds that out of the two million original inhabitants of Haiti, fewer than one hundred and fifty survived as a result of the suicides and slaughter.[18] In the end the Spaniards, faced with an embarrassing labor shortage, put a stop to the epidemic of suicides by persuading the Indians that they, too, would kill themselves in order to pursue them in the next world with even harsher cruelties.

The despair which ends with racial suicide is a peculiarly pure phenomenon and proportionately rare. Only under the most extreme conditions does the psychic mechanism of self-preservation go into reverse for a whole nation, unsanctioned by morality or belief and unswayed by zealotry. In a less pure, more complex culture, where death is accepted casually but beliefs are no longer simple and morality fluctuates, within limits, according to the individual, the question of suicide becomes urgent in another way. The supreme example is that of the Romans, who turned the ancient world's toleration of suicide into a high fashion.

The toleration began with the Greeks. The taboos against suicide which obtained even in Athens—where the corpse was buried outside the city, its hand cut off and buried separately—

were linked with the more profound Greek horror of killing one's own kin. By inference, suicide was an extreme case of this, and the language barely distinguishes between self-murder and murder of kindred. Yet in literature and philosophy the act passes more or less without comment, certainly without blame. The first of all literary suicides, that of Oedipus' mother, Jocasta, is made to seem praiseworthy, an honorable way out of an insufferable situation. Homer records self-murder without comment, as something natural and usually heroic. The legends bear him out. Aegeus threw himself into the sea—which thereafter bore his name—when he mistakenly thought his son Theseus had been slain by the Minotaur. Erigone hanged herself from grief when she discovered the murdered body of her father Icarius—thereby, incidentally, causing an epidemic of suicide by hanging among the Athenian women which lasted until the blood guilt was wiped out by the institution of the Aeora festival in honor of Erigone. Leukakas jumped off a rock in order to avoid being raped by Apollo. When the Delphic oracle announced that the Lacedaemonians would capture Athens if they did not kill the Athenian king, the reigning monarch Codrus entered the enemy camp in disguise, picked a quarrel with a soldier and allowed himself to be slaughtered. Charondas, the lawgiver of Catana, a Greek colony in Sicily, took his life when he broke one of his own laws. Another lawgiver, Lycurgus of Sparta, extracted an oath from his people that they would keep his laws until he returned from Delphi, where he went to consult the oracle about his new legal code. The oracle gave a favorable answer, which Lycurgus sent back in writing. He then starved himself to death so that the Spartans would never be absolved from their oath.[19] These suicides, like most of the others in ancient Greece, had one quality in common: a certain nobility of motive. So far as the records go, the ancient Greeks took their lives only for the best possible reasons: grief, high patriotic principle, or to avoid dishonor.

Their philosophic discussion of the subject is proportionately detached and balanced. The keys were moderation and high principle. Suicide was not to be tolerated if it seemed like an act of wanton disrespect to the gods. For this reason, the Pythagoreans rejected suicide out of hand since for them, as for the later Christians, life itself was the discipline of the gods. In the *Phaedo*, Plato made Socrates repeat this Orphic doctrine approvingly before he drank the hemlock. He used the simile—often to be repeated later—of the soldier on guard duty who must not desert his post, and also that of man as the property of the gods, who are as angry at our suicide as we would be if our chattels destroyed themselves. Aristotle used much the same argument, though in a more austere way: suicide was "an offense against the state" because, as a religious offense, it polluted the city and, economically, weakened it by destroying a useful citizen. That is, it was an act of social irresponsibility. Logically, this is no doubt impeccable. But it also seems curiously irrelevant to the act of suicide. It is not, I mean, a style of argument likely to impinge on the state of mind of a man about to take his own life. The fact that it was considered to be so cogent—Aristotle's huge authority apart—implies a curiously cool and detached attitude to the problem of suicide.

In contrast, Plato's arguments are less simple, more subtle. Socrates' sweetly reasonable tone repudiates suicide, yet at the same time he makes death seem infinitely desirable; it is the entry to the world of ideal presences of which earthly reality is a mere shadow. In the end, Socrates drinks the hemlock so cheerfully and has argued so eloquently for the benefits of death that he has set an example for others. The Greek philosopher Cleombrotus is said to have been inspired by the *Phaedo* to drown himself, and Cato read the book through twice the night before he fell on his own sword.

Plato also allowed for moderation in the other sense. He suggested that if life itself became immoderate, then suicide became a rational, justifiable act. Painful disease, or intolerable constraint were sufficient reasons to depart. And this, when the religious superstitions faded, was philosophical justification enough. Within a hundred years of Socrates' death, the Stoics had made suicide into the most reasonable and desirable of all ways out. Both they and the Epicureans claimed to be as indifferent to death as to life. For the Epicureans the principle was pleasure; whatever promoted that was good, whatever produced pain was evil. For the Stoics the ideal was vaguer, more dignified: that of life in accordance with nature. When it no longer seemed to be so, then death came as a rational choice befitting a rational nature. Thus, Zeno, the founder of the school, is said to have hanged himself out of sheer irritation when he stumbled and wrenched his finger; he was ninety-eight at the time. His successor Cleanthes died with equally philosophic aplomb. As a cure for a gumboil he was ordered to starve himself. Within two days the gumboil was better and his doctor put him back on an ordinary diet. But Cleanthes refused, "as he had advanced so far on his journey towards death, he would not now retreat"; he duly starved himself to death.

Classical Greek suicide, then, was dictated by a calm, though slightly excessive, reasonableness. In Athens, as in the Greek colonies of Marseilles and Ceos, where hemlock was developed and whose customs inspired Montaigne to his eloquent defense of noble suicide, the magistrates kept a supply of poison for those who wished to die. All that was required was that they should first plead their cause before the Senate and obtain official permission. The precepts were clear:

> Whoever no longer wishes to live shall state his reasons to the Senate, and after having received permission shall abandon life. If your existence is hateful to you, die; if you are overwhelmed by fate, drink the hemlock. If you are bowed with grief, abandon life. Let the unhappy man recount his misfortune, let the magistrate supply him with the remedy, and his wretchedness will come to an end.[20]

These early Stoics brought to the subject of their own death the same degree of nicety that Henry James reserved for morals. And this was appropriate, since the question of how they died became for them the final measure of discrimination. Plato had justified suicide when external circumstances became intolerable. The Greek Stoics developed and rationalized this attitude according to their ideal of life in accordance with nature. The advanced Stoicism of the later Roman Empire was a further development of Plato; the argument was essentially the same but now the circumstances were internalized. When the inner compulsion became intolerable, the question was no longer whether or not one should kill oneself but how to do so with the greatest dignity, bravery and style. To put it another way, it was an achievement of the Greeks to empty suicide of all the primitive horrors and then gradually to discuss the subject more or less rationally, as though it were not invested with much feeling, one way or another. The Romans, on the other hand, reinvested it with emotion, but in doing so, turned the emotions upside down. In their eyes suicide was no longer morally evil; on the contrary, one's manner of going became a practical test of excellence and virtue. On the night the Emperor Antoninus Pius died, the password, by his command, was *"aequanimitas."*[21]

I mentioned the belief that the more sophisticated and rational a society becomes, the further it travels from superstitious fears and the more easily suicide is tolerated. Roman Stoicism would seem to be the ultimate example of this. Stoic writing is full of exhortations to suicide, all of which embroider more or less elegantly on those Athenian precepts quoted above from Libanius. The most famous is Seneca's:

> Foolish man, what do you bemoan, and what do you fear? Wherever you look there is an end of evils. You see that yawning precipice? It leads to liberty. You see that flood, that river, that well? Liberty houses within them. You see that stunted, parched, and sorry tree? From each branch liberty hangs. Your neck, your throat, your heart are all so many ways of escape from slavery . . . Do you enquire the road to freedom? You shall find it in every vein in your body.

It is a beautiful and cadenced piece of rhetoric. But where most rhetoric is a protection from reality—a verbal armor the writer puts between himself and the world—Seneca finally practiced his precepts: he stabbed himself to avoid the vengeance of Nero, who had once been his pupil. His wife, Paulina, refused to be left behind and died with him in the same way.

One other example is enough to set the tone of the times. It is the advice of Seneca's ascetic friend Attalus to one Marcellinus, who was suffering from an incurable disease and was contemplating suicide:

> Be not tormented, my Marcellinus, as if you were deliberating any great matter. Life is a thing of no dignity or importance. Your very slaves, your animals, possess it in common with yourself: but it is a great thing to die honourably, prudently, bravely. Think how long you have been engaged in the same dull course: eating, sleeping, and indulging your appetites. This has been the circle. Not only a prudent, brave or a wretched man may wish to die, but even a fastidious one.[22]

Again, there was no gap between rhetoric and reality. Marcellinus took his friend's advice and starved himself to death, a "fastidious" answer to the wild indulgence of Tiberius' Rome.

In doing so, he also joined the company of some of the most distinguished men of the ancient world. I have already mentioned Socrates, Codrus, Charondas, Lycurgus, Cleombrotus, Cato, Zeno, Cleanthes, Seneca and Paulina. Among many others were the Greek orators Isocrates and Demosthenes; the Roman poets Lucretius, Lucan and Labienus, the dramatist Terence, the critic Aristarchus, and Petronius Arbiter, who was the most fastidious of them all; Hannibal, Boadicea, Brutus, Cassius, Mark Antony and Cleopatra, Cocceius Nerva, Statius, Nero, Otho, King Ptolemy of Cyprus, and King Sardanapalus of Persia. There was also Mithridates, who, to protect himself from his enemies, had immunized himself by years of swallowing small doses of poison. As a result, when he finally tried to take his own life by poison, he failed. And so on. John Donne's list of notable suicides of the classical world runs to three pages, including the witty comments; Montaigne produced a host of others. Both chose more or less at random from many hundreds of possibilities; and these, in turn, were only a fraction of those who died in the Roman fashion.

The evidence is, then, that the Romans looked on suicide with neither fear nor revulsion, but as a carefully considered and chosen validation of the way they had lived and the principles they had lived by. The supreme, and supremely perverse, example is that of Corellius Rufus, a nobleman who, according to Fedden, "put off committing suicide throughout the reign of Domitian, saying that he did not wish to die under a tyrant. Once this powerful Emperor was dead he took his own life with an easy mind, and as a free Roman."[23] To live nobly also meant to die nobly and at the right moment. Everything depended on the dominant will and a rational choice.

This attitude was reinforced by Roman law. There were no revenges, no degradation, no evidence of fear or horror. Instead the law was the law—practical. According to Justinian's *Digest,* suicide of a private citizen was not punishable if it was caused by "impatience of pain or sickness, or by another cause," or by "weariness of life . . . lunacy, or fear of dishonor." Since this covered every rational cause, all that was left was the utterly irrational suicide "without cause," and that was punishable on the grounds that "whoever does not spare himself would much less spare another."[24] In other words, it was punished because it was irrational, not because it was a crime. There were other exceptions, but they were even more strictly practical: it was a crime for a slave to kill himself for the simple reason that he represented to his master a certain capital investment. Like a car, a slave was guaranteed against faults: hidden physical blemishes, a suicidal or criminal nature. If he killed himself, or attempted to, within six months of his purchase he could be returned—alive or dead—to his old master and the deal was declared invalid.[25] In the same way, a soldier was considered to be the property of the state and his suicide was tantamount to desertion. Roman law, that is, took literally the two similes—the soldier and the chattel—which Socrates had used so eloquently. Finally, it was also an offense for a criminal to take his own life in order to avoid trial for a crime for which the punishment would be forfeiture of his estate. In this case, a suicide was declared to be without legal heirs. The relatives, however, were allowed to defend the accused as though he were still alive; if he was found innocent, they then retained their inheritance; if not, it went to the state. In short, in Roman law the crime of suicide was strictly economic. It was an offense against neither morality nor religion, only against the capital investments of the slave-owning class or the treasury of the state.

The icy heroism of all this is admirable, even enviable, but it also seems, at least from our perspective, curiously unreal. It seems impossible that life and behavior could ever be quite so rational, and the will, at the moment of crisis, quite so dependable. That the Romans were able to act as though they were indicates an extraordinary inner discipline—a discipline of the soul they did not believe in. But it also says something about the monstrous civilization of which they were part. I suggested earlier that only comparatively recently has death ceased to be casual and public. In imperial Rome this casualness reached that point of lunacy where the crowd, for its entertainment, would be satisfied with nothing less than death. Donne quotes a learned source who says that in one month thirty thousand men died in gladitorial shows.[26] Frazer says that at one time people would offer themselves for execution to amuse the public for five *minae* (about £50), the money to be paid to their heirs; he adds that the market was so competitive that the candidates would offer to be beaten to death rather than beheaded, since that was slower, more painful and so more spectacular.[27]* Perhaps, then, Stoic dignity was a last defense against the murderous squalor of Rome itself. When those calm heroes looked around them they saw a life so unspeakable, cruel, wanton, corrupt and apparently unvalued that they clung to their ideals of reason much as the Christian poor used to cling to their belief in Paradise and the goodness of God despite, or because of, the misery of their lives on this earth. Stoicism, in short, was a philosophy of despair; it was not a coincidence that Seneca, who was its most powerful and influential spokesman, was also the teacher of the most vicious of all Roman emperors, Nero.

Perhaps this is why Stoic calm was so easily assimilated into the religious hysteria of the early Christians. Rational suicide was a kind of aristocratic corollary of vulgar blood lust. Christianity, which began as a religion for the poor and rejected, took that blood lust, combined it with the habit of suicide, and transferred both into a lust for martyrdom. The Romans may have fed Christians to the lions for sport, but they were not prepared for the fact that the Christians welcomed the animals as instruments of glory and salvation. "Let me enjoy those beasts," said Ignatius, "whom I wish more cruell than they are; for if they will not attempt me, I will provoke and draw them by force."[28] The persecution of the early Christians was less religious and political than a perversion of their own seeking. For the sophisticated Roman magistrates, Christian obstinacy was mostly an embarrassment: as when the Christians refused to make the token gestures toward established religion which would save their lives or, failing that, refused to avail themselves of the convenient pause between judgment and execution in which to escape. Embarrassment moved into irritation when the would-be martyrs, student revolutionary tacticians before their day, responded to clemency with

---

*There is a case in the late eighteenth century of a man who advertised that he would commit suicide publicly in Covent Garden in order to raise money for his poverty-stricken family, provided he could find enough spectators willing to pay one pound each. But by this time brutal amusement was qualified by an even stronger taste for "the Pathetick." Nowadays, someone making a similar offer would qualify only for the nearest psychiatric ward, or as a suitable cause for treatment in the Theater of the Absurd.

provocation. And it finished with boredom: an African proconsul, surrounded by a mob of Christians baying for martyrdom, shouted to them, "Goe hang and drown your selves and ease the Magistrate."[29] Others, no less bored, were less forbearing. The glorious company of martyrs came to number thousands of men, women and children who were beheaded, burned alive, flung from cliffs, roasted on gridirons, and hacked to pieces—all more or less gratuitously, of their own free will, as so many deliberate acts of provocation. Martyrdom was a Christian creation as much as a Roman persecution.

Just as the early Christians took over the Roman religious festivals, so they also took over the Roman attitudes toward death and suicide, and in doing so, magnified them theologically, distorted them and finally turned them upside down. To the Romans of every class, death itself was unimportant. But the way of dying—decently, rationally, with dignity and at the right time—mattered intensely. Their way of death, that is, was the measure of their final value of life. The early Christians showed this same indifference to death but changed the perspective. Viewed from the Christian Heaven, life itself was at best unimportant; at worst, evil: the fuller the life, the greater the temptation to sin. Death, therefore, was a release awaited or sought out with impatience. In other words, the more powerfully the Church instilled in believers the idea that this world was a vale of tears and sin and temptation, where they waited uneasily until death released them into eternal glory, the more irresistible the temptation to suicide became. Even the most stoical Romans committed suicide only as a last resort; they at least waited until their lives had become intolerable. But for the primitive Church, life was intolerable whatever its conditions. Why, then, live unredeemed when heavenly bliss is only a knife stroke away? Christian teaching was at first a powerful incitement to suicide.

The early Fathers had another inducement, almost as powerful as heavenly bliss. They offered posthumous glory: the martyrs' names celebrated annually in the Church calendar, their passing officially recorded, their relics worshiped. Tertullian, the most bloodthirsty of the Fathers, who explicitly forbade his flock even to attempt to escape persecution, also proffered them the sweetest of recompenses, revenge: "No City escaped punishment, which had shed Christian blood."[30] The martyrs would peer down from Paradise and see their enemies tortured eternally in Hell.

But above all, martyrdom afforded certain redemption. Just as baptism purged away original sin, so martyrdom wiped out all previous transgressions. It was as much a guarantee of Paradise to the Christians as violent death was to the Vikings and the Iglulik Eskimos. The only difference was that the martyrs died not as warriors but as passive victims; the war they fought was not of this world and all their victories were Pyrrhic. We are back, by another route, with frivolous suicide.

Theologically, the argument was irresistible, but to respond to it required a zealotry which touched on madness. Donne remarked, unwillingly and with some embarrassment, "that those times were affected with a disease of this natural desire of such a death . . . For that age was growne so hungry and ravenous of it [martyrdom], that many were baptized onely because they would be burnt, and children taught to vexe and provoke Executioners, that they might be thrown into the fire."[31] It culminated in the genuine lunacy of the Donatists, whose lust for martyrdom was so extreme that the Church eventually declared them heretics. Gibbon elegantly described their weird and ambiguous glory:

The rage of Donatists was enflamed by a phrensy of a very extraordinary kind: and which, if it really prevailed among them in so extravagant a degree, cannot surely be paralleled in any country or in any age. Many of these fanatics were possessed with the horror of life and the desire of martyrdom; and they deemed it of little moment by what means or by what hands they perished, if their conduct was sanctified by the intention of devoting themselves to the glory of the true faith and the hope of eternal happiness. Sometimes they rudely disturbed the festivals and profaned the temples of paganism with the design of exciting the most zealous of the idolators to ravage the insulated honour of their Gods. They sometimes forced their way into the courts of justice and compelled the affrighted judge to give orders for their execution. They frequently stopped travellers on the public highways and obliged them to inflict the stroke of martyrdom by promise of a reward, if they consented—and by the threat of instant death, if they refused to grant so very singular a favour. When they were disappointed of every other resource, they announced the day on which, in the presence of their friends and brethren, they should cast

themselves headlong from some lofty rock; and many pre-
cipices were shown, which had acquired fame by the number
of these religious suicides.[32]

The Donatists flourished—if that is the word—in the fourth and
fifth centuries and inspired their contemporary, St. Augustine, to
the comment: ". . . to kill themselves out of respect for martyrdom
is their daily sport." But Augustine also recognized the logical
dilemma of Christian teaching: if suicide was allowed in order to
avoid sin, then it became the logical course for all those fresh from
baptism. That sophistry, combined with the suicide mania of the
martyrs, provoked him into arguments to prove suicide to be "a
detestable and damnable wickedness," mortal sin greater than any
that could be committed between baptism and a divinely ordained
death. I have already mentioned that the first of the arguments he
used was derived from the Sixth Commandment, "Thou shalt not
kill." Thus the man who killed himself broke this commandment
and became a murderer.* Moreover, if a man killed himself to
atone for his sins, he was usurping the function of the state and
the church; and if he died innocent in order to avoid sin, then he
had his own innocent blood on his hands—a worse sin than any he
might commit, since it is impossible for him to repent. Finally,
Augustine took over Plato's and the Pythagoreans' argument that
life is the gift of God, and our sufferings, being divinely ordained,
are not to be foreshortened by one's own actions; to bear them
patiently is a measure of one's greatness of soul. Thus, to take
one's own life proved only that one did not accept the divine will.
    Augustine's large authority and the excesses of the presump-
tive martyrs finally swung opinion against suicide. In A.D. 533 the
Council of Orleans denied funeral rites to anyone who killed
himself while accused of a crime. And in doing so, they were not

---

*It was this argument which was assimilated into civil law: "Up to this
day, we do not know what crime suicide constituted, whether a crime *sui
generis* or a particular instance of murder, the better view being that it was
the latter. Another interesting feature of that crime is the manner in
which it was formulated. In the case of all other offenses, the common law
defines the crime itself ('larceny is the felonious taking'; 'murder is the
unlawful killing'). But in suicide, not the crime but the criminal is defined:
'*felo de se* is *he who kills.*' Obviously, as was Christian doctrine, so was the
common law struggling with the dilemma of a crime in which the
aggressor and the object of aggression are united in one person."[33]

merely following Roman law which had been formulated to safeguard the state's rights to the suicide's inheritance. Instead, they were condemning suicide both as a crime in itself and also as a crime more serious than others, since ordinary criminals were still allowed a properly Christian burial. Thirty years later this seriousness was recognized without qualification by canon law. In 562 at the Council of Braga, funeral rites were refused to *all* suicides regardless of social position, reason or method. The final step was taken in 693 by the Council of Toledo, which ordained that even the attempted suicide should be excommunicated.

The door had slammed shut. The decent alternative of the Romans, the key to Paradise of the early Christians, had become the most deadly of mortal sins. Where St. Matthew recorded the suicide of Judas Iscariot without comment—implying by his silence that it in some way atoned for his other crimes—later theologians asserted that he was more damned for killing himself than for betraying Christ. St. Bruno, in the eleventh century, called suicides "martyrs for Satan," and two centuries later St. Thomas Aquinas sealed up the whole question in the *Summa;* suicide, he said, is a mortal sin against God, who has given his life; it is also a sin against justice and against charity. Yet even there, in what was to be the center of Christian doctrine, Aquinas takes his arguments from non-Christian sources. The sin against God derives ultimately, like Augustine's similar argument, from Plato. The sin against justice—by which he means the individual's responsibilities to his community—harks back to Aristotle. As for the sin against charity, Aquinas means that instinctive charity which each man bears toward himself—that is, the instinct of self-preservation which man has in common with the lower animals; to go against that is a mortal sin, since it is to go against nature.* That reason was first used by the Hebrew general Josephus to dissuade his soldiers from killing themselves after they had been defeated by the Romans. (He also used Plato's argument.)

---

* It isn't. Glanville Williams quotes a learned source to show that dogs sometimes commit suicide, "usually by drowning or by refusing food, for a number of reasons—generally when the animal is cast out from the household, but also from regret or remorse or even from sheer ennui. Animal suicide of these kinds is capable of being regarded as a manifestation of intelligence."[34]

But however un-Christian the sources of the arguments, suicide became, in the long, superstitious centuries between Augustine and Aquinas, the most mortal of Christian sins. Augustine had attacked suicide as a preventive measure: the cult of martyrdom had got out of hand and was, anyway, no longer relevant to the situation of the Church in the fourth century. Moreover, it was an offense against that respect for life as the vehicle of the soul which was the essence of Christ's teaching; to love one's neighbor as oneself makes no sense if to kill oneself is also permitted. Yet the fact remained that suicide, thinly disguised as martyrdom, was one of the rocks on which the Church had first been founded. So perhaps the absoluteness with which the sin was condemned and the horrors of the vengeance visited on the dead bodies of the suicides were directly proportional to the power the act exerted on the Christian imagination, and to the lingering temptation to escape the snares of the flesh by the shortest, most certain way. Thus when the Albigensians, in the early thirteenth century, followed the example of the early saints and suicidally sought martyrdom, they were thought only to have compounded the damnation which their other heresies had already earned them. In doing so, they justified the terrible savagery with which they were butchered.

Fedden believes that Augustine's teaching and canon law acted together as a catalyst which released all those primitive terrors of suicide which are repressed in more rational periods. Perhaps. But what also occurred was somehow more profound: what began as a preventive measure finished as a kind of universal character change. An act which during the first flowering of Western civilization had been tolerated, later admired, and later still sought as the supreme mark of zealotry, became finally the object of intense moral revulsion. When, in the late Renaissance, the question of the individual's right to take his own life once more arose, it seemed to be challenging the whole structure of Christian belief and morals. Hence the deviousness with which men like John Donne began once again to argue the case for suicide after a gap of more than a thousand years. Hence, too, the note of hoarse moral rectitude of their detractors, that earnest certainty which could dispense with argument because it had behind it the whole massive weight of the Church's authority. The increasingly outspoken and rational arguments of the philosophers—Voltaire, Hume, Schopenhauer—did more or less nothing to shake this moral certainty, although as time went on the pious denunciations became shriller, less assured, more outraged.

It took the counterrevolution of science to change all this. Henry Morselli, an Italian professor of psychological medicine and Durkheim's most distinguished predecessor in the use of statistics to analyze the problem of suicide, wrote in 1879: "The old philosophy of individualism had given to suicide the character of liberty and spontaneity, but now it became necessary to study it no longer as the expression of individual and independent faculties, but certainly as a social phenomenon allied with all the other racial forces." [35]

The shift is from the individual to society, from morals to problems. Socially, the gains were enormous: the legal penalties gradually dropped away; the families of successful suicides no longer found themselves disinherited and tainted with the suspicion of inherited insanity; they could bury their dead and grieve for them in much the same way as any other bereaved. As for the unsuccessful suicide, he faced neither the gallows nor prison but, at worst, a period of observation in a psychiatric ward; more often, he faced nothing more piercing than his own continuing depression.

Existentially, however, there were also losses. The Church's condemnation of self-murder, however brutal, was based at least on a concern for the suicide's soul. In contrast, a great deal of modern scientific tolerance appears to be founded on human indifference. The act is removed from the realm of damnation only at the price of being transformed into an interesting but purely intellectual problem, beyond obloquy but also beyond tragedy and morality. There seems to me remarkably little gap between the idea of death as a fascinating, slightly erotic happening on a television screen and that of suicide as an abstract sociological problem. Despite all the talk of prevention, it may be that the suicide is rejected by the social scientist as utterly as he was by the most dogmatic Christian theologians. Thus even the author of the entry on suicide in the *Encyclopaedia of Religion and Ethics* writes, with unconcealed relief: "Perhaps the greatest contribution of modern times to the rational treatment of the matter is the consideration . . . that many suicides are non-moral and entirely the affair of the specialist in mental diseases." The implication is clear: modern suicide has been removed from the vulnerable, volatile world of human beings and hidden safely away in the isolation wards of science. I doubt if Ogarev and his prostitute mistress would have found much in the change to be grateful for.

N O T E S

1. Quoted by E. H. Carr, *The Romantic Exiles* (Harmondsworth: Penguin Books, 1949), p. 389.
2. Both quotations from Glanville Williams, *The Sanctity of Life and the Criminal Law* (New York: Knopf, 1957, and London: Faber and Faber, 1958), p. 233.
3. See Emile Durkheim, *Suicide,* trans. by J. A. Spaulding and G. Simpson (New York: The Free Press, 1951, and London: Routledge and Kegan Paul, 1952), pp. 327–30.
4. Quoted by Giles Romilly Fedden, *Suicide* (London and Toronto, 1938), p. 224. I have leaned heavily and gratefully on this learned but unusually readable book.
5. Ibid., p. 223.
6. *The Connoisseur,* quoted by Charles Moore, *A Full Enquiry into the Subject of Suicide,* 2 vols. (London: Printed for J.F. and C. Rivington, 1790), Vol. I, pp. 323–24.
7. See Fedden, *op. cit.,* pp. 27–48, who gives many other examples.
8. Glanville Williams, *loc. cit.*
9. *The Times* of London, January 21, 1970. See also January 26 and 27, 1970.
10. John Donne, *Biathanatos,* Part 1, Distinction 3, Section 2 (New York: Facsimile Text Society, 1930), p. 58.
11. See Sigmund Freud, "Totem and Taboo," *Complete Psychological Works,* ed. by James Strachey, et al. (London: Hogarth Press, 1962), Vol. XIII, especially pp. 18–74.
12. J. G. Frazer, *The Golden Bough,* abridged ed. (New York: Criterion Books, 1959), p. 467.
13. See Moore, *op. cit.,* Vol. I, p. 147.
14. Rapin's *Introduction to the History of England,* quoted by Moore, *op. cit.,* Vol. I, p. 149n.

15. Gregory Zilboorg, "Suicide Among Civilized and Primitive Races," *American Journal of Psychiatry*, Vol. 92 (1936), p. 1,362.
16. See Durkheim, *op. cit.*, p. 218.
17. Zilboorg, *op. cit.*, p. 1,368.
18. J. Wisse, *Selbstmord und Todesfurcht bei den Naturvölkern* (Zutphen, 1933), pp. 207–8, quoted by Zilboorg, *op. cit.*, pp. 1,352–53.
19. See Fedden, *op. cit.*, pp. 55, 59.
20. Libanius, quoted by Durkheim, *op. cit.*, p. 330.
21. Fedden, *op. cit.*, p. 83.
22. Both these quotations: *ibid.*, pp. 79–80.
23. Ibid., p. 50.
24. Quoted by Helen Silving, "Suicide and Law," in *Clues to Suicide*, ed. by Edwin S. Shneidman and Norman L. Farberow (New York: McGraw-Hill, 1957), pp. 80–81.
25. See Fedden, *op. cit.*, p. 93.
26. See Donne, *op. cit.*, p. 54.
27. Quoted by Fedden, *op. cit.*, p. 84.
28. See Donne, *op. cit.*, pp. 64–65.
29. Ibid., p. 66.
30. Ibid., p. 60.
31. Ibid., pp. 63, 65.
32. Gibbon, *Decline and Fall of the Roman Empire*, Vol. III, p. 401, quoted by Moore, *op. cit.*, Vol. I, p. 290.
33. Helen Silving, in Shneidman and Farberow, *op. cit.*, pp. 81–82.
34. Glanville Williams, *op. cit.*, p. 226, quoting Perlson and Karpman, "Psychopathologic and Psychopathetic Reaction in Dogs," *Quarterly Journal of Criminal Psychopathology* (1943), pp. 514–15.
35. Henry Morselli, *Suicide* (London: C. K. Paul and Co., 1881), p. 3.

Conceptual
Issues

DID SOCRATES
COMMIT SUICIDE?

R. G. Frey

Frey claims that Socrates, in drinking the hemlock at the order of the Athenian court, did commit suicide. Frey's case rests upon an analysis of what it is to commit suicide and a demonstration of how the death of Socrates satisfies this analysis, despite the objections that Socrates was compelled to drink the hemlock and that death was his sentence for corrupting the youth of Athens.

R. G. Frey, educated in the United States and England, is senior lecturer in philosophy at the University of Liverpool. He has published papers in a large number of philosophical journals and is the author of Interests and Rights: The Case Against Animals *(Oxford University Press, 1980) and of* Aspects of Consequentialism *and* Modern Moral Vegetarianism: A Critical Assessment, *both in progress. He is also at work on several additional pieces on philosophical issues in suicide.*

It is rarely, if at all, thought that Socrates committed suicide; but such was the case, or so I want to suggest. My suggestion turns not upon any new interpretation of ancient sources but rather upon seeking a determination of the concept of suicide itself.

Suppose Sir Percy is cleaning his gun and that his finger slips on the trigger, as a result of which the gun discharges, mortally wounding him: does Sir Percy commit suicide? It seems reasonably clear that he does not: if killing oneself is a part of committing suicide, it is not the whole. What seems wanted is a reference to the fact that Percy did not intend to take his life; it is not killing oneself but killing oneself intentionally that constitutes suicide. (One must not construe the phrase "killing oneself intentionally" so narrowly, however, that a death can only be suicide if it is self-inflicted, as in drinking poison or cutting one's wrists; as I show elsewhere,[1] a death can be other-inflicted and still count as suicide, provided the victim has intentionally manipulated the circumstances and the other party to bring about his own death.)

If suicide, then, is killing oneself intentionally, then Socrates (I mean the Socrates of Plato's *Phaedo*) certainly did commit suicide. For he drank the hemlock knowingly, not unknowingly or in ignorance of what it was or what its effect on him would be, and intentionally, not accidentally or mistakenly; and he died as a result of his act of drinking the hemlock.

A number of ways in which one might try to avoid this conclusion come to mind; but each of them, I think, fails.

"Socrates did not want to die." It is apparent from Plato's narrative of Socrates's last hours with Phaedo and his friends that Socrates intends to drink the hemlock. At least ordinarily, however, an agent intends an act only if he knows he is doing it and wants to do it either as an end in itself or as a means to some further end. So unless one is prepared to say that Socrates did not intend to drink the hemlock, we can infer from the fact that he intended to drink it, together with his knowledge of what its effect on him would be, that he wanted to die, either as an end in itself or as a means to some further end. (It should perhaps be added, too, that in the early passages of the *Phaedo,* where Socrates expounds his view of what the philosopher's attitude towards death should be (61c–69e), he does betray a wish to die.) Of course, Socrates is known to have had a concern with the laws of Athens and their observance, and one might argue, I suppose, that though he foresaw as a consequence of drinking the hemlock (as his sentence) that he would die, what he wanted was not to die but to uphold the laws of Athens. It is equally plausible to argue, however, that Socrates wanted to die, sentenced, as he was, by the city to do so, in order to uphold—and be seen upholding—these very laws.

"Socrates was forced to drink the hemlock." This is simply untrue. He did not take the cup of hemlock reluctantly. Nor, after he had taken it, did he throw its contents to the floor. He did not drink the hemlock against his will: his jailers were not required to listen to his protests or pleas, and they did not have to hold him down and pour the hemlock down his throat. Even granted that he had to die, Socrates had a choice between drinking the hemlock willingly and having it, so to speak, force-fed; and only by choosing to be force-fed would Socrates have been forced to drink the hemlock, that is, compelled to die against his will.

"Socrates was under duress." Even if true, this fact is irrelevant, unless one is prepared to argue, what is almost certainly false, that duress vitiates choice. Socrates had to die, but he could die by his own hand, by taking and drinking the hemlock willingly, or by the hand of another, by having the hemlock force-fed. What duress Socrates is under pertains to his having to die, not to his having to die by his own hand.[2]

"The whole context in which Socrates drinks the hemlock, namely, his trial, the verdict and the drinking of hemlock as his sentence, is what is important; he does not commit suicide because he takes the hemlock in the context of an execution by the city of Athens." I agree that Socrates takes the hemlock as a result of his sentence, indeed, as his sentence, but I deny that intentionally taking one's life because it is one's sentence *ipso facto* precludes committing suicide. Suppose that the sentence for murder were a bit different, that every convicted murderer was allowed to live for twelve months from the date on which his sentence was passed, and could either take his own life within this period or else face the absolute certainty of a state execution at the end of twelve months: do not the murderers who intentionally take their own lives commit suicide? The fact that their sentence is as it is does not preclude their doing so; on the contrary, given that they have to die, they intentionally take their own lives and thereby make plain their decisions to commit suicide rather than to undergo state executions. True, their acts of intentionally taking their own lives can be described as "implementing their sentence" as well as "committing suicide"; but the use of the former description in no way bars the use of the latter to describe what they did.

"The time of Socrates's death is fixed by his sentence, and this is what is important; he does not commit suicide because he does not choose when to die." The assumption that choosing the time and moment of death is part of what it is to be a suicide is false. Suppose Sir Percy decides to commit suicide but simply cannot face cutting his wrists or shooting himself in the temple; instead, he plants hundreds of pounds of gelignite under his house and attaches the fuses to his telephone, so that, if his telephone rings, his house explodes; and then he sits down to wait. Percy will die whenever his telephone rings, but *he* does not know or determine (or perhaps even care) when that will be; and if, unknown to him, his telephone has been disconnected, then it may never ring. But if at some time or other it does ring, and if Percy does die, he has certainly committed suicide. Again, Captain Oates was aware that, in walking away from Scott's camp, he was walking to his death; and he could have been reasonably certain of dying soon. But he did not know or choose the moment of death, and in reaching hs decision to walk away, I doubt if he cared just *when* death would come. Thus, the fact that Socrates does not choose the time and moment of his death does not *ipso facto* preclude his committing suicide.

"Socrates died a noble and dignified death and suicide is ignoble and undignified." On the contrary; the fact that Socrates died a noble and dignified death does not show he did not commit suicide, but rather that suicide need not be ignoble and undignified.

NOTES

1. In R. G. Frey, "Suicide and Self-Inflicted Death," forthcoming in *Philosophy*.
2. It is true that, whether Socrates decides to die by his own hand or by that of another, his life will come to an end; and in these circumstances one might be inclined to say that "It's no choice whatever." But this means not that Socrates literally has no choice between these alternatives, but that they are horrible alternatives to have to choose between, with death the result whichever alternative he selects.

THE CONCEPT OF SUICIDE

Peter Y. Windt

Windt claims that muddle over the definition of "suicide" leads to confused thinking, and thus to confused social policy. Arguing that the concept of suicide is "open-textured," he provides a Wittgenstein-ian analysis of the concept "suicide" in terms of criteria, characteristics in virtue of which an event is a suicide, but which are neither necessary nor sufficient conditions.

Peter Windt is associate professor of philosophy at the University of Utah and former chairman of the department. He has spent the last several years, including one under a grant from the Rockefeller Foundation, working on problems in bioethics. He is particularly interested in issues concerning the ethics of (re)designing human nature; he also works on philosophical method, especially problems of informal logic, and on problems in epistemic justification.

The empirical study of suicide and the moral appraisal of cases of suicide depend in a variety of ways upon the analysis or definition of the concept of suicide. In what follows I shall argue that the concept of suicide is open-textured, briefly sketch a portion of its analysis, and touch upon consequences of that analysis for the study and appraisal of suicide.

By saying that the concept of suicide is open-textured, I mean that characteristics of cases of suicide may be found which are definitional, in the sense that they really are the characteristics by virtue of which an event is a suicide, but which are neither necessary nor sufficient conditions for an event's being a case of suicide—that is, for each such characteristic, cases of suicide may be found which do not have the characteristic, and cases may be found of events which have the characteristic but are not cases of suicide. Let us call such characteristics *criteria* of suicide.[1] If the concept of suicide is open-textured, then, it must involve some criteria. This is not to deny that some definitional characteristics of suicide may be necessary conditions, nor is it to deny that some complex combination of characteristics of suicide may constitute a sufficient condition. It is to deny that there is some nuclear set of characteristics which is to be found in all cases of suicide, and in no other cases.

The claim that a concept is open-textured need not indicate that it is arbitrary, vague, or inconsistent. While different criteria may be involved in different cases, we should expect to find similarities among the whole family of cases which justify their assimilation under a single concept. Such similarities will be the result of different combinations of criteria (and any necessary conditions) under different circumstances. And, because similarity is capable of degrees and variation, we might expect to find that some cases of suicide are paradigms, while others, though still genuine cases of suicide, exhibit various atypical characteristics. And we can expect to encounter borderline cases which are similar to typical cases of suicide in some respects, dissimilar in others, so that we simply do not know whether to count them suicides or not.

If, indeed, the concept of suicide is open-textured, its analysis should specify any necessary conditions, indicate criteria and the circumstances under which they are or are not significant, give paradigms, and say something about the general character of the similarities linking the various cases together. Let us turn now to that set of tasks.

It might be thought that death must occur in all cases of suicide. But where an attempt at suicide (say, by shooting) results in enough brain damage to destroy the personality, or where abuse of alcohol or other drugs produces radical destruction of memory and character, we sometimes are tempted to speak of suicide, even though the body survives. If calling such cases suicides is not mere metaphor or exaggeration, then death of the organism will not be a necessary condition of suicide (however, we might then make a case for death of the *person* as a necessary condition). To sidestep the debate about the nature of persons and the definition of death, let us suppose, tentatively, that death, either of the person or of the organism, is a necessary condition of suicide.[2]

If we concede that death is a necessary condition of suicide, then we also may want to concede that another necessary condition is the applicability of some reflexive description of the death. One such description would be that one has killed oneself. In other cases it is more appropriate to say one has gotten oneself killed; and in still other cases that one has let oneself be killed. For example, one may commit suicide by shooting oneself deliberately and with premeditation (killing oneself). Or one may commit suicide by ordering a servant to do the job (getting oneself killed). Or, on falling into a river, one may opt for suicide and refuse to swim (letting oneself be killed). One might even kill oneself by deliberately starting a fight, offering little resistance, and thereby letting oneself be killed (as intended), getting oneself killed, and committing suicide—all at once. Thus, while some cases of suicide might involve the deceased being killed by someone else or someone else's getting him killed or letting him be killed, the deceased also must kill himself or get himself killed or let himself be killed.

But the applicability of one or more of these descriptions is not a sufficient condition of suicide. One who drives into a rock wall, mistaking a late-evening shadow for a tunnel entrance, has killed himself. It is less natural to say he has gotten himself killed, and wrong to say he has let himself be killed. One who comes between a grizzly bear sow and her cubs while trying to photograph them may get himself killed, but not kill himself (the bear does that) nor let himself be killed (he puts up a good fight, under the circumstances). A prisoner may let himself be killed, rather than give information, but does not thereby get himself killed, nor kill himself. None of these cases should be counted as suicide.[3]

Then what other features distinguish suicide from other kinds of death? The literature on suicide mentions several factors: that death was caused by the actions or behavior of the deceased; that the deceased wanted, desired, or wished death; that the deceased intended, chose, decided, or willed to die; that the deceased knew that death would result from his behavior; that the deceased was responsible for his death. My contention is that all these factors are *criteria* of suicide, rather than necessary or sufficient conditions. To support that contention I shall sketch a set of circumstances in which a death occurs, and show that as we alter the details of the case, each of the factors listed can be shown to be neither necessary nor sufficient, but criterially significant under certain circumstances.

Let us suppose, then, that a man has gone hiking along a primitive trail which at one point employs a slender log as a bridge, crossing a very swift stream. At this point on the trail, he ventures out onto the log, falls into the stream, and drowns. What kinds of details about this case would determine that it was a case of suicide, and what kinds of details would determine that it was not? [4]

We should note that if he is in high spirits, generally satisfied with his lot, cheerfully thinking of his plans for the evening, loses his balance because the log shifts under his feet, and tries valiantly to swim to safety, then there will be no question of suicide and the death will be accidental. Or, if he is in despair, wants to die, has planned to do so at that spot by drowning, deliberately leaps from the log and makes no effort to swim, we will have no hesitation in calling his death a suicide. The cases which need careful consideration are those in between, in which only some of the factors in question are present.

Suppose our victim suffers from depression and wants to die, although he has formed no plans for his death. Accidentally, he slips on the log and falls in. But then he refuses to swim and lets himself drown. Here we have a suicide, but no significant causation by the deceased. On the other hand, suppose that he has no depression or inclination to die, but believes falsely that he can swim the stream safely. He leaps in to cool off and is drowned. Here his actions do cause his death, but it is not suicide. The difference between these two cases rests on the presence or absence of the desire to die and the decision to do so.

But now suppose that our victim has been suffering for some time from a recurring compulsion to commit suicide. He fears this compulsion, desires not to succumb to it, has sought aid in combatting it, but it grows in him as he hikes this day, and at the bridge it drives him into the water and to his death. Although this counts as a case of suicide, the very nature of the compulsion and his struggle with it indicates that he did not desire to die nor intend to do so. In fact, the compulsion operated against his will. Thus, wanting, willing, intending, or deciding to die are not necessary conditions of suicide. In this case we should note that the operant criteria seem to be that his actions did cause his death and that he *knew* that death would result from them. (We should distinguish this case from one in which he has a compulsion to jump without regard to consequences, in which he would have jumped compulsively but died accidentally as a result. Compulsive *suicide* requires knowledge of the fatal consequences likely to result from the compulsive behavior.)

If our victim has the intention or desire to die sometime that day but has not decided yet how it should happen, or has decided that it should happen, say, by poison, later on, then he might slip, fall off the log and drown by accident. But what if he specifically wants to or intends to die by jumping off the log and drowning? Suppose that, as he is poised to jump, composing himself and gathering his willpower, a fierce gust of wind upsets him and he falls (not jumps) into the stream. Confused by the unexpected shock of the cold water, he swims as strongly as he can for shore, but drowns anyway. Although he has died as he intended, his death is accidental.[5] Here the absence of fatal causation by the deceased is significant.

In these cases, whether or not a death due to compulsive behavior was suicide depended upon whether the deceased knew that the result of the compulsive behavior would be fatal. But such knowledge is not a necessary condition of suicide. Suppose that our victim is moody, depressed, and decides to leap from the log and try to swim the stream. He is not sure that he will survive, and not sure that he won't. If he does, he is prepared to take it as a good omen and thinks he will return to his normal life with renewed vigor. If he dies, he supposes that it will be just as well. He is leaving his fate up to chance, the gods, or whatever. Here he cannot be said to have known that he would die; nevertheless, we will count his death as a suicide. But, of course, the kind of knowledge in question is not sufficient to determine that a death is suicide: our victim may know perfectly well that falling into the stream would be fatal for him, fall accidentally, and not have committed suicide.

Finally, what of responsibility? Before considering examples, we should realize that the claim that a person is responsible for an event can mean many different things. It sometimes means that the person has caused the event for which he is responsible. Examples already given show that this sort of responsibility is criterial for suicide. Sometimes to say that a person is responsible is to say that he is rational, has an adequate grasp of reality, understands his situation, acts within acceptable parameters, and so on. Our victim might have been clearly not responsible in this sense (he may have been suffering from a variety of neuroses or incapacities) and still could have committed suicide by throwing himself from the log. Or, on the other hand, he could have been fully responsible in this sense and have died accidentally by falling from the log. Still, this sort of responsibility is not totally irrelevant to questions about suicide. For example, if our victim thought he could breathe water as easily as air, his killing himself by leaping into the stream would not be a case of suicide. But the significance of this kind of diminished capacity may be only that it reveals lack of knowledge or intention, and, thus, no new criterion is found here.

Again, we might consider whether a person is *morally* responsible, that is, morally liable for an action. If he were careless or negligent in attempting to cross the stream, then, our victim would be morally responsible for his accidental death. But he would not be morally responsible for the compulsive suicidal death already described. Since the question of one's moral liability often is a question of one's intentions, actions, and motives with respect to some behavior, and since intentions, causality, and motives are criterial for suicide, there will be a close connection between the determination of moral responsibility for some deaths and the determination that they are suicides.

It may be felt that there is still some other sense of responsibility in which it must be true of *all* suicides that the deceased is responsible for his own death. But I think this will turn out to amount to nothing more than a necessary condition already admitted tentatively, namely, that some reflexive description of the death be true. To say that the deceased killed himself, got himself killed, or let himself be killed, perhaps, is to attribute to him some minimal sort of responsibility for his death.

If the concept of suicide is open-textured, as I have argued, can anything be said generally about the similarities which knit the cases of suicide into a single family? It is tempting to reply that what all suicides have in common is just that they are suicides, and that the account of criteria, and the circumstances in which they are significant, *is* the account of the similarities which connect the various cases. That account, of course, should consider many more situations and circumstances than those given here, and, indeed, the account may be open-ended, so that some further elucidation of significant details always may be possible. But perhaps one useful, if rather vague, remark can be made about the similarities cases of suicide bear to one another.

In suicide we find a peculiar negation of the value of life. Of all persons, we should expect he whose life it is to be most sensitive to the value of a life; but in suicide, it is that very person who allows the value of his life to be overridden by other factors. The overriding of the value of the lives of others found in homicide is, somehow, less puzzling, perhaps even less awesome. To understand the suicide, we must understand how this negation of the value of one's own life is possible. But, of course, while this may say something about the way in which suicides are similar, it does not take us very far. The negation of the value of life occurs in too many ways. In some cases a life really may not be worth living further; in others delusion and irrationality may only make it seem so; in still others something of greater worth may be achieved by sacrificing life; and so on. The sense of negation of the value of life thus invoked is itself open-textured.

Failure to appreciate the open texture of the concept of suicide will result in distortion of our views as to what is and what is not suicide. Definition of the concept in terms of some nuclear set of characteristics may err in excluding some genuine cases of suicide from our consideration, or including cases which are not suicides, or distorting our conception of the nuclear features themselves, so that we may seem to find them just where our strong intuitions about what suicide is tell us they must be. The variety of ways in which such errors can occur is too great for thorough treatment here, but consider as an instance the following speculative scenario:

Suppose we became convinced that suicide could be defined, say, as self-caused death, where there is a wish to die on the part of the victim. Such a conviction would lead us to ignore the importance of intention or choice. In that case, we would refuse to count as suicides cases in which persons have no wish to die but intentionally do let themselves die, e.g., persons who refuse lifesaving medical treatment because they find the conditions of continued existence (impairment, suffering, etc.) worse than death itself. Such persons intend to die but need not *wish* to do so—they may find death the least undesirable of the choices available to them. Or, again, we might be led to count as cases of suicide cases of accidental death, e.g., a person who desires to die and unintentionally causes his own death by driving carelessly— the crucial error here being the supposition that there *must* be some causal connection between the desire and the death.

Or, what is ultimately most dangerous, we might begin to distort our conception of wishing or desiring, incorporating into it aspects of intention and causality. Thus, we might presume that intention to die always reveals a wish to die—in some cases so thoroughly suppressed that it can be detected in no other way save through the intentional self-destructive act. And we might attribute to the wish to die an exaggerated causal efficacy, so that where it is present and death occurs, we presume that it *must* have been the cause of death. But this distortion of what it is to wish to die, combined with the view that all suicides involve this wish, might tend to seduce us into regarding suicide as a medical or behavioral problem, its victims suffering from a desire with which they cannot cope and which will cause their destruction unless some intervention is successful. At this point suicidal behavior would be regarded as a symptom of an illness, and the questions simply would not be raised whether it is intentional or not, rational or not. And so we would not hesitate to intervene, to treat, to commit; for we would see ourselves as rescuing victims rather than as interfering with deliberate, intentional actions. And at this point we would have not only theoretical error but a risk of unjust treatment of persons.[6]

Now this scenario is far too speculative and simple to be an adequate account of any widely held theories or practices regarding suicide. It merely indicates ways in which an incorrect definitional stance on suicide can *tend* to contribute to error in such theories and policies. But the scenario is not sheer fantasy, either, for such tendencies have played a part in the development of some views of suicide which treat it as such, e.g., always having its origin in a death wish, or in depression, or even as always involving failure of the individual to cope with his situation. (This is to claim that in some situations death *is* the best method of coping.)

Of course, recognition of the open-textured character of the concept of suicide will not, by itself, insure accurate assessment and just treatment of suicides and suicidal individuals. But it is one step in the right direction.

NOTES

1. By way of contrast, consider the concept *even*, as it is applied to integers. Any integer which is *even* is a product of two and some integer, and any product of two and some integer is even. Thus the concept is completely defined in terms of necessary and sufficient conditions, without reference to criteria. It should be noted that there is considerable disagreement about what philosophers have meant by the terms "criterion" and "open texture." In stipulating what I mean here, I take no stand on, say, what Wittgenstein or Waismann may have meant elsewhere, although my choice of these terms is not merely coincidental.

2. The sorts of cases mentioned here could be viewed as borderline cases. Thus, where death of the organism has not occurred but was intended, and destruction of the personality has resulted from actions intended to produce death (common among attempted but "failed" suicides), we have considerable likeness to ordinary cases of suicide, but also some important unlikeness.

3. Contrast this view with that of Lebacqz and Engelhardt in "Suicide and Covenant," p. 84.

4. For brevity, in the cases that follow suicide will be contrasted only with *accidental* reflexively describable death. Cases can be found in which nonsuicidal reflexively describable death is not accidental but due to natural causes (he killed himself by overwork) or homicide (he got himself killed by seducing the wife of the man who shot him).

5. Could a sufficient condition of suicide be that one cause one's death precisely as one intends? Perhaps. But *how precise* must the intention be? Intending to die of old age and doing so does not constitute suicide; nor does intending to die in battle and being killed in battle.

6. See the selection by Szasz, "The Ethics of Suicide," p. 185.

SUICIDE AND
SELF-SACRIFICE

Robert M. Martin

Martin's objective is to discredit some of the "baroque attempts" of traditional and recent philosophers to distinguish morally permissible self-killings from those which are not permissible. He examines the ways in which various authors (Augustine, Aquinas, Kant, Holland, and Margolis) try to draw this distinction, and argues that their attempts are both contrived and inadequate. He finds that the principle of double effect, often used by Catholic moralists in connection with issues in abortion and euthanasia, succeeds in differentiating permissible from impermissible self-killings, but that it is itself indefensible as a moral prinicple.

Robert M. Martin, educated at Columbia University and the University of Michigan, teaches philosophy at Dalhousie University, Halifax, Nova Scotia. He has spoken on suicide to meetings of the Canadian Philosophical Association, the International Association for Suicide Prevention, and over the television network of the Canadian Broadcasting Corporation. His principal areas of publication are philosophy of language and analytic metaphysics.

THE PROBLEM

"Suicide" is often defined simply as "self-killing,"[1] or "an act of taking one's own life";[2] more careful definitions (ruling out the

48

accidental or coerced taking of one's life) are "intentional self-destruction,"[3] "the act or instance of taking one's own life voluntarily and intentionally."[4] In an important British legal decision, a judge ruled that

> every act of self-destruction is, in common language, described by the word suicide, provided it be the intentional act of a party knowing the probable consequences of what he is about. This is, I think, the ordinary meaning of the word . . .[5]

Other than the philosophical difficulties (which we shall ignore) with the terms "voluntarily" and "intentionally," there seems to be no problem here. Yet there is a considerable tradition of philosophical writing which wants to deny that a number of cases which fit all these definitions are in fact suicides; these writers maintain that all suicides are morally forbidden, but that the cases in question are not blameworthy and are not properly called suicides. Kant, for example, wants to count all suicides as violations of duty, but claims that

> those who fall on the field of battle are not suicides, but the victims of fate. Not only is this not suicide; but the opposite, a faint heart and fear of the death which threatens by the necessity of fate, is no true self-preservation; for he who runs away to save his own life, and leaves his comrades in the lurch, is a coward; but he who defends himself and his fellows even unto death is no suicide, but noble and high-minded.[6]

If we suppose that Kant's soldiers were fighting voluntarily, knowing that their actions were certain or very likely to result in death, then they would be committing suicide under those initial definitions; but Kant denies that they are suicides.

R. F. Holland denies that Socrates' act of drinking the hemlock was a suicide.[7] He also imagines an event

> at a grenade-throwing practice when one of the grenades is dropped and there is no time to throw it clear, whereupon an N.C.O. falls on the grenade and with his body shields the others from its effects.[8]

This man, according to Holland, is no suicide; neither was Captain Oates, the explorer with the Scott polar expedition, who, finding himself severely disabled and thus endangering the others by retarding their progress, walked out of their tent into a blizzard, and to his certain death.[9]

Joseph Margolis claims that

> a man may knowingly and willingly go to his death, be rationally capable of avoiding death, deliberately not act to save his life, and yet not count as a suicide. In this sense, we usually exclude the man who sacrifices his life to save another's, the religious martyr who will not violate his faith, the patriot who intentionally lays down his life for a cause.[10]

Looked at one way, the issue is a rather trivial one: whether or not the word "suicide" really refers to the cases these writers give, or whether the definitions quoted earlier, which seem to include all these cases under the term, are correct. This is simply a question of what the word "suicide" refers to. Ordinary language is not especially clear here; one does speak of a soldier's "suicide mission"; on the other hand, there is a strong tendency to refuse the label to those cases and to call them instead, perhaps, self-sacrifices. Possibly the moralists in this tradition find most suicides to be such horrible crimes that the very word "suicide" gets infested with negative magic, and rather than admit that certain acts of intentional, voluntary self-killing are acceptable or even praiseworthy suicides, they prefer to deny that those acts are called suicide. The question of definition is, however, uninteresting. More interesting are the questions: On what basis are Kant and the others distinguishing these two kinds of self-killing? And: Is this basis for distinction also a valid basis for difference in moral judgment? In order to concentrate on these problems and not to get stalled by nomenclature disputes and confusions, I shall normally use the words "self-killing" to refer to *all* cases and see if it is possible to find criteria to distinguish some self-killings from others in the way Kant and the rest want to.

THE SEARCH FOR CRITERIA: FAILURES

The necessity of distinguishing these two classes arose in our tradition simultaneously with the first widespread condemnation of self-killing; this is natural, since the function of the division of the class of self-killings into the two subclasses is supposed to be the marking of a moral distinction. Some people find it surprising to learn that there are few cultures and religions which give wholesale moral condemnation to self-killing, and that the view that the Everlasting had fixed His canon 'gainst self-slaughter was not even everlasting through the history of Christianity. The first general authoritative condemnation of self-killing comes from Augustine. He argues that self-killing is not permitted to the Christian *under any circumstances*[11] since it is a violation of the Sixth Commandment, "Thou shalt not kill."[12] He admits that God makes exceptions to this commandment—that it is not violated by

> those who have waged wars on the authority of God, or those who have imposed the death-penalty on criminals when representing the authority of the State in accordance with the laws of the State;

these act under a just law sanctioned by God, under the order of someone given authority by God, or by a specific direct command of God. The direct-command exception justifies Abraham, who was ready to kill his son, and, to the point here, Samson: when he

> destroyed himself, with his enemies, by the demolition of the building, this can only be excused on the ground that the Spirit, which performed miracles through him, secretly ordered him to do so.[13]

Similarly, Augustine excuses those women "venerated as martyrs in the Catholic Church" who killed themselves when they were about to be raped by pagans, on the grounds that they were, he supposes, acting under divine instruction; although he admits that it is difficult to tell whether someone is acting in obedience to a secret order direct from God rather than "through a human mistake."[14]

As an explanation of the difference between morally acceptable and unacceptable self-killing, what Augustine says clearly leaves much to be desired. Augustine perhaps helps us get some way in understanding why self-killing is prima-facie wrong (since it is killing and thus forbidden); but, seemingly at a loss to explain the exceptions to this rule, he lamely assumes that God gives special dispensations in those cases in which self-killing is morally acceptable, but can give no reason why that dispensation might have been given—i.e., can cite no feature of those cases which justifies a moral distinction and explains God's special dispensation. Kant argues that

> suicide is not inadmissible and abominable because God has forbidden it; God has forbidden it because it is abominable in that it degrades man's inner worth. . . .[15]

Socrates makes much the same point in more general terms when he argues that it is not the case that an act is just because it is loved by the gods; rather, it's loved by the gods because it's just.[16] One way of taking this point is that the fact that something has religious sanction does not justify or explain the moral evaluation that one wants to give it. Anyway, Augustine was reasoning circularly: the divine order to Samson was not mentioned in the Bible; the only reason Augustine has to think there was one is apparently that he believed Samson's act of self-destruction was morally permitted. Augustine fails, then, to give us any useful distinction between the two sorts of self-destruction, or any reason why we should give different moral evaluations to each sort. All he does is give a strongly worded general condemnation of self-killing:

> What we are saying, asserting, and establishing by all means at our command is this: that no one ought deliberately to bring about his own death . . .[17]

coupled with some unexplained exceptions, made so as not to condemn those who took their own lives but who were, rather, traditionally revered.[18]

Augustine's authority in the Church brought it about that, during the course of succeeding Church councils, his strong general condemnation of self-killing was incorporated into Church doctrine, where it has remained ever since. Aquinas added reasons why self-killing was wrong and made exceptions of exactly those cases Augustine did, quoting Augustine's reasons as the only "justification" of making these exceptions he could give.[19]

Kant, as we have seen, would not call suicides the self-killings he counted as morally acceptable. Kant writes:

There are many circumstances under which life ought to be sacrificed. If I cannot preserve my life except by violating my duties towards myself, I am bound to sacrifice my life rather than violate these duties. But suicide is in no circumstances permissible.[20]

and

Life is not to be highly regarded for its own sake. I should endeavour to preserve my own life only so far as I am worthy to live.[21]

Kant speaks of its being acceptable to *refrain from preserving* one's life (when preservation would also mean violation of duty), but he does not talk of acceptable self-killing as if it were a positive action. He speaks of the soldier who knowingly faces death and dies rather than fleeing, as a "victim of fate"; [22] whereas the unacceptable self-killer "disposes of his person." [23]

We have no right to offer violence to our nature's powers of self-preservation and to upset the wisdom of her arrangements. This duty is upon us until the time comes when God commands us to leave this life. Human beings are sentinels on earth and may not leave their posts until relieved by another beneficent hand.[24]

The hint here is that death may happen to one, but one is never allowed to caused it actively; so perhaps Kant is indicating that the only acceptable "self-killings" (as it were) are passive sufferings of death. He does not, however, explicitly offer this as a criterion to distinguish acceptable and unacceptable self-killings; but Holland does. Attempting to justify his exclusion of the action of Captain Oates from the class of unacceptable self-killings, Holland says that Oates's action can be distinguished from actions in the unacceptable class "at least partly" on the basis of "the distinction between doing and suffering":

If someone objects, "But he [Oates] killed himself," . . . I can say, "No; the blizzard killed him." Had Oates taken out a revolver and shot himself I should have agreed he was a suicide.[25]

Now, for a number of reasons, the "distinction between doing and suffering" will not do the job wanted of it here. Were Oates killed by a blizzard that had caught him by surprise when he wanted to live, and struggled to escape, it would make sense to say that he suffered death and did not act to kill himself; but in the case at hand, he performed an action which he knew would result in his death (leaving the tent and thereby exposing himself to the blizzard) intentionally and voluntarily. Of course, this is what makes it the case that there is an *action* of his, and not simply something happening to him. This try at absolving Oates from self-killing is absurd; Holland himself admits that there are problems with this way of looking at the case. He insists that a man who put his head on the railroad tracks is an unacceptable self-killer (suicide), even though he sees that it could be said of the railroad-track man, paralleling what Holland said of Oates, that he didn't kill himself—the train did it. Holland feels that saying that *this* man didn't kill himself would be a "sophistical absurdity," but nevertheless claims that "the blizzard killed Oates" is an acceptable way of looking at *that* case; yet he fails to give any good reason for looking at these two cases differently.[26]

Now, the *refraining from preventing X* is quite different from the mere *passive suffering of X;* and the former seems somewhat more to the point here. Perhaps what Kant was hinting at in those quotes was that unacceptable self-killings are positive actions and acceptable ones merely refrainings; Margolis, in the previous quote, also speaks in this way. This interpretation is lent some initial plausibility by the fact that a refraining is, at least, something one *does* and not simply what *happens* to him. An acceptable self-killing must at least be an *action.*

Religiously condoned self-killings do tend to take the form of refrainings: religious martyrs often die at the hands of others by refraining from escape or from resistance to their captors, or by starvation (refraining from eating); note also that a rather standard line of moral reasoning within the Catholic tradition would excuse some refrainings with bad effects when positive actions with those same bad effects are blamed. For example, it is sometimes argued that doctors are not permitted to commit euthanasia (e.g., by giving an injection) but may, under some circumstances, refrain from taking certain extraordinary measures to prolong life.[27]

The acting/refraining distinction is not itself without philosophical problems; even were it a clear and readily applicable distinction, however, it would not do what it's supposed to here. For one thing, many of the acceptable cases of self-killing seem to be cases of acting rather than of refraining: Socrates *drank* the hemlock, and Oates *walked* out of the tent. But even if one (perversely) were to construe all the cases counted as acceptable as refrainings and all the unacceptable ones as actings, it seems clear that the distinction wouldn't have the moral relevance needed. T. C. Kane sensibly writes:

> One can cause his own death voluntarily either by a positive act of self-destruction or by refusing or neglecting to do something known to be necessary for the preservation of one's life. The difference between a positive act and an omission is notable from a physical point of view, but it is of little moral consequence. To fail to do something physically and morally necessary to the preservation of life is the moral equivalent of a positive act of self-destruction. A man who bleeds to death because he will not close an open artery is no less a suicide than one who opens an artery with the intent of taking his own life.[28]

Holland continues his attempt to distinguish Oates from unacceptable self-killers by offering the following explanation of why he feels justified in saying "the blizzard killed Oates":

> The indirectness of what [Oates] did in relation to the onset of his death and the entrance of time as a factor are features of the case which help to put it for me in this perspective.[29]

I find it difficult to see how Holland can look at the taking of a long walk alone through an Antarctic blizzard as an "indirect" way of causing death; it is also unclear why the features of indirectness and lapse of time are supposed to reinforce the judgment that his death was a suffering and not an acting. Most central, however, is an objection that Holland himself immediately admits: that indirectness and time lapse may figure to exactly the same extent in the case that he will not excuse: the man who lays his head on the tracks. Holland says that these features, in the railroad-track case, "enter in, but not to the same effect because of the difference in the spirit and in the surroundings of what is done." To explain this he notes that a blizzard is a natural phenomenon and a train not; this, he says, "makes a difference"; but he immediately notes that

> a man who out of sorrow drowns himself might also perhaps be said to expose himself to a natural phenomenon, but again the context and the spirit of it are different.[30]

In what, perhaps, gives a hint of an adequate explanation, Holland adds:

> Oates simply walks away from his companions—and in the act of doing so becomes exposed to the blizzard: he needs to put distance between himself and them and he cannot do so in any other way. He is concerned only with their relief.[31]

Clearer, certainly, and perhaps more initially promising is the account of the difference proposed by Joseph Margolis. Admitting that his characterization may go "counter to some familiar judgments," he proposes that

> the suicide's overriding concern is to end his own life, not for the sake of any independent objective that, in principle, he might pursue in another way . . .[32]

and

> if an agent is presumed rational, then if he takes his own life or allows it to be taken for some further purpose that he serves instrumentally, then we normally refuse to say he has suicided.[33]

This seems relatively straightforward, but Margolis's applications of these criteria throw the matter into confusion. He treats as an example the case of a Buddhist monk who sets fire to himself to protest a war; Margolis assumes that the war might, in principle, have been protested in another way. This seems clearly enough to fit his characterization of nonsuicide; but he says

> he *may* be said to have suicided if resisting the war and influencing his countrymen are judged not to bear on what,

all things considered, proves to be the overriding characterization of what he did; and, if he is said to have suicided even
though he took his life in order to protest the war, then there
is no coherent way to view his act but as an act of protest-
suicide.[34]

I'm not sure I understand the complexities here. It seems to me,
though, if Margolis's criteria are taken at face value, they yield
peculiar results. What he appears to be saying is that suicide
(unacceptable self-killing) is self-killing when one has the intention
of causing his own death as a thing desired for its own sake,
whereas nonsuicide (acceptable self-killing) is self-killing when the
agent's actions are a means to some other end. But applying this in
the only obvious way, it would turn out that almost all cases of self-
killing fall into the second (nonsuicide, acceptable) category; for it
seems almost always to be the case that the person who wants to
kill himself doesn't simply desire death *per se:* rather, he wants to
die for some other reason, e.g., in order to avoid prosecution, to
end the unbearable pain, to teach someone else a lesson, and so
on. But these are exactly the cases that are ordinarily called suicide
and are condemned by the tradition as unacceptable self-killings.

✓ THE DOUBLE-EFFECT PRINCIPLE

The only distinction which roughly divides the examples
considered by the authors we have treated into the categories they
wanted to place them into is the one, recently formulated by
Catholic moralists, called the double-effect principle. The principle is used to distinguish certain cases of actions with bad effects
and good effects as morally permissible. The principle states that
an act which has bad consequences is permissible only when the
following conditions are met:

1. The act itself must be morally good or at least indifferent.
2. The agent may not positively will the bad effect but may
merely permit it. If he could obtain the good effect without the
bad effect, he should do so. The bad effect is sometimes said to be
indirectly voluntary.
3. The good effect must . . . be produced directly by the
action, not by the bad effect. . . .

4. The good effect must be sufficiently desirable to compensate for the allowing of the bad effect.[35]

The principle is intended to provide a halfway ground between a straightforward utilitarianism, which would simply consider the relative weights of the good and bad consequences of an action in order to make a moral judgment of it, and a variety of sterner moral positions, which would either deny the moral relevance of consequences to actions altogether or would judge immoral any action with bad consequences, no matter what other good consequences it had.

To illustrate the application of the principle, let us use the case of the soldier's jumping on the grenade. (1) The act of jumping on a live grenade *itself* (viewed apart from its *effects*, viz., the death of the agent and the saving of his buddies) is morally neutral. (2) The agent, we are to assume, does not "positively will" the bad effect, namely his own death; that is to say, he does not desire that event in and of itself; he would save his buddies without bringing about his own death if he could, but he cannot. (3) The good effect (the saving of his buddies) is produced directly by the action (the jumping on the grenade) and not by the bad effect (the soldier's death). It's not his death which causes them to be saved; it's his jumping on the grenade which causes both their being saved and his death. (4) Several people's being saved from death is sufficiently good (we are to assume) to compensate for the death of one.

The cases that are judged morally unacceptable, by this principle, include those (a) in which death in and of itself is desired; and (b) in which death, although not desired in and of itself, is desired as a means to an end, as a cause, no matter how good the intended effects. The person who shoots himself so that his life insurance policy can be paid to needy beneficiaries would not be justified, in this view, no matter how much good the payment of his life insurance would do—no matter, even, if it saved a dozen lives; for here the good effects (the payment of the policy and the good results of that) *are caused by* the bad effect (the death of the agent); so condition 3 is violated.

Now we can see, perhaps, why Holland wanted to say that Oates cannot be condemned since what he needed was "to put distance between himself and them, and he cannot do so in any other way. He is concerned only with their relief."[36] Holland, I suspect, is trying to indicate that Oates satisfies condition 2—that he doesn't "positively will" his own death. What he "positively wills" is the good result of the action, namely the freeing of the rest from the encumbrance he constituted; and that the only action Oates could have done, under the circumstances, which would have had this good effect was also an action that would lead to his death. This confirms the claim that Oates did not "positively will" his own death, for if there were some other way that Oates could have brought about the good effect and he did the act resulting in his death anyway, it would show that he "positively willed" his own death.[37]

We now can cope also with the case that gave Holland so much trouble—the man who put his head on the railroad tracks—since this case, if we assume the most "normal" set of accompanying circumstances and conditions, would be placed in the category of unacceptable self-killing by application of the double-effect principle. For, we can assume, the agent could not reasonably have intended any results of the action of putting his head there which he desired in themselves, *other* than his death or the results of his death. One could hardly imagine any other results of that act, in a typical case, which would be relevant to the agent's desires.

Margolis's cases now become somewhat clearer, too: "the man who sacrifices his life to save another's" would be exonerated by the principle, provided that it was not his death that caused the other to be saved, and the same for "the patriot who intentionally lays down his life for a cause." The "religious martyr who will not violate his faith," on the other hand, gives us some trouble, e.g., in the cases of Augustine's women who killed themselves to avoid rape by infidels and of the self-immolating Buddhist monk; for here it would seem that the good effect would be an effect of the death of the agent. By and large, however, the principle seems to sort things the way our authors wanted them sorted. This is perhaps the best principle of sorting available; I shall have something to say later concerning why there may be no better one for the cases we have had presented.

In contrast to the other principles of sorting that we have examined, the double-effect principle seems quite clearly statable and unambiguously applicable. The question I shall concentrate on, then, is whether application of the principle provides sufficient grounds for making the right sorts of moral discriminations.

I shall not, for the purposes of this consideration, question the assumption that death of the agent is always, in itself, a *bad* result of the act of self-killing, although this is questionable.[38]

The presentation of two examples of the application of the principle—not, this time, to cases of self-killing—may serve to cast some doubt, for some people, on its moral validity.

Example 1: The principle has sometimes been used to justify the infliction of pain by a doctor on a patient in the course of treatment (a bad result of the doctor's actions), since the cure is worth the pain, there is no less painful cure, the pain is not "directly willed" by the doctor but is rather a tolerated by-product of the treatment, and the pain is not the cause of the cure. Of course, it seems reasonable here to absolve the doctor of guilt for producing pain. But if one *needs* the principle to justify the infliction of pain here, then in a case similar except for the fact that the pain *is* the cause of the cure, the infliction of pain would *not* be justified. For example: some psychologists have had some success in treating tobacco addiction by having smoke blown into the patient's face every time he takes a puff on his cigarette. This extra dose of smoke soon becomes nauseating to the patient, and this pain acts as negative reinforcement to the patient's smoking, causing his future smoking to diminish or stop. The nausea caused by the doctor is a minor pain and the cure is a great good; but since the pain *causes* the cure, condition 3 is violated and the doctor's act is not justified. This is a peculiar moral result, since, I should think, most of us have the moral intuitions that the infliction of pain is justified in both circumstances (since we assume that it's necessary to the cure, the cure is worth it, the patient wants the cure, and so on). This objection to the principle of double effect holds, for a large class of cases involving negative reinforcement.

Example 2: A doctor has three patients, A, B, and C; each has a different failing organ. Patient D is also in the hospital for a checkup; he is found perfectly healthy, but the doctor orders that he be placed under total anesthesia, and while he is unconscious, the doctor removes from him the three healthy organs needed by A, B, and C, and transplants D's healthy ones into A, B, and C. This operation causes the saving from death of A, B, and C; but it also, of course, causes D's death. But the principle applies here: the good effect (the saving of three) is worth the bad effect (the death of one); the bad effect is not "directly willed" by the doctor;

there is no other way (under the circumstances) to get the good effect; and the bad effect does not *cause* the good effect—both are effects of the action of the multiple operation. Many people would, I think, count this as an absurd attempt at moral justification, but it is, I think, a correct application of the principle.[39] These examples cast doubt on the principle by showing the results of its application to be incompatible with some moral intuitions. It seems, then, not to provide grounds for a satisfactory distinction between morally blameworthy and morally permissible suicides.

The principle may be questioned more directly. Several of its presuppositions are at least controversial: the first condition of the principle presupposes the (problematic) distinction between an act itself and that act considered with regard to its consequences; and it assumes a blanket prohibition of all acts that are wrong in themselves, regardless of good consequences. The second condition bases the morality of an act on the will of the agent; this, also, of course, can be debated.

But the central peculiarity of the principle is its third condition: that given satisfaction of the other conditions, an act is permitted if the good and bad consequences were each caused by the act, but forbidden if the good consequences were caused by the bad. The difference is illustrated in the following diagram (in which arrows represent causal connections):

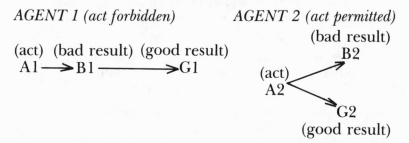

AGENT 1 (act forbidden)   *AGENT 2 (act permitted)*

What seems to be behind this position is the notion that one is forbidden to act on a will to do what's evil; and, it is supposed, Agent 1 wills evil in a way that Agent 2 does not. What is the difference here? Perhaps we are supposed to think that Agent 1 does A1 consciously trying to bring about the bad result, B1, since he knows that this will result, in turn, in the good result, G1; but that Agent 2, on the other hand, does not act trying to bring about B2. He does A2 wholly in order to bring about G2, although he expects and regrets the inevitable by-product of his action, B2. Thus moralists say that Agent 1 *directly wills* B1, whereas Agent 2 only *indirectly wills* B2.

But is there really a moral difference here? It seems to me that, morally speaking, we must put Agents 1 and 2 on exactly the same footing. Neither desires the bad result in itself; each tolerates it only because, under the circumstances, it is necessary for obtaining the good result. Each would have obtained his good result without the bad, had that been possible. There are natural senses of the words in which we can say that neither *wants* his respective bad result; yet each brings it about, unwanted, because of the greater good for which it is necessary. Again, in a different but equally natural sense, we can say that *both* agents want their respective bad results, but that these are only "conditional" wants: both want them only because and insofar as they are necessary for the good.

Why say that Agent 1 wills B1 in some way that Agent 2 does not will B2? The rationale for this may be the supposition that one may will an event only as an end in itself or as a means to (or cause of) something else desired as an end. But it seems to me that these examples show that one may will an event in neither of these ways but instead as merely a condition necessary under the circumstances for an end.

(A third sort of causal setup, incidentally, in which a bad result may be necessary for a good one, is the following:

$$\text{(act)} \qquad \text{(good result)} \qquad \text{(bad result)}$$
$$A3 \longrightarrow G3 \longrightarrow B3$$

I wonder what the principle would say about *this* case?)

My conclusion, then, is that there is no good reason to think of Agent 1 as willing the bad result in a way that Agent 2 does not also. As far as morality is concerned, then, Agent 1 is no worse than Agent 2, and the principle's distinction has no moral relevance.

Concluding Remarks

So far I have been searching through attempts at distinguishing self-killings into two sorts such that there are clear criteria for the distinction, the paradigm examples are sorted as they have traditionally been, and the distinction provides grounds for a putative moral difference. I have claimed that only the principle of double effect gives clear criteria and sorts cases in something like the traditional way, but that it does not provide grounds for a moral distinction. I shall conclude with some remarks concerning the source of this apparent lack of good distinction, and some suggestions on what such a good distinction might be.

I feel that the messiness and inadequacy of the discussions I have dealt with arise from a conflict between two moral dispositions that are incompatible with one another, but both of which, it is intended, the distinction should serve. These two dispositions are: one, that it is felt that killing, perhaps especially self-killing, is absolutely wrong, and so wrong that it is forbidden no matter what good might result from it. This rather theoretical position is contradicted, it seems to me, by the practical judgment that some self-killings are so noble in aim that they must be justifiable and even laudable. This conflict requires a good deal of sophistical squirming to make it seem to disappear; but it seems to me that one must either (implausibly) forbid *all* self-killing or allow self-killing when the extrinsic aims are good enough to override (what we have been assuming to be) the intrinsic badness of the act. I believe, despite the strange maneuvers the debate historically has taken, that it is this latter position that the moralists in the tradition have taken. Examination of the paradigm cases of self-killing shows that, *by and large,* the acceptable ones are cases in which the self-killer had a noble aim—either the accomplishing of some effect of great benefit to others (the soldier who jumped on the grenade, Captain Oates, the person who yields his place in the lifeboat, etc.) or the accomplishing of an act otherwise judged morally good (religious martyrs, hunger strikers). The ones judged morally bad are usually rather selfish in nature: the man who kills himself because he can't stand the physical or mental pain he would otherwise have to suffer. In the familiar, standard moral view, the former cases would be called heroic and generous, the latter selfish and cowardly.

Maurice Van Vyve distinguishes between what he calls acts of *suicide* (unacceptable self-killing) and *sacrifice* (what he has the tendency to think are acceptable acts, despite official Catholic doctrine) thus:

To sacrifice oneself is to accomplish one's duty, to be "engagé" to the end, to renounce life for a greater good; to commit suicide is to give it up out of egoism, to give up in the face of one's duty. Diametrically opposed moral attitudes.[40]

He recognizes that this is not the same distinction as the one made using the double-effect principle. Now, since he feels that the word "suicide" carries with it the implication of moral disapproval, he wants to reserve it for those cases of self-killing which he thinks are to be disapproved of; he excuses (consistently with Catholic doctrine) cases of "indirect" self-killing which satisfy the double-effect criteria, but, in conflict with that doctrine, also excuses "directly willed" self-killing for the greater good; and he still condemns self-killing for selfish motives. He calls the first class of actions "passive sacrifice," the second "active sacrifice," and the third "suicide."

Issues of nomenclature aside, Van Vyve's relevance to us is his intuition that directly willed, unselfish, morally acceptable self-killing is possible. If this is our moral judgment, then the double-effect principle has no relevance—we simply must judge whether the suicide's extrinsic motives were good enough to overrule the prima-facie badness of self-killing, and may ignore altogether the intricacies of direct and indirect volition. I have left untouched the questions of whether self-killing is intrinsically prima-facie bad; and, if it is, what sorts of goods are good enough to overrule this badness. What I am suggesting is that the real distinction between acceptable and unacceptable self-killings be made on the basis of these considerations and not on the basis of any of the rather baroque attempts at distinction made by the authors we have considered. I suggest that the considerations I have offered for distinguishing between acceptable and unacceptable self-killings are in fact the ones we use and the ones that have been responsible, by and large, for the initial sorting out of cases, either explicitly or intuitively. The only reason I can see that these criteria were not accepted by the writers we have looked at as the operative ones is that they wanted the results of their search for criteria to be consistent, somehow, with Augustine's doctrines, which were based on the conflicting desires at once to make *all* self-killing immoral while accepting generous, principled self-killing as laudable.[41]

NOTES

1. Glanville Williams, "Suicide," *The Encyclopedia of Philosophy*, ed. Paul Edwards (New York: Macmillan and The Free Press, 1967), Vol. 8, p. 43.
2. *The Oxford English Dictionary*, Vol. X, p. 121.
3. Edward Westermarck, "Suicide: A Chapter in Comparative Ethics," *The Sociological Review*, Vol. I (1908), p. 12.
4. "Suicide," *Encyclopaedia Brittanica*, Vol. 17, p. 777. Essentially the same definition is given in *Webster's Collegiate Dictionary*, *The American Heritage Dictionary*, and others.
5. B. Rolfe, in *Clift v. Schwabe* (1846) 3.C.B., 464. Cited and affirmed by *In re Davis*, decd. (1968) 1 Q.B., 72.
6. Immanuel Kant, "Suicide," *Lectures on Ethics*, tr. Louis Infield (New York: Harper Torchbooks, 1963), pp. 150–1.
7. R. F. Holland, "Suicide," in *Talk of God*, Royal Institute of Philosophy Lectures (London: Macmillan 1967–68; New York: St. Martin's Press, 1969), p. 75, Vol. 2.
8. Ibid., pp. 78–9.
9. Ibid., p. 79.
10. Margolis, *Negativities* (Columbus, Ohio: Charles E. Merrill, 1973), pp. 23–4, from the chapter on "Suicide."
11. Augustine, *City of God*, Book I, Article 27.
12. Ibid., Article 20.
13. Ibid., Article 21.
14. Ibid., Article 26.
15. Kant, *Lectures on Ethics*, op. cit., p. 154.
16. Plato, *Euthyphro*, 10A–11B.
17. Augustine, *City of God*, Article 26.
18. Some historical background may help explain this curious position. To the very early Christians, life was unimportant and death for the person free from sin meant salvation and bliss; martyrdom especially guaranteed redemption and the attainment of paradise. John Donne reports:

    For that age was growne so hungry and ravenous of [martyrdom], that many were baptized onely because they

> would be burnt, and children taught to vexe and provoke
> Executioners that they might be thrown into the fire.
> *(Biathanatos,* 1646, Part I, Dist. 3, Sect. 2)

Gibbon describes the Donatists, a fourth- and fifth-century
Christian sect, declared heretical largely through the efforts of
Augustine, thus:

> Many of these fanatics were possessed with the horror of
> life and the desire of martyrdom; and they deemed it of
> little moment by what means or by what hands they
> perished, if their conduct was sanctified by the intention
> of devoting themselves to the glory of the true faith and
> the hope of eternal happiness. Sometimes they rudely
> disturbed the festivals and profaned the temples of
> paganism with the design of exciting the most zealous of
> the idolators to revenge the insulted honour of their
> Gods. They sometimes forced their way into the courts of
> justice and compelled the affrighted judge to give orders
> for their execution. They frequently stopped travellers
> on the public highways and obliged them to inflict the
> stroke of martyrdom by promise of a reward, if they
> consented—and by the threat of instant death, if they
> refused to grant so very singular a favour. *(The Decline
> and Fall of the Roman Empire,* Chap. xxi.)

A theory advanced to explain both the earlier flourishing of these
practices and the later efforts of the Church to end them has to do
with practical political advantage: the extreme and fanatic gesture
is appropriate for a revolutionary minority at its struggling
beginnings; but when that group is well established (by Augustine's time), a high birth and survival rate is more important to
its spread.

19. St. Thomas Aquinas, *Summa Theologica,* 2a2ae, 64.5.
20. Kant, *Lectures on Ethics, op. cit.,* p. 151.
21. Ibid., p. 150.
22. Ibid.
23. Ibid., p. 149.
24. Ibid., p. 154.
25. Holland, "Suicide," *op. cit.,* p. 80.

26. Ibid.
27. A good attack on this sort of reasoning is presented by Jonathan Bennett, "Whatever the Consequences" *(Analysis,* 26, 1966).
28. T. C. Kane, "Suicide," in *New Catholic Encyclopedia* (New York: McGraw-Hill, 1967), Vol. XII, p. 782.
29. Holland, "Suicide," *op. cit.,* p. 80.
30. Ibid.
31. Ibid. Holland claims that the condemnation of suicide and the distinction between justified self-killing and suicide are justified by a religious "picture"; he does not, however, succeed in explaining exactly what this "picture" amounts to. In a truly extraordinary passage he allows that the atheist, as well as the believer, might have a negative reaction to someone's shooting himself, but that the atheist's reason could only be that the act "would have been ugly, unpleasant, and messy, and hence a course to be rejected out of fastidiousness" (p. 81).
32. Margolis, *Negativities, op. cit.,* pp. 26–7.
33. Ibid., p. 28.
34. Ibid., p. 27.
35. F. J. Connell, "Principle of Double Effect," *New Catholic Encyclopedia* (New York: McGraw-Hill, 1967), Vol. IV, p. 1021.
36. Holland, "Suicide," *op. cit.,* p. 80.
37. Closer examination of the case, however, raises doubts whether even this works. It was, after all, his *death,* not his walking out of the tent, that resulted in the disencumbering of his party; for if they had not known him to be dead, they would, we expect, have searched for him and thus have lost still more time from forward progress.
38. I have argued against this assumption in an address to the meetings of the Canadian Philosophical Association, June 1975, revised portions of which appear in this volume under the title "Suicide and False Desires."
39. This example was used against the principle in the discussions by Leonard Geddes, "On the Intrinsic Wrongness of Killing Innocent People," *Analysis,* 33, no. 3 (January, 1973), pp. 93–7, and R.A. Duff, "Intentionally Killing the Innocent," *Analysis* 34, no. 1 (October 1973), pp. 16–19. James G. Hanink. ("Some Light on Double Effect," *Analysis* 35, no 5 [April, 1975], pp. 147–151) argues that it misapplies the principle; I don't agree, but I can't go into this debate here.

40. "La notion de suicide," *Revue Philosophique de Louvain,* 52, no. 36 (1954), p. 603, my translation.
41. The author wishes to express his gratitude to his colleague, Dr. Susan Sherwin, for suggestions and criticisms that have greatly influenced this article.

The
Morality of
Suicide

SUICIDE: SOME THEOLOGICAL REFLECTIONS

P. R. Baelz

Speaking from a Christian perspective, Baelz reviews the traditional moral religious objections to suicide. He argues that although suicide is often a kind of killing which we must condemn, like murder, it may also sometimes be a kind of killing, like that done in self-defense, which may be morally permissible, particularly when circumstances threaten to destroy a man's humanity before death itself supervenes. His article contains an extensive review of both the theological and secular arguments traditionally employed to oppose suicide.

Educated at Dulwich College, Cambridge, the Rev. Canon P. R. Baelz has been Fellow and Dean of Jesus College, Cambridge; University Lecturer in Divinity at Cambridge; and has recently moved from Oxford, where he was Canon of Christ Church and Regius Professor of Moral and Pastoral Theology, to become Dean of Durham. His publications include Prayer and Providence *(1968),* Christian Theology and Metaphysics *(1968),* The Forgotten Dream *(1975), and* Ethics and Belief *(1977).*

"A strong feeling against suicide seems to be the spontaneous deliverance of moral consciousness, wherever the Christian view of life, with its ideas of discipline, education, or moral probation, and its sense of responsibility to a divine Father, is accepted." [1]

71

Rashdall's judgment cannot be gainsaid. Such a feeling has been general, if not universal. Furthermore, it has persisted even in some of those who have been unable to find a reasonable basis for it. By and large Christians have felt a moral repugnance to suicide, even though they have also felt a moral regard for a willingness to go to certain death as an act of martyrdom or of self-sacrifice for a greater good. Nor are such feelings to be despised simply because they are feelings. They may reflect a certain sensitivity to moral dimensions which have not yet been brought to the level of explicit understanding. It is not necessarily irrational to believe something to be the case even though no reasons are immediately forthcoming. On the other hand our feelings are not infallible guides to right action. They need to be carefully and continually scrutinized. If they arise within an outlook on life which is governed by a distinctive set of beliefs, it is important to test both the connections between feelings and beliefs and the validity of the beliefs themselves. Our feelings have the habit of persisting even when we no longer hold to the beliefs which originally supported them. Again, they may get attached, as it were, to the wrong object. For example, they may get attached to certain specific actions which in certain circumstances expressed certain values but which in other circumstances no longer express these same values, and in such a case we might wish to say that the proper object of the feelings was the set of values rather than the species of action. In short, our moral feelings are an essential part of our moral equipment, but moral reflection is no less necessary for the good life.

Sometimes it is thought sufficient, in order to rule out suicide, simply to appeal to a principle of the sanctity of life, a principle which most men might be expected, in theory if not in practice, to espouse. Such an appeal, however, marks the beginning rather than the end of argument. First, the principle must presumably be narrowed to the sanctity of *human* life. Immediately we face the problem what is to count as human life. Is it to be defined in biological terms or in personal terms? If the former, then perhaps after all we ought to extend the principle to cover animal as well as human life. If the latter, then we shall find ourselves asking the question whether there are stages in the development and decline of the human animal when it is not or no longer a human person. I raise these questions only to show that the principle of the sanctity of life is not as clear as it first appears to be. Secondly, the principle itself is often admitted to allow exceptions. In certain circumstances it is generally reckoned permissible to take life, for example, in self-defence, in the pursuit of a just war, or even in capital punishment. In the last instance there has been a gradual change in moral judgment. Many people no longer believe that capital punishment is morally justifiable. Human life ought not to be taken unless there are morally good reasons for taking it, and the alleged reasons for capital punishment are no longer held to be morally persuasive. Thirdly, an appeal to the sanctity of human life may mean no more than that human life ought not to be taken unless there are morally persuasive reasons for taking it. This does not at once rule out suicide, although it does place the *onus probandi* on anyone who would wish to affirm the moral permissibility of suicide in certain circumstances. On the other hand it may implicitly be appealing to certain theological considerations. The original meaning of the word "sanctity" certainly suggests that this is the case. The task then is to draw out these theological considerations and to make as clear as possible precisely what they are.

Christians have not always explicitly condemned suicide. For example, there is no such explicit condemnation in the New Testament.[2] But silence should not be counted as consent. It is possible that the matter did not seem to call for any moral comment. It may not have arisen. Or the contemporary Jewish condemnation of suicide, if such there was, as indeed seems to be the case, may have been taken over by the early Christians without question. We cannot be certain. Furthermore, we must be careful not to draw the wrong conclusions from the fact, if fact it is, that the early explicit condemnation of suicide by Christian writers was occasioned by a wholesale rejection of a pagan way of life in which suicide was permitted if not encouraged, or by a movement among certain groups of Christians to court death in order to win a martyr's crown, fleeing this evil world for the joys of heaven. The condemnation of suicide may indeed have been occasioned by circumstances which no longer obtain, but reasons were given by Augustine and others for such condemnation, and it is the validity of these reasons which must be examined. They may hold good even though circumstances have changed. Continuity and development are features of Christian moral insight as they are of non-Christian moral insight. Experience and reflection may lead to change in moral judgment or it may not. A simple appeal to history will not settle a moral issue.

Various types of reason have been given for the condemnation of suicide. Since Christians have not usually claimed a monopoly of moral insight, they have availed themselves of arguments which have their origin in a non-Christian context as well as of arguments which are specifically Christian. Let us, for convenience sake, call the first group of arguments secular and the second group Christian.

The secular arguments can be summarized under two main headings—first, that suicide is wrong because it is contrary to self-love; and secondly, that it is wrong because it is an offence against society. Neither set of arguments seems to be compelling.

As regards self-love, it might be argued that suicide, far from being contrary to self-love, is in fact an inordinate expression of it to the exclusion of all other claims. In fact, some forms of suicide have been condemned on the charge of selfishness. It may be admitted that human beings have a strong instinct for self-preservation and that to that extent suicide is "unnatural." But the instinct of avoiding pain is equally deep-rooted and, if we are to believe Freud, there may even be a "natural" death-wish in human beings. Furthermore, it is not easy to see how moral judgments are to be derived from the presence or absence of instincts. These may provide the material for moral judgments, but in what sense do they provide the norms? There has been a long and venerable tradition in the history of Christian moral theology which has developed the idea that reflection on the given nature of man can provide us with a notion of man's proper end and that from this notion can be deduced certain moral conclusions concerning what he may or may not do as he follows or deviates from the path which leads to that end. His freedom of choice is morally circumscribed by what nature or the Lord of nature intends him to be. Thus certain types of action can be proscribed as contrary to nature. This tradition of Natural Law is highly complex and cannot be assessed in a few words. My own view is that, despite its difficulties, it ought not to be completely rejected. We must have some notion of what it is to be a proper man, and empirical facts are highly relevant to any such notion which is to command our respect. However, it must be admitted that the further we proceed from general principles to the consideration of specific types of

action, the more room there is for honest disagreement. And
theologians have themselves on occasion admitted that the resources of revelation may be needed in order to understand
clearly what the Natural Law dictates. If Stoics believed that
suicide might be according to reason and so according to nature, it
would appear that the decisive considerations lay with the total
view of man, the world and God rather than directly with the
more obvious empirical facts of man's physical and psychological
make-up.

The second set of arguments is based on the view that suicide
is an offence against society. This may be taken in a variety of
ways. It may be taken to mean no more than that a man has
certain obligations to others which override any desire that he may
himself have to take his own life. If so, the nature and extent of
these obligations must be spelled out in detail and their strength
assessed. Or it may be taken to mean that individuals belong to
something greater than themselves called Society, that their very
existence in some sense or other augments the greatness of
Society, and that only Society has the right to dispose of the lives
of its members. Such a view is incompatible with a belief that the
individual has certain rights of his own by virtue of his humanity
rather than by derivation from the allegedly prior and essential
rights of Society. There may be a conflict of claims, but if there is
then each conflict has to be examined on its own merits and no
appeal to the rights of Society will automatically settle the issue.
However we may interpret the notion of an offence against
society, it is not easy to see that in all conceivable or even likely
cases the suicide of one is bound to cause harm to others.
"Suppose that it is no longer in my power to promote the interest
of society; suppose that I am a burden to it; suppose that my life
hinders some person from being more useful to society: in such
cases, my resignation of life must not only be innocent, but
laudable."[3] Such arguments as Hume's are not easy to rebut, at
least in the ethical framework in which Hume operates. Consequently most Christian writers have argued against suicide from
within a framework of Christian belief and have urged that it is
always against the will of God. Dietrich Bonhoeffer went so far as
to affirm: "It becomes quite clear that a purely moral judgment on
suicide is impossible, and indeed that suicide has nothing to fear
from an atheistic ethic. The right to suicide is nullified only by the
living God."[4] This may be something of an exaggeration. There

are what may be called common-sense moral arguments against suicide, but it may well be concluded that these are not valid in all circumstances. Before moving to the specifically theological scene we shall mention one or two of such common-sense considerations.

For example, suicide may be condemned as an act of cowardice. This, however, is not so much to condemn the act of suicide as such as the motive from which it is committed. It is the agent who is to be blamed. But suppose that it were the case, as surely it might be, that the agent's motives were not cowardly, would suicide in that case be permissible or even praiseworthy? Even were the suicide deliberately escaping from present or expected pains, it would still remain an open question whether his action were cowardly or not. Cowardice is partly an evaluative term, not a straightforwardly descriptive one. The coward runs away from situations which he *ought not* to run away from. To run away from some situations may be a sign of prudence rather than of cowardice. Discretion is the better part of valour! And when it comes to the pains of death, which everyone would agree ought to be alleviated as far as possible, accusations of cowardice may well be thought to be beside the point. Having said this, I cannot forbear quoting the remark of W. R. Inge, who ended his arguments in favour of modifying the traditional Christian view of suicide with the confession: "At the same time I hope, inconsistently perhaps, that if I were attacked by a painful illness I should have patience to wait for the end, and I do not think I should wish anyone near and dear to me to act otherwise." [5]

Other common-sense objections are that suicide is irrevocable, or that would-be suicides have later recovered their *joie de vivre* and have been glad that they did not put the idea into action. It may be concluded from these considerations that suicide ought in general to be discouraged, since the future course of our lives is never completely predictable. It may also be argued that suicide ought in all cases to be ruled out of court, on the grounds that more good will be achieved in this way than if the decision were left to the individual who might more often than not misjudge the situation. On the other hand it is difficult to resist the suggestion that now or in the future there may be *some* cases in which, for example, medical prognosis concerning the nature and progress of a terminal illness may be as good as certain. In such cases, if suicide is irrevocable and final, so too is death itself.

To my mind the strongest common-sense argument against suicide is that it would cause injury to others. That we ought to consider others as well as ourselves is a fundamental principle of morality. Who these "others" are, the extent of their claims upon us, the nature of the "injury" which a suicide might cause, are all debatable matters. Different people will judge differently. In some cases the injury done to others may be accounted minimal, in others grave. But if we are to decide the morality of suicide after this fashion, what are we to say in cases in which it might be argued that suicide would be of benefit to others, that they might thereby be released from an intolerable burden? Would it in such cases become permissible or even obligatory? On a strictly utilitarian scheme of ethics it is difficult to avoid answering this question in the affirmative. The action is justified by the end it subserves. Suicide becomes self-sacrifice. But are there not limits to this utilitarian procedure? Are there not actions, for example, dehumanizing actions, which ought to be forbidden even though it appears that the consequences of so acting will produce greater good than the consequences of refraining from the action? Might not the person for whose sake I am prepared to take my own life say to me that there are some burdens, even "intolerable burdens," which he would rather not do without if the only alternative is to be relieved of them by my suicide? Some burdens we may be willing to accept out of love. We may go on to reflect that it is morally right to accept them out of loyalty, and in so doing we may reject certain ways of getting rid of these burdens as morally wrong. What I am suggesting is that in human relationships there are "canons of loyalty" which should guide our moral decisions, and that these may be more fundamental than the utilitarian is prepared to admit. The texture of our common life is made up not only of utilitarian considerations, but also of covenanted relationships which are held to be good in themselves and to be the expression of our fundamental humanity. To call attention to these relationships does not immediately answer the moral question concerning suicide. It does, however, I suggest, put it in a somewhat different light. If, furthermore, as Christians believe, men stand in a covenanted relationship with God who is both their Creator and their Redeemer, it may be that suicide begins to take on a rather different aspect from any which we have so far considered. To these distinctively theological matters we must consequently now turn.

In the main Christians have believed that suicide is an act of disobedience or disloyalty towards God, to whom they have given their unqualified allegiance. The will of God is for them in all things paramount. But how in general do they claim to know what the will of the Lord is, and on what grounds in particular do they believe that he has proscribed the act of suicide?

Appeal may be made to the scriptures, or to natural law, or to the teaching authority of the Church. Of these the appeal to the scriptures is primary. Even the Roman Catholic communion, which places greater weight than other communions on the magisterial office of the Church, will wish to affirm that its authoritative moral pronouncements have their origin and basis in the scriptures—they are not simply self-authenticating. Natural law, too, as we have already seen, requires the illumination of the scriptures if the power of reason is to operate without impediment. The scriptures, then, are fundamental. But what do the scriptures tell us?

The interpretation of the scriptures is a vexed question which it is impossible even to attempt to deal with here. Their study by critical and historical methods has not left them untouched. For most if not all Christians they remain authoritative, but the precise nature of that authority is a matter on which differing views are held. Even were we to continue to look upon them as the express words of God, containing his commandments and ordinances, the question of suicide would not be immediately settled. As has been frequently pointed out, there is no explicit condemnation of suicide to be found in them. Augustine, among others, argued that suicide was contrary to the sixth commandment, "Thou shalt do no murder," but it is open to question whether suicide was included under that prohibition. To call suicide self-murder is but to beg the question. And even Augustine had to admit to the possibility of exceptions to the general proscription of suicide. In the case of Samson he appealed to a special divine ordinance superseding but not in general abrogating the sixth commandment. His detractors might say that he was thereby making the best of a bad case! A further argument which Augustine used was that suicide precluded the possibility of repentance; but to this it may be replied, without any appeal to unknown opportunities for repentance in an after-life, that if suicide is not divinely forbidden, no repentance is called for. Again, the question is begged.

More common today than an immediate appeal to the

scriptures is an appeal through the scriptures, for example, to the doctrine of God as Creator. The doctrine in itself does not seem to carry with it any moral commands or prohibitions. No immediate deductions concerning the moral life can be compellingly made. But it is said that since God is our Creator, it is not for us to determine the bounds of our mortal life. "The Lord giveth, the Lord taketh away: blessed be the name of the Lord." Here we must tread cautiously. Certainly Christians will want to say that life, as the whole created order, is a gift from God and ultimately depends on him. On the other hand they will equally want to say that men are called to exercise their freedom responsibly under God and to be his "fellow-workers." The problem concerns the bounds which their obedience to God and dependence on him place upon the exercise of their freedom. These bounds have been drawn differently in different ages. Take the parallel doctrine of God as Provider. It was once argued that God set each of us in his appointed social station, and that this set limits to the sphere in which he might exercise his responsible Christian liberty. Few would espouse such a view today. Furthermore, most Christians would agree that it is right to have some say in the question when another human life should begin. They accept the claims of responsible parenthood, even if they may differ concerning the ways in which such responsibility is to be exercised. Nor is there any objection to attempts to prolong life beyond the normal span of threescore years and ten, or even fourscore years. That God is our Creator, that there is a dimension of sheer givenness to all creaturely existence, that we owe him the allegiance of heart and mind—these are all important and basic Christian beliefs; but they do not tell us in what ways it is fitting that we should express our allegiance, nor do they mark out what is right and what is wrong in any specific situation. Further principles are necessary. It is the task of moral theology to set forth these principles and to suggest their application. In the end in any particular situation the individual must exercise his own conscientious judgment and make his own moral decision. There are wide differences of opinion not only between different Churches, but also between different moral theologians within the same Church, concerning the way in which the interplay of doctrine, principle and individual judgment is to be understood.

With a Christian context the doctrine of God as Creator is given fuller meaning in relation to the further doctrines of God as

Redeemer and Sanctifier. In particular, the concept of the divine will is given further characterization in terms of the person, work and teaching of Jesus Christ. The nature of the divine activity and of the human response appropriate to such activity finds perfect expression in this man. Thus God is love, Father of Jesus Christ, and those who recognize him as such are called to offer a fitting response of loving obedience in relation to him and of loving care in relation to their fellow-men. Love embodied and exemplified in Jesus Christ—such is the ultimate norm of responsible Christian commitment. But how such love shall be expressed in the particular decisions confronting men and women in concrete, complex and sometimes tragic situations is a question which admits of no agreed answer.

There are those who would argue that love is not only the ultimate norm but also the only principle to which appeal needs to be made. If this means more than an appeal to intention and motive—and however important these may be they cannot in themselves determine the morality of an action—it would seem to mean that any action is morally justifiable if its consequences are such that love would approve them in preference to the consequences of any other possible action. However, it is by no means always clear what ends love dictates. Nor is it certain that consequences, either actual or expected, are the only relevant considerations in judging the morality of a particular action. The emphasis on persons rather than rules is salutary; but persons inhabit a world of relationships, and loyalty to these personal structures may proscribe some actions whatever their apparent consequences. It is not for nothing that we speak of some actions as inhuman. Perhaps within a Christian context we should speak of others as ungodly. If suicide were such as to deny the fundamental relational structure between man and God, then suicide might be an action to be universally forbidden. Serious moral reflection demands a careful discrimination between different types of action which might at first glance appear identical. For example, we discriminate between different kinds of homicide, between, say, murder on the one hand and killing in self-defence on the other. The question to hand is precisely what are the characteristics of suicide, itself a form of homicide, and what is our moral evaluation of these characteristics. Is it a kind of killing which we must condemn, like murder, or is it a kind of killing which may be morally permissible, like killing in self-defence?

To explore this issue we have to ask how death itself is to be characterized within a horizon of Christian meaning. It is not simply a natural occurrence, although it is certainly that, and in terms of nature it may even be said that death serves life and to that extent is good, for in dying living things make room for other living things. Nor from a Christian viewpoint is it possible to claim an inalienable right to death on the grounds that my life is my own and I may do with it whatsoever I please. In death as in life a Christian has to do with God. Death has a godward dimension as well as manward and natural dimensions. How, then, is a Christian to understand it?

One line of thought has proceeded on the assumption that death, at least man's death, is the divinely appointed consequence of sin. It is possible to argue on that basis that, if death is a punishment for sin, it is not for the sinner to anticipate that punishment and make himself his own executioner, thus "cheating justice." An argument like this, however, depends for its validity on a highly doubtful concept of the justice of God, and we need not consider it any further.

Nevertheless, it may still represent a valid insight to describe death as man's "last enemy." It is the final disordering and destruction of a human being and his world. Thus "the Christian . . . accepts death as that signal occasion when he is finally to prove the love and power of God in Christ. He sees death as the last and crucial occasion for the testing of his faith, where victory is to be won in Christ and his redemption fulfilled."[6] Because death is the destruction of himself and all his powers the faith which conquers death must be a faith which throws itself entirely upon the being and love of God, a faith which finds a meaning in death not in anything which man can achieve but only in what God can achieve. Adherence to God is through acceptance and passivity. "At that last moment when I feel I am losing hold of myself and am absolutely passive within the hands of the great unknown forces that have formed me . . . O God, grant that I may understand that it is You (provided only my faith is strong enough) who are painfully parting the fibres of my being in order to penetrate to the very marrow of my substance and bear me away within Yourself."[7]

For the Christian, then, death signifies the ultimate helplessness of man before God and his ultimate dependence on God. His faith bids him wait upon God in patience and hope. It is this insight, I suggest, that finds expression in W. R. Inge's hope, quoted above, "that if I were attacked by a painful illness I should have patience to wait for the end, and I do not think I should wish anyone near and dear to me to act otherwise." Quite clearly suicide might in certain instances be the expression of a refusal to trust in God, an embracing of death for its own sake, a form of self-justification, a desertion to the enemy. A final act of despair is substituted for a waiting in hope. If such is the intrinsic character of deliberate suicide, it can readily be understood why it has been forbidden in the Christian tradition. But has it necessarily this character?

This is not an easy question to answer. It might be argued that, if death ought for the Christian to be a passion, something that he undergoes in utter dependence on God, then suicide, which makes of death an action, something that he performs himself in his own freedom, is *ipso facto* wrong, whether it expresses a deliberate rejection of God or not. It is not the motive which makes the action wrong: it is wrong in itself, whatever the motive. In face of death all other considerations should give way to a simple and faithful waiting on the course of events. Certainly a man should act with prudence and concern for others in preparing for death. Equally certainly everything should be done to alleviate the pains of death. But when the time to die comes all action should yield to passive dependence upon God. Was not this the way in which Jesus himself suffered unto death and "learned obedience"?

To this it might be replied that the reality of our ultimate dependence upon God is not impugned by the responsible exercise of our freedom of choice. The dialectic of freedom and dependence, of action and passion, of doing and suffering, is far more subtle than has been suggested. Certainly in death there is a final passion, and for victory over death we must wait upon God. But does this necessarily mean that we must in all circumstances wait upon the course of events which we call dying? If it is certain that the natural course of events will result in my being robbed of my proper humanity through the onset of pains greater than I can bear or the degradations of imbecility, is a decision to end my life before nature does it for me incompatible with my acknowledging my ultimate and total dependence on God? If my disintegration as a human being occurs before death, is there still any sense in speaking of either action or passion, self-determination or waiting on God?

If a Christian is convinced that suicide is in all cases a contravention of the declared law of God or of the canons of loyalty which the structure of our relationship with God prescribes, then he must eschew even the thought of suicide. If, however, he is not convinced that either is necessarily the case, then he must attempt to specify the conditions under which it is permissible. Alternatively, he may decide that although suicide is not in itself necessarily a failure of loyalty to God or a declaration of our duty towards him, the risk of its being an expression of such disloyalty or disobedience is so great that it ought to be universally forbidden. If he thinks it right to attempt to specify conditions under which it may be permitted, it is likely that he will wish to circumscribe these with considerable stringency, limiting them to cases in which the process of dying threatens to destroy a man's humanity before death itself supervenes. . . .

N O T E S

1. Hastings Rashdall, *The Theory of Good and Evil* (Oxford: Clarendon Press, 1906), Vol. I, p. 210.
2. Even the suicide of Judas, if such it was (but cf. Acts I:18f. with Matt. 27:5), is not explicitly condemned. It was his betrayal of Jesus rather than the manner of his death which constituted his grave sin and evoked the real horror.
3. David Hume, "On Suicide," *The Philosophical Works of David Hume* (Edinburgh: Printed for A. Black and W. Tait, 1826), Vol. IV, p. 566.
4. *Ethics*, ed. Eberhard Bethge (New York: Macmillan, 1965), p. 172.
5. *Christian Ethics and Modern Problems* (New York, London: G. P. Putnam's Sons, 1930), p. 373.
6. Archbishop of Canterbury, *Ought Suicide to Be a Crime?* (Westminster: The Church Information Office, 1959), p. 28.
7. Pierre Teilhard de Chardin, *Le Milieu Divin* (Paris: Éditions du Seuil, 1957), pp. 69f.

SUICIDE AND COVENANT

Karen Lebacqz and H. Tristram Engelhardt, Jr.

Claiming on libertarian grounds that persons might have a prima facie *right to commit suicide, Lebacqz and Engelhardt maintain that this right is nevertheless usually overridden by contravening duties, which grow out of our covenantal relations with others. However, there may be a right to suicide in at least three kinds of cases: voluntary euthanasia, "covenantal" suicide, and symbolic protest, for in these cases suicide would affirm the covenants we have with others.*

Karen Lebacqz is associate professor of Christian ethics at the Pacific School of Religion and is a former member of the National Commission for the Protection of Human Subjects of Biomedical and Behavioral Research. H. Tristram Engelhardt, Jr. is Rosemary Kennedy Professor of the philosophy of medicine at the Kennedy Institute of Ethics, Georgetown University; he is author of Mind/Body: A Categorical Relation *(Martinus Nijhoff, 1973) and coeditor of the series* Philosophy in Medicine *(D. Reidel).*

At a fundamental level, questions of the ethical acceptability of suicide are questions of the value of life and the dignity of freedom. . . . Our argument is simply this: That which gives humans their unique worth is the fact that they can be respected, blamed or praised for their actions because they are rational free agents.[1] Respect for persons as free moral agents should entail that they be allowed to choose that which endows their lives with meaning as long as such choice will not seriously affect the freedoms of others or violate prior agreements between persons. That is, persons have a *prima facie* right to seek out their own values. The right is a *"prima facie"* one in this sense: persons are to be held to have that right until there is evidence to the contrary— e.g., covenants by which they cede some liberty.

With respect to suicide, therefore, we hold that persons are the best judges of the proper balance of values in their lives. An element of respecting others is respecting their right to take their lives in the absence of any contravening duties. Persons should be permitted to take their own lives when they have chosen to do so freely and rationally and when there are no other duties which would override this freedom.

There is thus nothing in principle morally wrong with suicide.[2] But to say that one has a *prima facie* right to take one's own life is not to say that it is always morally justifiable to do so. It means rather that one has a right to take one's life until a contravening moral obligation obtains. The question of suicide is therefore at root a question of distributive justice— of the proper distribution of benefits and burdens, the proper balancing of personal good and social obligation.

As human beings, we exist in mutual relationships of responsibility. Perhaps the strongest reason that can be given in opposition to suicide is that it violates our covenantal obligations to others. It breaks through the faithfulness we owe to those around us. A critic might agree with us, therefore, that there is a *prima facie* right to kill oneself, but might argue that the right to suicide is nonetheless always defeated by the claims of others.

This argument does not turn on whether bad consequences follow from the act of suicide. It is not a consequentialist or teleological argument. . . . Rather, the argument is that suicide is wrong because it violates certain *prima facie* duties of covenant-fidelity—such as gratitude, promise-keeping, and reparations. For example, parents choosing to have children make an implicit promise to provide for them, just as children who are provided for have obligations of gratitude to their parents. Suicide destroys the possibility of keeping the promise to care or the obligation of showing gratitude. Insofar as it violates these duties the right to suicide is overridden.[3] Suicide is wrong when it violates obligations of covenant-fidelity.

If suicide is wrong when it violates obligations of covenant-fidelity, then it may be right when it does not violate such obligations. We propose that there are at least three circumstances in which suicide might be right.

1. Voluntary Euthanasia. There are circumstances in which normal obligations of covenant-fidelity cease because their fulfill-ment is impossible.[4] Under certain life circumstances, such as terminal illness accompanied by great pain, it may be impossible to fulfill normal covenant obligations to one's family and friends. If so, these obligations cease and thus the right to dispose of one's own life is not contravened by any restraining duties. In these circumstances, the right to suicide cannot be defeated because the circumstances themselves defeat the possibility of fulfilling any obligation to others.[5]

2. "Covenantal" Suicide. If the first instance in which suicide is morally justifiable is that in which covenantal obligations cease to exist, the second is that where the suicide itself fosters rather than violates covenantal obligations. Suicide need not be covenant-breaking; it can be covenant-affirming.

There are two types of covenant-affirming suicide. The first is the "suicide pact" or joint suicide in which marriage partners, close friends, or others who live in covenantal relationship bind themselves "even unto death." The second is the "self-sacrificial" suicide of one who chooses to die rather than to burden her family or friends.[6] (For example, one who kills herself rather than deplete family resources with expensive medical treatment affirms the covenant with her family in so doing.)

Whether any particular instance of "covenantal" suicide is justifiable depends on the extent to which it fulfills rather than violates other covenantal obligations. An act of suicide which fosters some covenants at the expense of others might still be wrong. But in cases where the act does not violate the *prima facie* duty of covenant-fidelity, it is not *prima facie* wrong.

3. "Symbolic Protest." In the first two instances of justifiable suicide, the suicide was not judged to be wrong either because the duty of covenant-fidelity ceased or because it was supported by suicide. But are there any cases where the suicide appears to violate covenants but may yet be justifiable? We propose that there is at least one such case: that of suicide as "symbolic protest." Suicide is occasionally used as an act of symbolic protest against great evil and injustice—e.g., against war or imprisonment—and

is meant to support in a radical fashion respect for persons generally.[7]

In such cases, suicide appears to violate one's immediate obligations of covenant-fidelity, since family and friends may be abandoned in order to make symbolic protest. However, the intention of the act is to protest those institutions and structures which undermine the very conditions that make human life and covenant-fidelity possible. When suicide as symbolic protest provides a significant contribution to the struggle against forces which would destroy the freedom of others, taking one's own life can be at root an affirmation of the dignity of persons.[8] We might say that in this form of suicide, the individual aligns herself with more basic loyalties than those to family and friends—namely the community of moral agents. The need to struggle for justice may in circumstances be more compelling than obligations to one's immediate family and friends.[9]

Viewed within the perspective of justice, therefore, there are at least three instances in which suicide may be right: Those in which *prima facie* obligations of covenant-fidelity cease to exist, those in which the suicide fulfills *prima facie* obligations of covenant-fidelity, and those in which obligations of covenant-fidelity are superseded by demands of justice on a larger scale.[10]

NOTES

1. To say this is not to deny the value of human life *per se* but to suggest that the meaning of human life goes beyond mere physical existence. We take moral agency and covenant-fidelity as central to the meaning of human life. (Cf. Paul Ramsey, *The Patient as Person* [New Haven, Conn.: Yale University Press, 1970], p. xii: "covenant-fidelity is the inner meaning and purpose of our creation as human beings.")

2. In the preceding portions of this paper, not included in this volume, Lebacqz and Engelhardt have surveyed the major teleological and deontological arguments against suicide, and have concluded that general arguments against suicide do not succeed.—Ed.

3. It is for this reason that Brandt (this volume, p. 117) suggests

that suicide is not simply a choice of one's own future, but a choice of "world" futures. In choosing to foreclose certain future states for oneself, one also chooses to alter the nature of one's covenantal relationships. Suicide therefore points to the nature of human relationships. The central theological problem raised by suicide is not death *per se,* but abandonment, or breach of covenant-fidelity.

4. Sir William David Ross, *Foundations of Ethics* (London: Oxford University Press, 1939), p. 109.

5. Our position here stands in sharp contradistinction to that of Eike-Henner Kluge *(The Practice of Death* [New Haven, Yale University Press, 1975], p. 121), who claims that suicide is morally justifiable only when the life of the individual is, in her own eyes, "unwanted and unliveable." To say, as we do here, that one's situation is such that one cannot fulfill covenant obligations is not to say that life has ceased altogether to have value or that the remaining life of the individual is "not worth living." An individual may affirm the value of her life and yet choose freely to end it provided that there are no restraining duties.

6. Because of the importance of covenant-fidelity, however, we would agree with Michael Walzer ("Consenting to One's Own Death: The Case of Brutus," in Marvin Kohl, ed., *Beneficent Euthanasia* [New York: Prometheus, 1975], p. 104), that the concurrence of friends and others with whom one stands in covenantal relationship should be sought.

7. Such acts of symbolic protest should not be labelled irrational: "The broad evidence suggests that those who go on hunger strikes [in jail] are well aware of what they are doing and in fact pursue their course even to the point of death in order to exert pressure on their captors and to bear witness to something they believe to be important." (T. Beeson, "Sacrificial Suicides," *Christian Century* 91 [Sept. 18, 1974], p. 836.)

8. J. D. McCaughey, in "Suicide: Some Theological Considerations," *Theology* 70 (Feb. 1967), p. 68, argues that Christians should be cautious about suicide because as Christians they are called to affirm life and resurrection over death and destruction. The kind of suicide described here is precisely such an affirmation. Not all suicide, therefore, is a denial of faith. (Cf. L. V. Stein, "Faith, Hope and Suicide," *Journal of Religion and Health* 10 [July 1971], p. 216.)

9. Though it may be permissible to take one's life in such circumstances, it does not follow that it is obligatory. It is one thing to hold that one always has a right to contribute to the general good of moral agents, but it is not obligatory to give one's life as a contribution. Giving one's life is generally regarded as an act of supererogation, not of obligation.

10. Our position is more restrictive than that proposed by Bertram and Elsie Bandman ("Rights, Justice and Euthanasia," in Kohl, *Beneficent Euthanasia*). They argue that rational persons have the right to decide to live or die, and that only another's right to live outweighs one's right to decide to die. Thus suicide is wrong *only* if another is dependent on one for life itself. This prohibition of suicide is very limited. There are very few instances in which others are dependent on oneself *alone* for their continued existence. The *prima facie* obligation of covenant-fidelity proposed here encompasses more than the physical survival of one's dependents, and thus the requirements of distributive justice are more restrictive than those proposed by the Bandmans.

APOLOGIA FOR SUICIDE

Mary Rose Barrington

Barrington, an advocate of rational suicide and the notion of "planned death," argues that humane and advanced societies must embrace this notion—much as traditional pride in extensive procreation has given way to the concept of planned birth—in a world increasingly crowded, and increasingly populated by those who are old and no longer have great desire to live. She argues in detail for the psychological comfort the notion of "planned death" would give to the elderly, who might foresee and welcome their own deaths rather than waiting to be "passively suppressed."

Mary Rose Barrington is a Solicitor of the Supreme Court of Judicature of England, and the administrator of a group of almshouses for the aged. She is a past chairman of the London-based Voluntary Euthanasia Society (now re-named EXIT—The Society for the Right to Die with Dignity) and honorary secretary of the Animal Rights Group.

Of the many disagreeable features inherent in the human condition, none is more unpalatable than mortality. Many people declare that they find the concept of survival and immortal life both inconceivable and preposterous; but they will usually admit to a minimal pang at the thought of being snuffed out in due course and playing no further part in the aeons to come. That aeons have already passed before they were born is a matter that few people take to heart, and they tend on the whole to be rather glad not to have experienced the hardships of life before the era of the Public Health Acts and pain-killing drugs. To cease from being after having once existed seems altogether different and altogether terrible. This is an odd conclusion, bearing in mind that whereas before birth one must be reckoned to have had no effect on the course of events at all, the very act of birth and the shortest of lives may produce incalculable and possibly cataclysmic effects by indirect causation. Viewed in this light we might all be filled with satisfaction to think that our every move will send ripples of effects cascading down time. In fact, speculations of this kind do little if anything to satisfy the immortal longings, and even though being remembered kindly by others is generally felt to be something of a comfort, absolute death remains absolutely appalling. Many people who have no religious convictions save themselves from despair by filing away in their minds some small outside chance that they might, after all, survive, perhaps as some semi-anonymous cog in a universal system; many others resolutely refuse to give any thought to death at all.

If human convictions and behaviour were a direct function of logical thinking, one would expect that the more firmly a person believed in the survival of his soul in an existence unhampered by the frequently ailing body, the more ready he would be to leave this world and pass on to the next. Nothing of the sort appears to be the case, at least for those whose religion is based on the Old Testament. Self-preservation is presented in such religions as a duty, though one that is limited by some inconsistent provisos. Thus a person may sacrifice his life to save others in war, or he may die a martyr's death in a just cause; but if he were to reason that there was not enough food in the family to go round, and therefore killed himself to save the others from starvation (a fate, like many others, considerably worse than death), this would be regarded as the sin, and erstwhile crime, of suicide. Whether performed for his own benefit or to benefit others, the act of suicide would be condemned as equivalent to breaking out from prison before the expiry of the term fixed, a term for which there can be no remission.

The old notions about suicide, with an influence still lingering on, are well summarized by Sir William Blackstone in his famous *Commentaries on the Laws of England* (1765–9): "The suicide is guilty of a double offence: one spiritual, in invading the prerogative of the Almighty and rushing into his immediate presence uncalled for; the other temporal, against the King, who hath an interest in the preservation of all his subjects."[1]

Religious opposition to suicide is of decreasing importance as people become ever more detached from dogmas and revelationary teachings about right and wrong. The important matter to be considered is that while the humanist, the agnostic or the adherent of liberal religion seldom condemns suicide as a moral obliquity, he appears on the whole to find it as depressing and horrifying as the religious believer for whom it is sinful. There are many reasons for this, some good, and some regrettable.

Indoctrination against suicide is regrettably to be found at all levels. In itself the tendentious expression "to commit suicide" is calculated to poison the unsuspecting mind with its false semantic overtones, for, apart from the dangerous practice of committing oneself to an opinion, most other things committed are, as suicide once was, criminal offences.[2] People are further influenced by the unhappy shadow cast over the image of suicide by the wide press coverage given to reports of suicide by students who are worried about their examinations, or girls who are upset over a love affair, or middle-aged people living alone in bed-sitting-rooms who kill themselves out of depression—troubles that might all have been surmounted, given time. In pathetic cases such as these, it is not, as it seems to me, the act of suicide that is horrifying, but the extreme unhappiness that must be presumed to have induced it. Death from despair is the thing that ought to make us shudder, but the shudder is often extended to revulsion against the act of suicide that terminates the despair, an act that may be undertaken in very different circumstances.

The root cause of the widespread aversion to suicide is almost certainly death itself rather than dislike of the means by which death is brought about. The leaf turns a mindless face to the sun for one summer before falling for ever into the mud; death, however it comes to pass, rubs our clever faces in the same mud, where we too join the leaves. The inconceivability of this transformation in status is partly shot through with an indirect illumination, due to the death of others. Yet bereavement is not death. Here to mourn, we are still here, and the imagination boggles at the notion that things could ever be otherwise. Not only does the imagination boggle, as to some extent it must, but the mind unfortunately averts. The averted mind acknowledges, in a theoretical way, that death does indeed happen to people here and there and now and then, but to some extent the attitude to death resembles the attitude of the heavy smoker to lung cancer; he reckons that if he is lucky it will not happen to *him*, at least not yet, and perhaps not ever. This confused sort of faith in the immortality of the body must underlie many a triumphal call from the hospital ward or theatre, that the patient's life has been saved—and he will therefore die next week instead of this week, and in rather greater discomfort. People who insist that life must always be better than death often sound as if they are choosing eternal life in contrast to eternal death, when the fact is that they have no choice in the matter; it is death now, or death later. Once this fact is fully grasped it is possible for the question to arise as to whether death now would not be preferable.

Opponents of suicide will sometimes throw dust in the eyes of the uncommitted by asking at some point why one should ever choose to go on living if one once questions the value of life; for as we all know, adversity is usually round the corner, if not at our heels. Here, it seems to me, a special case must be made out for people suffering from the sort of adversity with which the proponents of euthanasia are concerned: namely, an apparently irremediable state of physical debility that makes life unbearable to the sufferer. Some adversities come and go; in the words of the Anglo-Saxon poet reviewing all the disasters known to Norse mythology, "That passed away, so may this." Some things that do not pass away include inoperable cancers in the region of the throat that choke their victims slowly to death. Not only do they not pass away, but like many extremely unpleasant conditions they cannot be alleviated by pain-killing drugs. Pain itself can be controlled, provided the doctor in charge is prepared to put the relief of pain before the prolongation of life; but analgesics will not help a patient to live with total incontinence, reduced to the status of a helpless baby after a life of independent adulthood. And for the person who manages to avoid these grave afflictions there remains the spectre of senile decay, a physical and mental crumbling into a travesty of the normal person. Could anything be more reasonable than for a person faced with these living deaths to weigh up the pros and cons of living out his life until his heart finally fails, and going instead to meet death half-way?

It is true, of course, that, all things being equal, people do want to go on living. If we are enjoying life, there seems no obvious reason to stop doing so and be mourned by our families and forgotten by our friends. If we are not enjoying it, then it seems a miserable end to die in a trough of depression, and better to wait for things to become more favourable. Most people, moreover, have a moral obligation to continue living, owed to their parents while they are still alive, their children while they are dependent, and their spouses all the time. Trained professional workers may even feel that they have a duty to society to continue giving their services. Whatever the grounds, it is both natural and reasonable that without some special cause nobody ever wants to die *yet*. But must these truisms be taken to embody the whole truth about the attitude of thinking people to life and death? A psychiatrist has been quoted as saying: "I don't think you can consider anyone normal who tries to take his own life."[3] The abnormality of the suicide is taken for granted, and the possibility that he might have been doing something sensible (for him) is not presented to the mind for even momentary consideration. It might as well be argued that no one can be considered normal who does not want to procreate as many children as possible, and this was no doubt urged by the wise men of yesterday; today the tune is very different, and in this essay we are concerned with what they may be singing tomorrow.

There is an obvious connection between attitudes to birth and to death, since both are the fundamentals of life. The experience of this century has shown that what may have appeared to be ineradicably basic instincts can in fact be modified in an advanced society, and modified not merely by external pressures, but by a corresponding feedback movement from within. Primitive people in general take pride in generating large families, apparently feeling in some deep-seated way that motherhood proves the femaleness of the female, and that fatherhood proves the maleness of the male, and that the position in either case is worth proving very amply. This simple pride is not unknown in advanced countries, although public applause for feats of child-bearing is at last beginning to freeze on the fingertips, and a faint rumble of social disapproval may be heard by an ear kept close to the ground. The interesting thing is that it is not purely financial considerations that have forced people into limiting their progeny, and least of all is it the public weal; people have actually come to prefer it. Women want to lead lives otherwise than as mothers; men no longer feel themselves obliged to assert their virility by pointing to numerous living tokens around them; and most parents prefer to concentrate attention and affection upon a couple rather than a pack. The modification in this apparently basic drive to large-scale procreation is now embraced not with reluctance, but with enthusiasm. My thesis is that humane and advanced societies are ripe for a similar and in many ways equivalent swing away from the ideal of longevity to the concept of a planned death.

It may be worth pausing here to consider whether the words "natural end," in the sense usually ascribed to the term, have much bearing on reality. Very little is "natural" about our present-day existence, and least natural of all is the prolonged period of dying that is suffered by so many incurable patients solicitously kept alive to be killed by their disease. The sufferings of animals (other than man) are heart-rending enough, but a dying process spread over weeks, months or years seems to be one form of suffering that animals are normally spared. When severe illness strikes them they tend to stop eating, sleep and die. The whole weight of Western society forces attention on the natural right to live, but throws a blanket of silence over the natural right to die. If I seem to be suggesting that in a civilized society suicide ought to be considered a quite proper way for a well-brought-up person to end his life (unless he has the good luck to die suddenly and without warning), that is indeed the tenor of my argument; if it is received with astonishment and incredulity, the reader is referred to the reception of recommendations made earlier in the century that birth control should be practised and encouraged. The idea is no more extraordinary, and would be equally calculated to diminish the sum total of suffering among humankind.

This will probably be taken as, or distorted into, a demand for the infliction of the death penalty on retirement. And yet the bell tolls for me no less than for others. Apart from the possibility that he may actually have some sympathy for the aged, no one casting a fearful eye forward into the future is likely to advocate treatment of the old that he would not care to see applied to himself, lest he be hoist with his own petard. It cannot be said too many times that so long as people are blessed with reasonable health, reasonable independence and reasonable enjoyment of life, they have no more reason to contemplate suicide than people who are half their age, and frequently half as sprightly as many in their seventies and eighties today. Attention is here being drawn to people who unfortunately have good reason to question whether or not they want to exercise their right to live; the minor infirmities of age, and relative weakness, and a slight degree of dependence on younger people who regard the giving of a helping hand as a natural part of the life-cycle, do not give rise to any such question. The question arises when life becomes a burden rather than a pleasure.

Many middle-aged people are heard to express the fervent wish that they will not live to be pain-ridden cripples, deaf, dim-sighted or feeble-minded solitaries, such that they may become little else than a burden to themselves and to others. They say they *hope* they will die before any of these fates descend upon them, but they seldom affirm that they *intend* to die before that time; and when the time comes, it may barely cross their minds that they could, had they then the determination, take the matter into their own hands. The facile retort will often be that this merely goes to show that people do not really mean what they say and that like all normal, sensible folk, they really want to live on for as long as is physically possible. But this, I would suggest, is a false conclusion. They mean exactly what they say, but the conditions and conditioning of society make it impossible for them to act in accordance with their wishes. To face the dark reality that the future holds nothing further in the way of joy or meaningful experience, and to face the fact without making some desperate and false reservation, to take the ultimate decision and act upon it knowing that it is a gesture that can never be repeated, such clear-sightedness and resolution demand a high degree of moral strength that cannot but be undermined by the knowledge that this final act of self-discipline would be the subject of head-shakings, moralizings and general tut-tutting.

How different it would be if a person could talk over the future with his family, friends and doctors, make arrangements, say farewells, take stock of his life, and know that his decision about when and how to end his life was a matter that could be the subject of constructive and sympathetic conference, and even that he could have his chosen ones around him at the last. As things are at present, he would always be met with well-meant cries of "No, no, you mustn't talk like that," and indeed anyone taking a different line might feel willy-nilly that his complicity must appear unnatural and lacking in affection. We feel that we *ought* to become irrational at the idea that someone we care for is contemplating ending his own life, and only the immediate spectacle of intense suffering can shock us out of a conditioned response to this situation. The melancholy result is that a decision that cries out for moral support has to be taken in cheerless isolation, and if taken at all is usually deferred until the victim is in an advanced state of misery.

But supposing the person contemplating suicide is not in fact undergoing or expecting to undergo severe suffering, but is merely an elderly relation, probably a mother, in fragile health, or partially disabled, and though not acutely ill is in need of constant care and attention. It would be unrealistic to deny the oppressive burden that is very often cast on the shoulders of a young to middle-aged person, probably a daughter, by the existence of an ailing parent, who may take her from her career when she is a young woman in her thirties or forties, and leave her, perhaps a quarter of a century later, an elderly, exhausted woman, demoralized over the years by frequently having had to choke back the wish that her mother would release her by dying. Even in a case such as this, human feeling does demand, I would think, that the younger person must still respond to intimations of suicide with a genuinely felt, "No, no."

But what of the older person's own attitude? Here we arrive at the kernel of the violent and almost panic-stricken reaction of many people to the idea of questioning whether it is better, in any given situation, to be or not to be. For if there is no alternative to continued living, then no choice arises, and hence there can be no possibility of an older person, who is a burden to a younger person, feeling a sense of obligation to release the captive attendant from willing or unwilling bondage, no questioning of the inevitability of the older person's living out her full term. But what if there were a real choice? What if a time came when, no longer able to look after oneself, the decision to live on for the maximum number of years were considered a mark of heedless egoism? What if it were to be thought that *dulce et decorum est pro familia mori*? This is a possibility that makes many people shrink from the subject, because they find the prospect too frightful to contemplate. Is it (to be charitable) because they always think themselves into the position of the younger person, so that "No, no" rises naturally to their lips, or is it (to be uncharitable) because they cannot imagine themselves making a free sacrifice of this sort?

This very controversial issue is, it may be remarked, outside the scope of voluntary euthanasia, which is concerned exclusively with cases where a patient is a burden to *himself*, and whether or not he is a burden to others plays no part whatever. The essence of voluntary euthanasia is the co-operation of the doctor in making crucial decisions; the "burden to others," on the contrary, must make all decisions and take all responsibility himself for any actions he might take. The issue cannot, however, be ignored, because the preoccupation of many opponents of voluntary euthanasia with its supposed implications, suggests that few people have any serious objection to the voluntary termination of a gravely afflicted life. This principal theme is usually brushed aside with surprising haste, and opponents pass swiftly on to the supposed evils that would flow from making twilight existence optional rather than obligatory. It is frequently said that hard-hearted people would be encouraged to make their elderly relatives feel that they had outlived their welcome and ought to remove themselves, even if they happened to be enjoying life. No one can say categorically that nothing of the sort would happen, but the sensibility of even hard-hearted people to the possible consequences of their own unkindness seems just as likely. A relation who had stood down from life in a spirit of magnanimity and family affection would, after an inevitable period of heart-searching and self-recrimination, leave behind a pleasant memory; a victim of callous treatment hanging like an accusing albatross around the neck of the living would suggest another and rather ugly story. Needless to say, whoever was responsible would not in any event be the sort of person to show consideration to an aged person in decline.

Whether or not some undesirable fringe results would stem from a free acceptance of suicide in our society, the problem of three or four contemporaneous generations peopling a world that hitherto has had to support only two or three is with us here and now, and will be neither generated nor exacerbated by a fresh attitude to life and death. The disabled, aged parent, loved or unloved, abnegating or demanding, is placed in one of the tragic dilemmas inherent in human existence, and one that becomes more acute as standards of living rise. One more in the mud-hut is not a problem in the same way as one more in a small, overcrowded urban dwelling; and the British temperament demands a privacy incompatible with the more sociable Mediterranean custom of packing a grandmother and an aunt or two in the attic. Mere existence presents a mild problem; disabled existence presents a chronic problem. The old person may have no talent for being a patient, and the young one may find it intolerable to be a nurse. A physical decline threatens to be accompanied by an inevitable decline in the quality of important human relationships—human relationships, it is worth repeating, not superhuman ones. Given superhuman love, patience, fortitude and all other sweet-natured qualities in a plenitude not normally present in ordinary people, there would be no problem. But the problem is there, and voluntary termination of life offers a possible solution that may be better than none at all. The young have been urged from time immemorial to have valiant hearts, to lay down their lives for their loved ones when their lives have hardly started; it may be that in time to come the disabled aged will be glad to live in a society that approves an honourable death met willingly, perhaps in the company of another "old soldier" of the same generation, and with justifiable pride. Death taken in one's own time, and with a sense of purpose, may in fact be far more bearable than the process of waiting to be arbitrarily extinguished.[4] A patient near the end of his life who arranged his death so as, for example, to permit an immediate transfer of a vital organ to a younger person, might well feel that he was converting his death into a creative act instead of waiting passively to be suppressed.

A lot of kindly people may feel that this is lacking in respect for the honourable estate of old age; but to insist on the obligation of old people to live through a period of decline and helplessness seems to me to be lacking in a feeling for the demands of human *self*-respect. They may reply that this shows a false notion of what constitutes self-respect, and that great spiritual qualities may be brought out by dependence and infirmity, and the response to such a state. It is tempting in a world dominated by suffering to find all misery purposeful, and indeed in some situations the "cross-to-bear" and the willing bearer may feel that they are contributing a poignant note to some cosmic symphony that is richer for their patience and self-sacrifice. Since we are talking of options and not of compulsions, people who felt like this would no doubt continue to play their chosen parts; but what a truly ruthless thing to impose those parts on people who feel that they are meaningless and discordant, and better written out.

What should be clear is that with so many men and so many opinions there is no room here for rules of life, or ready-made solutions by formula, least of all by the blanket injunction that, rather than allow any of these questions to be faced, life must be lived out to the bitter end, in sickness and in health, for better or for worse, until death brings release. It is true that the embargo on suicide relieves the ailing dependent of a choice, and some would no doubt be glad of the relief, having no mind for self-sacrifice. But in order to protect the mildly disabled from the burden of choice, the severely sick and suffering patient who urgently wants to die is subjected to the same compulsion to live. The willingness of many people to accept this sheltering of the stronger at the expense of the crying needs of the incomparably weaker may be because the slightly ailing are more visible and therefore make a more immediate claim on sympathy. Everyone knows aged and dependent people who might find themselves morally bound to consider the advisability of continuing to live if an option were truly available; the seriously afflicted lie hidden behind hospital windows, or secluded from sight on the upper floors of private houses. *They* are threatened not with delicate moral considerations, but with the harder realities of pain, disease and degeneration. Not only are they largely invisible, but their guardians are much given to the issuing of soothing reports about, for example, the hundred thousand or more patients who die of cancer every year, reports in which words like "happiness" and "dignity" are used liberally, and words like "pain" and "humiliation" tactfully suppressed. Let us not be misled by the reassuring face so often assumed by doctors who would have us believe that terminal suffering is just a bad fairy tale put out by alarmist bogey-men. One can only hope that the pathetic human wrecks who lie vomiting and gasping out their lives are as sanguine and cheerful about their lamentable condition as the smiling doctor who on their behalf assures us that no one (including members of the Euthanasia Society) really wants euthanasia. . . .

Here again it must be made clear that what is needed is the fostering of a new attitude to death that should ultimately grow from within, and not be imposed from without upon people psychologically unable to rethink their ingrained views. The suffering and dying patients of today have been brought up to feel that it is natural and inevitable, and even some sort of a duty, to live out their terminal period, and it would do them no service to try to persuade them into adopting an attitude that to most of them would seem oppressive, as aimed against them rather than for their benefit. If people have an ineradicable instinct, or fundamental conviction, that binds them to cling to life when their bodies are anticipating death by falling into a state of irrevocable decay, they clearly must be given treatment and encouragement consistent with their emotional and spiritual needs, and kindness *for them* will consist of assurances that not only is their suffering a matter of the greatest concern, but that so also is their continued existence. It is future generations, faced perhaps with a lifespan of eighty or ninety years, of which nearly half will have to be dependent on the earning power of the other half, who will have to decide how much of their useful, active life is to be devoted to supporting themselves through a terminal period *"sans* everything," prolonged into a dreaded ordeal by ever-increasing medical skill directed to the preservation of life. It may well be that, as in the case of family planning, economic reality will open up a spring, the waters of which will filter down to deeper levels, and that then the new way of death will take root. The opponents of euthanasia conjure up a favourite vision of a nightmare future in which anxious patients will be obsessed with the fear that their relatives and doctors may make surreptitious plans to kill them; the anxiety of the twenty-first century patient may, on the contrary, be that they are neglecting to make such plans . . . focusing attention on practical steps, how is this to be brought about? Should schoolchildren be asked to write essays on "How I Would Feel if I Had to Die at Midnight" or compositions envisaging why and in what circumstances they propose to end their lives? The answer may well be that they should. An annual visit to a geriatric ward might also be in order. The usual argument against facing up to such reality is that life is long and death is short, and that dwelling on an unfortunate aspect is morbid and best shunned. . . . But instant death is granted to few, and the others would be well advised to expect to be an unconscionable time a-dying, and partly a-dying, and be prepared to meet the challenge not only of death, but of the unconscionable time preceding it. I would contend that the true end of education should be to prepare the pupil to learn in the course of life to orientate all knowledge and experience within the framework of a life bounded by decline and death, and to regard a timely and possibly useful death as the summation of the art of living. Pending the comfort of a death-conditioned society, a recommended exercise for the individual who is minded to reconcile himself to dying is a constant making and remaking of wills. An evening spent distributing largesse, followed by the clearing of the desk, the answering of letters and the paying of accounts, has the effect of a direct invitation to the Almighty to take you while you are in the mood to add your final touch to the day's work.

It is, of course, all too easy to make light of death when it seems far from imminent, and all too easy for someone who has had a satisfying life to say that other people, who may have had very little happiness, must learn to accept that their one and (ostensibly) only life must now cease. It may well turn out that we who insist on the right to come to terms with death before life becomes a burden may, when the time comes, be found to fail in our resolute purpose, and may end our lives by way of punishment in one of the appalling institutions provided by the state for the care of the aged. The failure may be due to physical helplessness coupled with the refusal of others to give the necessary help, or it may be due to a moral failure ascribable to personal weakness and the pressures of society, pressures that sometimes take a form too oblique to be recognized as twisters of the mind. Ending with a further complaint about linguistic misdirection, my final objection to tainted words is that a patient ending his own life, or a doctor assisting him to end it, is said to "take life," just as a thief "takes" property with the intention of depriving the owner of something he values. Whatever it is that is taken from a dying patient, it is nothing he wants to keep, and the act is one of giving rather than taking. The gift is death, a gift we shall all have to receive in due course, and if we can bring ourselves to choose our time for acceptance, so much the better for us, for our family, for our friends and for society.

NOTES

1. Sir William Blackstone, *Commentaries on the Laws of England,* 18th edition, ed. Arthur Ryland (London: Sweet, Pheney, Maxwell, Stevens & Sons, 1829), Vol. IV, p. 189.

2. Professor Flew points out the greater virtues of the French *"se suicider."* See Antony Flew, "The Principle of Euthanasia," in A. B. Downing, ed., *Euthanasia and the Right to Death* (London: Peter Owen, 1969), p. 46, n. 13. We should perhaps be grateful not to be burdened with an expression like the German *"Selbstmord,"* i.e., "self-murder."

3. Reported in *The Observer* (June 26, 1967).

4. It will be noted that reference is made here in all cases to the aged. In a longer exposition I would argue that very different considerations apply to the young disabled who have not yet enjoyed a full life span, and who should be given far greater public assistance to enable them to enjoy life as best they can.

THE ETHICS OF NOT-BEING: INDIVIDUAL OPTIONS FOR SUICIDE

Colleen D. Clements

Clements takes issue with the notion of rational suicide by arguing that rational calculation is something that takes place within life, and presupposes a fundamental, "yea-saying" attitude toward life and the universe. But, for Clements, there is no way to justify preferring a "yea-saying" to a "nay-saying" attitude. She examines the implications of this claim for suicide intervention, for medical models of suicide, and other ways in which a yea-saying society responds to a nay-saying, suicidal individual.

Colleen Clements, who specializes in the clinical aspects of medical ethics, is a Division Fellow in the Department of Pediatrics (Genetics) at the University of Rochester Medical Center.

A philosophic analysis of suicide poses one preanalytic risk which is rarely articulated because it is so closely tied to a major primitive assumption in philosophy: that man is importantly a rational animal only. This is really one of the unexamined primitives of much historical and contemporary ethics, from Aristotle (who tempered it) to John Rawls. My contention will be the heretical one that to analyze the ethics of suicide in terms of such an assumption concerning the overriding rational nature of man is to add little but confusion to the subject.

I am not thinking in terms of merely blatantly psychotic suicidal behavior. The risk is more extensive than that category alone, and I would hold that not all suicides would fit that designation. I am contending that suicidal judgments must be viewed as affect or attitudinal stances and that these are primary stances having precedence over rational analysis. Suicides which are not disguised and dishonest manipulations are acts based on a fundamental attitude concerning the universe, a primary nay-saying, to lean on Nietzsche's term. To approach them in terms of social roles and responsibilities, hedonic calculi, moral imperatives of consistency, and so on is to put the cart before the horse. Before all valuation (ethical, cognitive, and esthetic), human beings have an attitude concerning their existence in the world. This affect may be the result of conditioning or learning, or the result of biochemical differences in the brain, or the result of willingness to project oneself into the future—some of the possible causal interpretations—but whichever alternative causation, it is a yea-saying or nay-saying attitude (or various mixtures of both) which cannot be evaluated in terms of cognitive (rational) values since it is the precondition for all values.[1]

What we need is to get the horse in front of the cart before we can go anywhere with an analysis of suicide. I want to maintain that the attitude of affect is arational and has motivational priority. With whatever degree of sophistication or analysis of one's relationship to the rest of existence, one commits suicide because one no longer wants to relate to this particular existence; one becomes a nay-sayer. My contention is that the stance of affirmation or negation is a primary affect which cannot be philosophically either justified or rejected, since philosophizing implies the acceptance of cognitive values which are based on an affirmative stance and therefore cannot be used to arbitrate in the choice between affirmation and negation. I can have no reason to accept or reject a negative attitude toward existence, since reason is relevant only within an affirmative stance and, by the same argument, can also not be used to accept or reject an affirmative attitude. We beg the question, in other words.

Why is reason dependent on an affirmative stance? Because cognitive values are preferences themselves and imply future potentialities. We prefer to be noncontradictory because we like to feel we can rely on identity to help us segment our experience. We like to feel that way because segmenting our experience seems to facilitate our functioning in time in our world, to make it more pleasant for us, to aid in our future projections and allow us to avoid some of our past mistakes. Furthermore, the majority of us who preferred to structure our experience in terms of identity and from it noncontradiction have had a better survival record than those of us who did not, as the final bottom line. But who cares about future experiences of pleasure or pain, or survival records, or functional potential, except those with an affirmative attitude toward existence—the quick and not the dead or those wishing to be so. So cognitive values depend for their development and continuance on the yea-sayers among us, and they are one way of expressing the affirmative attitude. To call on them, then, to justify or refute either the affirmative or negative affect is to give them a function they can't possibly serve.

I don't wish to imply a dichotomy between affect and reason, just the motivational priority of affect and the valuational priority of affect. Reason can influence and generate affect to some extent (although if psychoanalysis were right, perhaps less than we would like to think), but only the affirmative affect can generate reason, and in this spiral, the affect has priority. For every reason one can muster to terminate life ("he killed himself because of rational considerations based on his situation"), one can give another for continuing to put up with one's conditions ("he didn't kill himself because all these options, though restricted, were still open to him")—*if* one wished to do so. Even persons in severe constant pain, with severely restricted options, have chosen to live as long as possible, producing reasons for doing so because they still wanted to live. Other persons, with what most of us would consider broad and exciting options, have chosen to kill themselves because only one need out of many was not being satisfied. Were any of them rational or irrational? My argument is that they were all arational or nonrational, exhibiting a (probably the) primary affect, which is not amenable to our rational evaluation. When we begin to discuss the very primary level of affirmation and negation, however, we are at the ultimate first choice, prior to values. In a real sense, an individual who does not value existence does not value anything at all, and to apply tools of cognitive values to this primary affect is to deny him his validity in a totally arbitrary fashion.

Further in the paper, I will modify or clarify this point. Yea-sayers can and do assign rational justification to their activities, but when they attempt this assignment to nay-sayers, to suicidal behavior which is a nay-saying stance, such considerations are actually meaningless. Yea-sayers may assign good and bad reasons for someone else's suicide within their own affirmative stance, although this has and should have limited application. But when they themselves make a choice to negate existence, they are no longer in the affirmative stance and all values, cognitive included, become impossible. Further, their implication that such cognitive values be accepted by the suicide himself (if he were in his "right" mind?) is contradictory.

This caveat necessitates considering two aspects of the analysis of suicide: (1) the individual's perception of his relationship to the universe and the resulting affect, and (2) the consensus of individuals concerning the human species' relationship to the universe. If emphasis, for example, is placed only on (2), we could arrive at the following plausible position in medical ethics. If all suicidal behavior is by definition part of a mental illness syndrome, and mental illness is understood as undesirable variation from a mental health norm, then the very classification of behavior as suicidal implies that the behavior is always undesirable. Further, the social dynamics of the sick role seem to require that an individual who assumes it has an obligation to seek help to restore himself to the norm, an antisuicidal attitude. To commit suicide is to violate the rules of the sick role. The application of the traditional sick role model to suicide seems definitely peculiar on this point: the suicidal patient does not perceive suicide as an undesirable solution or option but on the contrary remains actively determined on this option. I will have more to say about this further on, since it may seem to be analogous to mental illness in general, and there are some implications that may be problematic as a result.

Still emphasizing (2), suicide makes a statement that is profoundly disturbing to most modern societies, where the social consensus maintains an affirmative attitude toward the universe and existence. This is true of both Western versions of Judeo-Christian tradition and of dialectical materialist traditions, for example. Howard Parsons writes that the human condition is such that it produces an affirmation of life; that in spite of certain destructive urges, the dominant trend is life-preserving and affirming.[2] Such optimism and future orientation makes suicide a basically incoherent and unethical act for most Marxists, as well as a threatening one since it challenges their very basic optimism. While some, like Adam Schaff, may see possibilities for nay-saying,[3] the Marxist emphasis on social roles and responsibilities and the future-oriented optimism of the dialectic stress the attitude of the social consensus as the only approved affect *vis à vis* existence. I still recall correspondence with Marxists which involved their reaction to a rather pessimistic scenario involving future levels of environmental pollution. What was demanded by them was a call to arms and promise of eventual victory, a committed yea-saying even concerning the future. One described the gloomy scenario as emanating from the kind of attitude a man in the last stages of stomach cancer might have; another called on the ash can of history. To maintain an individual's option to express a nay-saying attitude, (1), in the face of such a consensus approving the yea-saying attitude (another attitudinal stance) is a herculean undertaking.

The Judeo-Christian position on suicide has tended to center on the sanctity of individual human life as contrary to suicidal behavior. The equating of quality with quantity which such a position implies has only recently been challenged. It is interesting that starting from an asocial perspective, contrary to the Marxist emphasis on a social interpretation, the Judeo-Christian view nevertheless arrives at a similar conclusion.

Yea-sayers need to remember that the universe exhibits disorganization as well as organization—systems breakdown and entropy as well as systems buildup and neg-entropy—and to realize it is the human being who gives preference to continued organization, not nature. We have no rational argument which can demonstrate that neg-entropy is superior to entropy, nor do I think such an argument can be marshaled even in theory.[4] The universe exhibits both characteristics; as Freud perceived, the human individual manifests both a drive for self-preservation and a drive for self-destruction. Self-preservation or systems buildup and maintenance is not the only aspect of either human nature or the universe; self-destruction or systems disintegration is as integral and as basic to both.

In fact, we tend to do a peculiar thing, as yea-sayers, to would-be suicides, which I feel should be guarded against. The suicide declares that a life of pain and suffering (physical or psychic) has no meaning left for him, yet those sharing the affirmative attitude often wish to require the would-be suicide to continue to exist because his existence, which has no meaning left for him, has meaning for them. This strikes me as an instrumental-only use of a human being, a strangely sadistic position which has some disturbing parallels in religious sacrifice.

An alternative option to such an ethical evaluation of suicide is to consider it in terms of a medical management problem, the clinical perspective. The Talcott Parsons sick role model is a poor fit when applied to suicide, specifically in terms of two requirements: (1) recognition that to be ill is inherently undesirable, and (2) obligation to get well. The role already prejudges that a negative attitude is not the norm and must be changed. One of the prime difficulties in the use of such a sick role model with categories of variant or abnormal is to determine the parameters of such variance or deviation from the norm, and to justify the norm as the only acceptable value. In some suicidal actions this is relatively easy (affect disorders due to biochemical imbalance or transient stress); in others it would be extremely difficult (suicidal affect based on considerations of degenerative illness, consistently narrowing options or possibilities, persistent serious questioning of life's worth).

From a pragmatic viewpoint the practice of expanding the medical sphere to include larger and larger areas is a dangerous undertaking: (1) if the sick role fit is poor, the reputation of medicine suffers from inability to effect cures, (2) the model already has problems with protection of patients' "rights" (read: needs and interests) and is a poor model for guaranteeing protection of individual interests when physician/patient relationships are bureaucratized or institutionalized, (3) the establishment of health norms and proper functioning is not a well-developed area of medicine and yet is a prerequisite for establishing proper parameters, and (4) as broader and broader areas are included, the rigor of clinical diagnosis and labeling can become more and more diffuse.

Use of this model for suicide has also been criticized because the act of taking one's life is seen as a peculiar threat to physicians who have a primary value of saving life and tend to handle death in general not very well. This may be oversimplistic, but in my experience it occurs frequently enough to consider it. We should keep in mind, however, that many experienced physicians have come to terms with the inevitability of winning the battle and losing the war and that their disengagement from dying patients may not be so much a question of inability to face defeat in a battle against death as personal grief and involvement with their patients. After all, even loving families often withdraw from the dying member in self-defense.

Granting a primary medical attitude of affirmation of life, however, we are back to the social consensus affect I previously discussed. I did not dismiss its importance then, but pointed out that it was one pole of a basic situation in tension and should not be stressed to the exclusion of the other pole, individual basic affect. This does not mean that conditioning, learning, persuasive techniques can not be attempted with would-be suicides. It does mean that after a point, after persistent maintenance of the negative attitude, one should perhaps respect individual variation and give up pressing one's affirmative attitude. The medical model shares the tension of the social consensus model. It too must finally come to grips with the primacy of the affirmative and negative attitudes, although unlike philosophy, it has better tools to deal with attitudes and does not have the primitive assumption that man is importantly only a rational animal. It can deal with suicidal behavior on the affect level, therefore, where it is actually localized, and sometimes effect an attitudinal (not a cognitive) change. The only suggestion I make is that foolish persistence in the face of inability to effect change in a particular situation is not to be commended in the least, and perhaps even negatively evaluated.

But does this buy us consequences we would rather not have, especially in terms of the similarity between the suicide's refusal to share our belief he ought to continue to live and the psychotic's refusal to share our belief that he ought to abandon his delusions and get well? Are we even more extreme here than Szasz, and does our position on suicide also entail emptying the wards? First, there is a significant difference between suicidal wishes and categories of mental illness, although suicide may be a component of those categories. The earnest would-be suicide wishes to stop existing (at least in this time, place, and mode). The psychotic may look at his universe very differently from the norm, but he may or may not wish to continue to exist—his affirmative or negative stance is not automatically defined by his psychosis, even in an affect disorder like depression, where suicide is often but not necessarily a component. We tend to think the psychotic's perception of reality is badly skewed from the norm, with certainly a component of affect disorder as well, whereas the suicide's affect is badly skewed from the norm, with perhaps a component of reality distortion. So while the medical model tends to blend the two abnormal patterns, we need to be careful that statements applying to the affirmative or negative affect not be extended automatically to reality perception.

However, it is true that sane/insane depends in part on a social consensus norm of what is reality. The important factor here is that we assume only *successful* social norms will have any staying ability, or to bring it back to the base of all values, survival value. Again we find ourselves in the affirmative attitude, and if the mentally ill also share that attitude and wish to survive, we can use that as justification for treating them and returning them to the norm. That norm we do assume is an approximation of some reality we are part of and act within, so that there are feedback mechanisms to indicate error or success in our approximations. I would not like to defend those assumptions here, but granting them, in treating these mental illnesses we are trying to help other yea-sayers survive and function well. That seems a reasonable agenda that does not involve the problem that suicide does. We can apply cognitive values (in terms of normal standards for apprehending reality) to psychotics who share our affirmative attitude toward existence.

We haven't, therefore, emptied the wards; but have we discharged all suicidal patients? Is that a consequence of my argument, which, though it is less extreme, somehow strikes us as inhumane? And here my answer can only be yes and no: (1) No, we cannot rationally, from some neutral position beyond the affirmative or negative stance, assign value to existence and disvalue to nonexistence. We can have an affect concerning existence or nonexistence, and if we have an affirmative affect we can then construct values, but we can't communicate in valuational (and as a subset, rational) language with the would-be suicide. A psychiatrist who told a patient, "You ought to live," would not be a very good psychiatrist, which is a very simple observation. So we have no really rational reason for preventing or treating suicides, and we shouldn't fool ourselves that we do. (2) Yes, we are in a social consensus of yea-sayers, and we have needs, interests, and values that are interwoven in a social transaction with individual nay-sayers. We must act on our values, and finally on our own affect, and we are humanly justified in that action—arationally justified. All I ask is that our interests be recognized as involving compassion, which is a broader demand than it seems. When prevention and treatment become more cruel than allowance, it is our own value which is being threatened, our selves which are being lessened by our disregard for the worth (including the possibility of being ultimately different in affect) of a fellow member of our species.[5]

Now to attempt some conclusions. Suicide, seen as the behavioral expression of a negative attitude, is inherent in the human situation, always a possible option. It can be generated by overwhelming impulses divorced from reality, or it can contain cognitive components such as rational perception of the environment and relevant probable events. There are too many varieties of suicidal attitudes to comfortably use one broad term to cover them all. On the one hand, there are reality-tested types such as altruistic suicides, suicides in situations of physiologically or psychologically painful terminal illnesses, suicides of existential despair, and suicides as the lesser of two evils. On the other hand, there are suicides of clearly psychotic individuals, suicides committed at a temporary moment of overwhelming emotional stress, suicides that are manipulative gambles, suicides that are ambivalent. But in the final analysis, all of them presuppose yea- or nay-saying, and there can be no ethical evaluation of systems maintenance versus systems destruction.

One can make some value statements, however. (1) The threat of suicide invokes a social response that cannot be denied (the social-consensus affect). It may be difficult for society to deal with such a rejection of the value of existence, and therefore it is socially important that a response be made, that there be an expression of the consensus attitude that existence can be meaningful. The natural response is to rescue the would-be suicide, and this response is quite a legitimate one, except in rare cases where there is no possibility for continued minimal functioning (e.g., terminal illnesses). There can be no valid reason for blocking the expression of the social-consensus attitude, but there are valid reasons why it cannot be overriding.

(2) The individual cannot and does not exist in a social vacuum. Because of the relational network of which the individual is part, a suicide will almost always have harmful consequences to other individuals. The children of suicides have a lifelong problem coping with the event. The significant others in the network can be seriously damaged by guilt or a sense of failure. Famous suicides can result in social chain reactions. Since the act is irreversible, it is difficult to modify the effects. Furthermore, Aristotle was partially correct: society invests in each individual, and loses that investment with suicides. This again is not an overriding, absolute sanction, but it represents the one social pole and needs to be seriously considered.

(3) In some cases suicide can be an aggressive, hostile act rather than a simple negation of individual existence. This also needs to be made explicit in terms of the harm done to others. The potential suicide should be aware of this component and consider it in his willingness to engage in such destructive behavior. The social consensus again is free to express its concern for preservation of its affirming members and can translate that concern into protective action. Nay-saying is not a license to harm those with affirmative attitudes, though it is not a prohibition either. But those who affirm existence can set values for their own self-preservation and happiness and can certainly act on those values. If someone else's suicidal act does seriously threaten those values, they can take the necessary measures to safeguard them. The problem arises when acts are unrealistically perceived as threatening, unnecessarily curtailed, or handled with lack of respect and compassion for that particular bit of general existence the yea-sayers are supposed to be affirming—the nay-saying individual.

(4) The possible ambivalent nature of suicide can justify medical intervention for the first attempt. It is frequently the case either that preserving and destroying attitudes unstably alternate, or that a momentary destructive urge can override the more consistent preservative urge. The difficulty in accepting self-reports and in ascertaining the attitude consistent with the patient's overall reality certainly allows for even heroic medical intervention initially. But after a reasonable intervention period, the individual needs to have his needs and desires recognized—his

individual affect cannot validly be forever submerged in a medical or social consensus. In understanding and compassion we may have to let our "erring" brothers and sisters go in peace.

(5) This kind of mature understanding of man's relationship to existence can only occur if society, and physicians as part of society, have come to actual grips with the problem and thus have developed honest, affirming attitudes which are not profoundly threatened by nay-saying suicides. Too many of us only tenuously and in an unexamined way affirm existence, and thus are profoundly shaken by suicide and overreact by ruthlessly suppressing or punishing the negative attitude. While this is psychologically understandable, it cannot be philosophically justified.

(6) The individual, finally, has an option to act out the negative attitude by committing suicide, although the option is qualified by the tension of the social consensus and the fact that man is a social species. Society in terms of the affirmative consensus has the qualified option to attempt to prevent suicides. The physician has a similar qualified option to intervene, heroically if necessary. No one has the option to impose involuntary restraint for long periods of time, with unsuccessful attempts at affect manipulation, unless definite risk of very significant harm to others can be clearly demonstrated.

NOTES

1. See my "Death and Philosophic Diversions," *Philosophy and Phenomenological Research* xxxix (No. 4, June 1979), pp. 524–36.
2. Howard Parsons, *Humanism and Marx's Thought* (Springfield, Ill.: Charles C. Thomas, 1971).
3. Adam Schaff, *Marxism and the Human Individual* (New York: McGraw-Hill, 1970).
4. Colleen Clements, "Stasis: the Unnatural Value," *Ethics* 86 (No. 2, Jan. 1976), pp. 136–44.
5. I am indebted to Dr. Morton S. Rapp, Dept. of Psychiatry, University of Toronto, for his helpful comments and criticisms.

The
Rationality
of Suicide

THE RATIONALITY OF SUICIDE

Richard B. Brandt

Brandt argues on utilitarian grounds that the decision to end one's life can be rational. He discusses how a person might go about deciding whether suicide is the best thing for himself, but shows ways in which depression can distort this rational decision process. He then argues briefly that intervention to prevent suicide may be justified if the decision to die has clearly been an irrational one, but that there is also an obligation to assist a person whose decision to end his life has been made rationally.

    Educated at Cambridge, Tübingen, and Yale, Richard Brandt has taught philosophy both at Swarthmore College and, since 1964, at the University of Michigan. He has been President of the American Society of Politics and Legal Philosophy, President of the American Philosophical Association, and the John Locke Lecturer at Oxford University. He is the author of Ethical Theory *(1959),* Value and Obligation *(1961), and* A Theory of the Good and the Right *(Oxford 1979). The paper from which this selection is taken was written in response to a request from Edwin Shneidman, dean of American suicidologists, for a "philosopher's view" of suicide.*

"Suicide" is conveniently defined, for our purposes, as doing something which results in one's death, either from the intention of ending one's life or the intention to bring about some other state of affairs (such as relief from pain) which one thinks it certain or highly probable can be achieved only by means of death or will produce death. It may seem odd to classify an act of heroic self-sacrifice on the part of a soldier as suicide. It is simpler, however, not to try to define "suicide" so that an act of suicide is always irrational or immoral in some way; if we adopt a neutral definition like the above we can still proceed to ask when an act of suicide in that sense is rational. . . .

1. WHETHER AND WHEN SUICIDE IS BEST OR RATIONAL FOR THE AGENT

If I were asked for advice by someone contemplating suicide, it is to this topic, I believe, that I would be inclined primarily to address myself. Some of the writers who are most inclined to affirm that suicide is morally wrong are quite ready to believe that from the agent's own selfish point of view suicide would sometimes be the best thing for him, but they do not discuss the point in any detail. I should like to get clear when it is and when it is not. Not that we can hope to get any simple conclusions applicable to everybody. What I hope to do is produce a way of looking at the matter which will help an individual see whether suicide is the best thing for *him* from the point of view of his own welfare—or whether it is the best thing for someone being advised, from the point of view of that person's welfare.

It is reasonable to discuss this topic under the restriction of two assumptions. First, I assume we are trying to decide between a *successful* suicide attempt, and no attempt. A person might try to commit suicide and succeed only in blinding himself. I am assuming that we need not worry about this possibility, so that the alternative is between producing death and continuing life roughly as it now is. The second assumption I am making is that when a person commits suicide, he is dead; that is, we do not consider that killing himself is only a way of expediting his departure to a blissful or extremely unpleasant afterlife. I shall assume there is *no* afterlife. I believe that at the present time potential suicides deliberate on the basis of both these assumptions, so that in making them I am addressing myself to the real problem as prospective suicides see it. What I want to produce is a fresh and helpful way of looking at their problem.

The problem, I take it, is a choice between future world-courses: the world-course which includes my demise, say, an hour from now, and several possible ones which contain my demise at a later point. We cannot have precise knowledge about many features of the latter group of world-courses. One thing I can't have precise knowledge about is how or when I shall die if I do not commit suicide now. One thing is certain: it will be sometime, and it is almost certain that it will be before my one-hundredth birthday. So, to go on the rational probabilities, let us look up my life expectancy at my present age from the insurance tables, making any corrections that are called for in the light of full medical information about my present state of health. If I do not already have a terminal illness, then the choice, say, is between a world-course with my death an hour from now, and several world-courses with my death, say, twenty years from now. The problem, I take it, is to decide whether the expectable utility to me of some possible world-course in which I go on for another twenty years is greater than or less than the expectable utility to me of the one in which my life stops in an hour. One thing to be clear about is: we are not choosing between death and immortality. We are choosing between death now and death some (possibly short) finite time from now.

Why do I say the choice is between *world*-courses and not just a choice between future life-courses of the prospective suicide, the one shorter than the others? The reason is that one's suicide has some impact on the world (and one's continued life has some impact on the world), and that how the rest of the world is will often make a difference to one's evaluation of the possibilities. One is interested in things in the world other than just one's self and one's own happiness. For instance, one may be interested in one's children and their welfare, or in one's future reputation, or the contribution one might make to the solution of some problems, or in the publication of a book one is finishing with its possible clarifying effects on the thinking of a profession, and so on.

What is the basic problem for evaluation? It is the choice of the expectably *best* world-course. One way of looking at the evaluation, although in practice we cannot assign the specific numbers it is suggested we assign, is this: We compare the suicide world-course with the continued-life world-course (or several of them), and note the features with respect to which they differ. We then assign numbers to these features, representing their utility to us if they happen, and then multiplying this utility by a number which represents the probability that this feature will occur. (Suppose I live, and am certain that either P or Q will occur, and that it is a 50:50 chance which; then I represent this biography as containing the sum of the utility of P multiplied by one-half and the utility of Q multiplied by one-half.) We then sum these numbers. The sum will represent the expectable utility of that world-course to us. The world-course with the highest sum is the one that is rationally chosen. But of course it is absurd to suppose that we can assign these numbers in actual fact; what we can actually do is something in a sense simpler but less decisive.

If we look at the matter in this way, we can see that there is a close analogy between an analysis of the rationality of declaring bankruptcy and going out of business. In the case of the firm, the objectives may be few and simple, and indeed for some boards of directors the only relevant question is: Will the stockholders probably be better off, or worse off, financially, if we continue or if we declare insolvency? More likely the question considered will be a bit more complex, since an enlightened firm will at least wonder what will happen to its officers and employees and customers and even possibly the general public if it goes out of business, and how their utilities will be affected. There is another difference: When the firm goes out of business, none of the people involved goes out of business (unless some officer, etc., kills himself).

Perhaps a closer analogy, if we want an analogy, to this choice between world-courses is the choice between a life-course in which I get twelve hours' sleep tonight, and one in which I do some one (the best) of the various possibilities open to me. The difference between the cases is that, to make the analogy more exact, I have to ignore the fact that I shall waken.

Since, as I have suggested, we cannot actually assign numbers in the way suggested, so as to compare expectable utilities, what then *is* the basic question we can and should answer, in order to determine which world-course is best, from the point of view of our own welfare? Certainly the question has to do with what we do or shall, or under certain circumstances would, *want* to happen, or want not to happen. But it is not just a question of what we prefer *now*, doubtless with some clarification of the other possibilities being considered. The reason for this is that we know that our preferences change, and the preferences of tomorrow (assuming we can know something about them) are just as legitimately taken into account in deciding what to do now as the preferences of today. The preferences of any future day have a right to an equal vote as to what we shall do now; there is no reason for giving special weight to today's preference, since any reason that can be given today for weighing heavily today's preference can be given tomorrow for weighing heavily tomorrow's preference. So, given this symmetry of reasons, the preferences of any time-stretch have a rational claim to an equal vote. Now the importance of that fact is this: we often know quite well that our desires, aversions, and preferences are going to be very different after a short span of time, from what they now are. When a person is in a state of despair—perhaps brought about by a rejection in love, or by discharge from a long-held position—nothing but the thing he cannot have seems desirable; everything else is turned to ashes. Yet we know quite well that the passage of time may reverse all this; after a time the grass may look green again and things in the world that are available to us will look attractive. So, if we were to go on the preferences of today, when the emotion of despair seems more than we can stand, we might find death preferable to life; but if we allow for the preferences of the weeks and years ahead, when many goals will be enjoyable and attractive, we might find life much preferable to death. So, if a choice, or what is best, is to be determined by what we want not only now but later (and later desires on an equal basis with the present)—as it should be— then what is the best or preferable world-course will often be quite different from what it would be if the choice, or what is best for one, were fixed by one's desires and preferences now. It may be hard to look to the future and see what one's attitudes are likely to be, but that is necessary if one's evaluation is to be rational.

Of course, if one commits suicide there are no future desires or aversions which may be compared with present ones, and which should be allowed an equal vote in deciding what is best. In that respect the status of the course of action which results in death is different from any other course of action we may undertake.

I do not wish to suggest the rosy possibility that it is often or always reasonable to believe that next week I shall be more interested in living than I am today, if today I take a dim view of continued existence. Quite on the contrary, when a person is seriously ill the probabilities are that he will continue to feel worse until sedations become so extensive that he is incapable of emotional reaction toward anything, one way or the other. Thus sometimes when on the basis of today's attitudes I must say that I prefer death to life, I shall find no reason to think that tomorrow the preference order will be reversed—rather, if anything, I can know that tomorrow I shall prefer death to life more strongly. When this situation obtains, I may do better by choosing the world-course which contains my own life span as short as possible.

The argument is often used—and it may as well be introduced in this connection as any other—that one can never be *certain* what is going to happen, and hence one is never rationally justified in doing anything as drastic as taking one's life. And it is true that certainties are hard to find in this life; they do not exist even in the sciences, if we are strict about it. Unfortunately for the critic who makes use of this line of argument, it works both ways. I might say, when I am very depressed about my life, that one thing I am certain of is that I am now very depressed and prefer death to life, and there is only some probability that tomorrow I shall feel differently; so, one might argue that if one is to go only by certainties, I had better end it now. No one would take this seriously. We always have to live by probabilities, and make our estimates as best we can. People sometimes argue that one should not commit suicide in order to escape the excruciating pain because a miraculous cure for one's terminal disease might be found tomorrow. And it is true that such a cure could, as a matter of logical possibility, be found tomorrow. But if everyone had argued in that way in the past hundred years, all of them would have waited until the bitter end and suffered excruciating pain; the line of argument that ignores probabilities and demands certainty would not have paid off in the past, and there is no reason to think it will pay off much better in the future. Indeed, if the thought were taken generally that probabilities should be ignored when they are short of certainty, in practical decisions, it can be demonstrated that the policy for action *cannot* pay off. A form of much the same argument is the assertion that if you are alive tomorrow you can always decide to end it all then, if you want to; whereas if you are dead tomorrow, you cannot then decide that it is better to live. The factual point is correct, of course. But the argument has practical bearing only if there is some reason to think that tomorrow you might want to live; and sometimes it is as nearly certain as matters of this sort can be, that you will not. It is true, of course, that one can always bear another day; so why not put it off? This argument, of course, can be used for every day, with the result that one never takes action. One would think that, as soon as it is clear beyond reasonable doubt not only that death is now preferable to life, but also that it will be every day from now until the end, the rational thing is to act promptly.[1]

Let us not pursue the question whether it is rational for a person with a painful terminal illness to commit suicide; obviously it is. However, the issue seldom arises, and few patients of this sort do so. With such patients matters get worse only slowly so that no particular time seems the one calling for action; they are so heavily sedated that it is impossible for the mental processes of decision leading to action to occur; or else they are incapacitated in a hospital and the very physical possibility of ending their lives is not available. Let us leave this gruesome topic and turn to the practically more important problem: whether it is rational for persons to commit suicide for some other reason than painful terminal physical illness. Most persons who commit suicide do so, apparently, because they face some nonphysical problem which depresses them beyond their ability to bear. It is to them that the above point, about the rational necessity of taking into account attitudes one will have next week, is primarily addressed.

If we look over a list of the problems that bother people, and some of which various writers have regarded as good and sufficient reasons for ending life, one finds (in addition to serious illness) things like the following: some event which has made one feel ashamed or has cost one loss of prestige and status; reduction to poverty as compared with former affluence; the loss of a limb or of physical beauty; the loss of sexual capacity; some event which makes it seem impossible that one will achieve things by which one sets store; loss of a loved one; disappointment in love; the infirmities of increasing age. It is not to be denied that such things can be serious blows to one's prospects of happiness.

In deciding whether, everything considered, one prefers a world-course containing one's early demise as compared with one in which this is postponed to its natural terminus, there are various plain errors to be avoided—errors to which a person is especially prone when he is depressed. Let us forget for a moment the relevance to the decision of preferences that we may have tomorrow, and concentrate on some errors which may infect our preference as of today, and for which correction or allowance must be made.

In the first place, depression, like any severe emotional experience, tends to primitivize one's intellectual process. It restricts the range of one's survey of the possibilities. One thing that a rational person will do is compare the world-course containing his suicide with his *best* alternative. But his best alternative is precisely a possibility he may overlook if, in a depressed mood, he thinks only of how badly off he is and does not contemplate plans of action which he has not at all considered. If a person is disappointed in love, it is possible to adopt a vigorous plan of action which carries a good chance of acquainting him with someone he likes at least as well; and if old age prevents one from continuing the tennis games with one's favorite partner, it is possible to learn some other game which provides the joys of competition without the physical demands.

There is another insidious influence of a state of depression; on one's planning. Depression seriously affects one's judgment about probabilities. A person disappointed in love is very likely to take a dim view of himself, his prospects, and his attractiveness; he thinks that, because he has been rejected by one person, he will probably be rejected by anyone who looks desirable to him. In a less gloomy frame of mind he would make, quite correctly, different estimates. Part of the reason for such gloomy probability estimates is that depression tends to repress one's memory evidence which supports a non-gloomy prediction. Thus a rejected lover tends to forget all the cases in which he has elicited enthusiastic response from ladies in relation to whom he has been the one who has done the rejecting. Thus his pessimistic self-image is based upon a highly selected, and pessimistically selected, set of data. Even when he is reminded of the data, however, he is apt to resist an optimistic inference. Even if he knows enough about the logic of inductive inference to know that the rational thing to do is project the frequency of past experiences into the future, basing one's estimate of the probability of a future event on the frequency of that event in the past, he is apt, doubtless sometimes with some reason, to reject the conclusion, for instance, on the ground that past experiences are unrepresentative and cannot be relied upon for a prognosis of the future. Obviously, however, there is such a thing as a reasonable and correct prognosis on the basis of an accurate account of past experience, and it is the height of irrationality not to estimate the future on that basis.

Another kind of distortion of the look of future prospects is not a result of depression, but is quite normal. Events distant in the future feel small, just as objects distant in space look small. The prospect of them does not have the effect on motivational processes that it would have if it were an event in the immediate future. Rat-psychologists call essentially this fact the "goal-gradient" phenomenon; a rat, for instance, will run faster toward a food-box when he is close enough so that he can actually see it, and does not do as well when he can only represent it in some nonperceptual way, as presumably he does in the early stages of a maze. Similarly, a professor will accept an invitation to give a lecture or read a paper a year ahead, which he would not dream of accepting only a month ahead; the vision of the work involved somehow does not seem as repellent at the greater distance. Everyone finds it hard to do something disagreeable now, even for the sake of something more seriously important at a future date; the disagreeable event now tends to be postponed, unless one makes one's self attend to the importance of the event which is thereby jeopardized. In the case of a person who has suffered some misfortune, and whose situation now is an unpleasant one, this phenomenon of the reduction of the motivational size of events more distant in time has the effect that present unpleasant states are compared with probable future pleasant ones, as it were by looking at the future ones through the wrong end of binoculars. The future does not elicit motivation, desire, or preference in relation to its true size. So, at the time of choice, future good things are apt to play less of a role than is their due. A rational person will, of course, make himself see the future in its proper size, and compensate for this feature of human psychology.

Another serious source of error in estimating the potential value to us of possible future outcomes of various courses of action is the very method we sometimes must use, and naturally tend to use, in determining how much we do or will want them or like them when they occur. It is true that sometimes we can and do rely on memory; we can recall, with something less than perfect reliability, how much we enjoyed certain situations in the past (but sometimes we must correct projections from these recollections by information about how we have changed as persons with the effect that we may be able to meet these situations better or worse—say, a night's camping out—and enjoy them more or less, in future). But most frequently what we do, and sometimes the only thing we can do, is simply imagine as vividly as we can what a certain situation would be like, and notice whether it now seems attractive, whether we are now drawn toward it and enthusiastic about it, or not. Unfortunately the reliability of this subjective test, as an indicator of how much we shall want or enjoy a certain kind of thing tomorrow, is seriously affected by the frame of mind in which we make it. Something which in fact we should much like in the future may utterly fail to stir us or even repel us, in a depressed or disappointed frame of mind; its favorable features either escape attention or simply fail to set the motivational machinery into motion which would make it seem attractive. Just as the sight of a good steak leaves us cold when we have just finished a hearty meal (presumably because chemical processes in the hypothalmus desensitize the relevant nervous channels or at any rate block the stimuli from having their ordinarily arousing effects), so the percept of a charming woman and *a fortiori* the mere thought of her will not elicit enthusiastic response from the rejected lover. Sorrow or depression simply shuts off or turns down the motivational machinery on which we customarily rely for deciding whether we will want, or enjoy having, certain things. Except, of course, the thing about which we are depressed; with it, the process is reversed. If there is something we have lost, or are debarred from getting, those of its features which normally strike us as unpleasant or unfavorable are excluded from attention or at any rate lose their repulsive force; whereas a halo is cast upon the features of the object which have been liked or wanted, rather as if the good features were now seen under a microscope and appear much larger than in real life. Why this should be so is not obvious. But even rats, it has been shown, will run harder for something which they have been frustrated in getting, than they run in ordinary circumstances. There is something about being frustrated in getting something which makes it look much better than it ordinarily does.

It is obvious that if we are trying to determine whether we now prefer, or shall later prefer, the outcomes in one world-course to the outcomes of another (and this is leaving aside the question of the weight of the votes of preferences at a later date), we have to take into account these infirmities of our "sensing" machinery. To say this does not tell us what to do about it, since to know that the machinery is out of order is not to tell us what results it would give us if it were working. One maxim of many wise people is to refrain from making important decisions in a stressful frame of mind; and one of the "important" decisions one might make is surely suicide. But, if decisions have to be made, at least one can make one's self recall, as far as possible, how one reacted to outcomes like the ones now to be assessed, on occasions in the past when one was in a normal frame of mind. Such reactions, however rough and defective in reliability, are at least better than the feeble pulses of sensing machinery which is temporarily out of order.

Most suicides which are irrational seem to be suicides of a moment of despair. What should be clear from the above is that a moment of despair should be, if one is seriously contemplating suicide, a moment of reassessment of one's goals and values, a reassessment which the individual must realize is very difficult to make objectively, because of the very quality of his depressed frame of mind. Let us consider in an example what form such a reassessment might take, based on a consideration of the "errors" we have been considering.

Suppose the president of a company is ousted in a reorganization and, to make matters as bad as possible, let us suppose he has made unwise investments so that his income from investments is small and, to cap it off, his wife has eloped with another man. His children are already grown, and he is too old to hope for election to a comparable position in another business. So his career and his home life are gone. Here we have the makings of a suicide. Let us suppose his pessimistic estimates are right: that there is no comparable future open to him in business, and that his wife is really gone. The prospect is one of uninteresting employment, if any; loneliness and no affection from a wife; moving from a luxurious home into a modest apartment; inability to entertain his friends in the manner to which he has been accustomed; and so on. Is all this bearable?

Obviously the man has to find a new mode of life. If he is an interesting man he can count on finding a woman with whom he can be close and who can mean as much to him as his wife actually did; or he may even find that he can become close to several persons of real interest, possibly resulting in an experience enriched beyond his imagination, as compared with the confines of traditional married life. The matter of career is more serious. Even Kant, who condemned suicide in all cases, says (inconsistently, I think) that a man unjustly convicted of a crime, who was offered a choice between death and penal servitude, would certainly, if honorable, "choose death" rather than "the galleys. A man of inner worth does not shrink from death; he would die rather than live as an object of contempt, a member of a gang of scoundrels in the galleys." [2] Kant may have been right about what it is rational to do, in this extreme instance. Would death be better for the ex-president of a company, than accepting a job, let us say, as a shoe salesman? There are 'some compensations in the latter. An intelligent man might find himself interested in engaging in conversation a variety of customers from all walks of life. He can try out his psychological knowledge by devices to play on the vanity of women as a motivation for buying expensive shoes. The prospect might seem unattractive. But, if he wants to be rational, he will not fail to get a full view of the various things about the job which he might enjoy—or which he might enjoy, after a time, when he had got over contrasting them with a past career which is no longer open to him. He will hopefully not forget that as a shoe salesman he will not require sleeping pills because of company problems which he cannot get off his mind. If he understands human nature and his own, he may be able to see that while this job is not as desirable as the post he lost, after a time he can enjoy it and be happy in it and find life worth living. Other reflections which this man may have, relevant to his initial impulse to end it all, will come to mind—applications of the distinctions made above.

At this point David Hume was not his usual perspicuous self—nor was Plato before him.[3] For Hume speaks of the propriety of suicide for one who leads a hated life, "loaded with pain and sickness, with *shame and poverty*."[4] Pain and sickness are one thing; they cannot be enjoyed and cannot be escaped. But shame and poverty are another matter. For some situations Hume might be right. But Hume, accustomed as he was to the good things of life, was too short with shame and poverty; a life which he would classify as one of shame and poverty might be a happy life, inferior to Hume's life style, but still preferable to nothing.

A decision to commit suicide may in certain circumstances be a rational one. But a person who wants to act rationally must take into account at least the various possible "errors" mentioned above, and make appropriate rectifications in his initial evaluations.

2. THE ROLE OF OTHER PERSONS

We have not been concerned with the law, or its justifiability, on the matter of suicide; but we may note in passing that for a long time in the Western world suicide was a felony, and in many states attempted suicide is still a crime. It is also a crime to aid or encourage a suicide in many states; one who makes a lethal device available for a suicidal attempt may be subject to a prison sentence—including physicians, if they provide a lethal dose of sedatives.[5]

The last-mentioned class of statutes raises a question worth our consideration: what are the moral obligations of other persons toward those who are contemplating suicide? I ignore questions of their moral blameworthiness, and of what it is rational for them to do from the point of view of personal welfare, as being of secondary concern. I have no doubt that the question of personal interest is important particularly to physicians who may not wish to risk running afoul of the law; but this risk is, after all, something which partly determines what is their moral obligation, since moral obligation to do something may be reduced by the fact that it is personally dangerous to do it.[6]

The moral obligation of other persons toward one who is contemplating suicide is an instance of general obligation to render aid to those in serious distress, at least when this can be done at no great cost to one's self. I do not think this general principle is seriously questioned by anyone, whatever his moral theory; so I feel free to assume it as a premise. Obviously the person contemplating suicide is in great distress of some sort: if he were not, he would not be considering seriously terminating his life.

How great a person's obligation is to one in distress depends on a number of factors. Obviously a person's wife, daughter, and close friend have special obligations to devote time to helping this sort of person—to going over his problem with him, to thinking it through with him, etc.—which others do not have. But that anyone in this kind of distress has a moral claim on the time of anyone who knows the situation (unless there are others more responsible who are already doing what should be done) is obvious.

What is there an obligation to do? It depends, of course, on the situation, and how much the second person knows about the situation. If the individual has decided to terminate his life if he can, and it is clear that he is right in this decision, then, if he needs help in executing the decision, there is a moral obligation to give him help. If it is sleeping pills he needs, then they should be obtained for him. On this matter a patient's physician has a special obligation, from which all his antiquated talk about the Hippocratic oath does not absolve him. It is true that there are some damages one cannot be expected to absorb, and some risks which one cannot be expected to take, on account of the obligation to render aid. But the cowardice and lack of social responsibility of some physicians can be excused only by conviction of a charge of ignorance.

On the other hand, if it is clear that the individual should not commit suicide, from the point of view of his own welfare, or if there is a presumption that he should not (when the only evidence is that a person is discovered unconscious, with the gas turned on), it would seem to be the individual's obligation to intervene, and prevent the successful execution of the decision, see to the availability of competent psychiatric advice and temporary hospitalization, if necessary. Whether one has a right to take such steps when a clearly sane person, after careful reflection over a period of time, comes to the conclusion that an end to his life is what is best for him and what he wants, is very doubtful, even when one thinks his conclusion a mistaken one; it would seem that a man's own considered decision about whether he wants to live must command respect, although one must concede that this could be debated.

The more interesting role in which a person may be cast, however, is that of adviser. It is often important to one who is contemplating suicide to go over his thinking with another, and to feel that a conclusion, one way or the other, has the support of a respected mind. One thing one can obviously do, in rendering the service of advice, is to discuss with the person the various types of issues discussed above, made more specific by the concrete circumstances of his case, and help him find whether, in view, say, of the damage his suicide would do to others, he has a moral obligation to refrain, and whether it is rational or best for him, from the point of view of his own welfare, to take this step or adopt some other plan instead.

To get a person to see what is the rational thing to do is no small job. Even to get a person, in a frame of mind when he is seriously contemplating (or perhaps has already unsuccessfully attempted) suicide, to recognize a plain truth of fact may be a major operation. If a man insists, "I am a complete failure," when it is obvious that by any reasonable standard he is far from that, it may be tremendously difficult to get him to see the fact. The relaxing quiet of a hospital room may be a prerequisite of ability to think clearly and weigh facts with some perspective.

But there is another job beyond that of getting a person to see what is the rational thing to do; that is to help him *act* rationally, or *be* rational, when he has conceded what would be the rational thing.

How either of these tasks may be accomplished effectively may be discussed more competently by an experienced psychiatrist than by a philosopher. But it may not be inappropriate to point out that sometimes an adviser can *cure* a man's problem, in the course, or instead, of giving advice what to do about it. Loneliness and the absence of human affection (especially from the opposite sex) are states which exacerbate any other problems; disappointment, reduction to poverty, etc., seem less impossible to bear in the presence of the affection of another. Hence simply to be a friend, or to find someone a friend, may be the largest contribution one can make either to helping a person be rational or see clearly what is rational for him to do; this service may make one who was contemplating suicide feel that there is no longer a future for him which it is impossible to face.

NOTES

The paper from which this excerpt is taken was written while the author was a Fellow at the Center for Advanced Study in the Behavioral Sciences, and also a Special Fellow in the Department of Health, Education and Welfare.

1. A patient who announces such a decision to his physician may expect amazement and dismay. The patient should not forget,

however, that except for the area of the physical sciences his physician is likely to be almost a totally ignorant man, whose education has not proceeded beyond high school. The physician is not a reliable source of information about anything but the body.

Physicians are also given to rosy prognoses about the absence of pain in a terminal illness. The writer once had some bone surgery, and after a night of misery listened to a morning radio program entitled "The Conquest of Pain," in which hearers were assured that the medical profession had solved the problem of pain and that they need not give a second thought to this little source of anxiety.

2. *Lectures on Ethics* (New York: Harper Torchbooks, 1963), p. 155.
3. *The Laws,* Bk. IX.
4. "On Suicide." This essay was first published in 1783, and appears in collections of Hume's works.
5. For a proposal for American law on this point see the *Model Penal Code,* Proposed Official Draft, The American Law Institute, 1962, pp. 127–8; also Tentative Draft No. 9, p. 56.
6. The law can be changed, and one of the ways in which it gets changed is by responsible people refusing to obey it and pointing out how objectionable it is on moral grounds. Some physicians have shown leadership in this respect, e.g., on the matter of dispensing birth control information and abortion laws. One wishes there were more of this.

IRRATIONAL SUICIDE

David J. Mayo

Mayo holds that arguments for the acceptance of the notion of rational suicide may increase the number of tragic, irrational ones as well. He points out that there are situations—including acute depression—in which people abandon their ordinary commitment to being as rational as they can, and he suggests that widespread acceptance of suicide as a realistic option in some circumstances might encourage suicide in such cases, even when it is not rational.

David Mayo was educated at Reed College and the University of Pittsburgh, and is now a member of the Department of Philosophy at the University of Minnesota/Duluth. His interests include value theory and medical ethics, and he has recently published a paper on brain death. He has been a member of the American Philosophical Association's Committee on Philosophy and Medicine, and has edited that group's newsletter.

Many contemporary philosophers argue that under certain conditions suicide would be a moral and rational act. But to espouse this view is to wield a double-edged sword, for if it is going to encourage suicide among those for whom it would be rational, it may also do so among those for whom it would be a tragic, irrational mistake. My concern in this paper will be to look briefly at some of the dangers lurking there.

Brandt,[1] one of the most articulate spokespersons for rational suicide, is particularly concerned to warn against the ways in which people "in a state of despair" are apt to go astray when they undertake to make a rational decision on the basis of future consequences of their actions. Such persons, he notes, are particularly apt to overlook certain possible courses of action which might lead them from their present despair. Further, they are apt to assign unrealistically low probabilities to the likelihood that their actions will produce desirable consequences. Finally, they may well deny the possibility of experiencing happiness in the future, because they fail to project themselves beyond their present despair and inability to find happiness in certain kinds of experiences now—rather like the man who goes to the market just after he has eaten a huge meal, only to find there is nothing he thinks he'll enjoy eating tomorrow. Brandt spells out these pitfalls because he feels they are not trivial and must be guarded against; I agree. Nevertheless one is left with the impression that Brandt feels that awareness of them is apt to be adequate safeguard against them. Whether this is the case I leave for the reader to decide—preferably during a moment when he is not "in a state of despair."

The case considered by Brandt and others examining the issue of rational suicide is that of a person who is trying to be rational but who fails because his judgment is in some way clouded. My primary concern is with a different case, namely that of the person in such a state of despair that he simply abandons any serious commitment to making rational decisions. I concede most of us normally manifest such a commitment: we are usually moved to reconsider a situation, for instance, if someone we respect accuses us of being irrational. But I wish to argue that this is by no means universally the case. I suggest that an integral feature of acute despair is often that such a commitment is totally lacking.[2] The person in such a condition is one of the most obvious examples of someone for whom being reasonable may have no appeal whatsoever.[3] Worse yet is the fact that there seem to be situations which not merely incline people to be unreasonable, but virtually require it.

The sorts of situations I have in mind involve human commitments, which may require some kind of irrationality if they are to be respected. Loyalty may involve such commitments; so may love, in its various manifestations.[4] Consider, for instance, the familiar case of the mother who believes that her young child is exceptionally bright. Rather than viewing this belief as deplorable because it is irrational (which it almost always is), most of us are inclined to see it as commendable because it is evidence of the depth of the mother's love and devotion.

Again, imagine the case of someone mourning the loss of a love. The grieving-mourning process has more than a psychological dimension; it has an intentional one as well. That is, it may also be viewed as a final expression of a commitment to the lost one, which contains irrational cognitive components. This process strikes us as entirely appropriate, even though it may involve a refusal to accept certain facts which will be obvious to any outside observer. For instance, the intense feelings of loss which the mourner is experiencing will subside, cease to preoccupy him, and perhaps disappear entirely. Yet while it is probably true that someone who has just lost a spouse after thirty years of happy marriage will feel quite a bit better in a few weeks, be going to baseball games and laughing with friends again in a month, and perhaps even be looking for a new spouse within a year or so, it would be a gross impropriety to confront the mourner with such claims, and for him it would be an unthinkable display of "bad faith" with the lost love to find comfort in assenting to them.

By the same token the sixteen-year-old who is shattered when his first love leaves him for someone else is not disposed to listen to (true) claims about how this happens to most of us when we lose our first love, how he's certain to get over it and probably forget all about her, and how the chances are excellent that he'll find another about whom he'll feel just as strong and with whom he'll laugh someday over memories of his present distress. Indeed, from his point of view, to accept the assimilation of his case to a universal pattern, or to entertain seriously the possibility of forgetting all about his unrequited love and finding someone else, would constitute a profound betrayal of the very feelings for the first girl which are causing him so much anguish—again, "bad faith." The fact that this must happen eventually if he is to get on with his life does not negate the fact that we respect, and indeed expect, a period of mourning of which irrational pessimism is to be an integral part.

The ubiquity of such situations suggests that philosophical arguments in favor of rational suicide, even if they are accompanied by warnings of the ways in which reason may go astray, provide little safeguard against irrational suicide: the propensity to irrationality, especially in the kinds of interpersonal relationships which often occasion suicide, appears after all to be something we respect, even when it serves as a basis for action.

Do these considerations give reason for withdrawing philosophical arguments favoring the possibility of rational suicide and instead arguing against all suicide whatsoever, so as to prevent increases in irrational suicide? Perhaps those who argue for widespread acceptance of rational suicide—Barrington, for instance[5]—should ask themselves whether the benefits they see resulting from such a change in public attitude mightn't be outweighed in the long run by the costs which might accrue by way of an increased number of irrational suicides. Or perhaps the doctrine of rational suicide manifests the same paradoxical feature which is often attributed to the thesis of ethical egoism, namely that for those who believe it, it becomes a matter of moral obligation to keep it dark.

N O T E S

1. "The Rationality of Suicide," in this volume, p. 117.
2. I avoid use of the term "depression" here because in some circles it seems to beg the very question at issue. I have in mind the Szaszian point that the remark that someone is depressed, or suffering depression, is viewed not merely as a remark about that person's despair or unhappiness, but as a quasi-medical classification of the person as someone who (like the measles victim) is suffering from some kind of illness—in this case "mental illness." Thus one can be led down the primrose path of medical paternalism from the judgment that someone is very depressed, to the judgment that he is "suffering acute depression," to the judgment that he is "mentally ill," to the judgment that he is an "invalid" in the medical sense. This in turn may lead to a decision that his legal-moral rights can properly be abridged, since he is incompetent to make valid decisions.
3. Another obvious example is a young person who is euphorically happy because he is in love. This contempt for reason seems to occur equally in persons experiencing "highs" and

those experiencing "lows." Persons who are elated, jubilant, or experiencing a rush of exhilaration may well greet charges that they are being unreasonable with disdain. They acknowledge that they are being unreasonable—by taking unnecessary chances, for instance—but are untouched by that realization. "Being reasonable" may strike them as a rather dry, cautious, and unrewarding procedure which does not interest them at all at that moment.

4. This, surely, is part of the force of the adage "Love is blind."
5. Mary Rose Barrington, "Apologia for Suicide," this volume, p. 90.

ON CHOOSING DEATH

Philip E. Devine

Devine argues that death cannot be chosen rationally. He claims that death could be a rational choice only if it involved choosing the best among alternatives which can be known and compared, but that because death manifests a "logical opaqueness," it precludes such a comparison.

Educated at Yale and Berkeley, Philip Devine now teaches philosophy at the University of Scranton. He is the author of The Ethics of Homicide *(Cornell, 1978), from which this paper is taken, and of papers on the ontological argument for the existence of God. He is currently working on a book on ethical theory.*

A celebrated Epicurean argument runs as follows: since death is annihilation, since (in Aristotle's phrase) "nothing is thought to be any longer good or bad for the dead,"[1] it follows not that death is the greatest of all evils but that death is no evil at all. Fear of death is irrational, because there is nothing of the appropriate sort—no state or condition of ourselves as conscious beings—to be afraid of in death.[2] This Epicurean argument supports the common contention that death may sometimes be an object of rational choice.

I wish to discuss critically this view, and to attempt to support the claim (for which the testimony of sensitive persons is overwhelming) that there is something uncanny about death, especially one's own.[3] I do not want to deny that a suicide can be calmly and

138

deliberately, and in that sense rationally, carried out. But then someone might calmly and deliberately do something blatantly foolish or even pointless, and it is sometimes rational to act quickly and with passionate fervor. But if, as seems plausible, a precondition of rational choice is that one know *what* one is choosing, either by experience or by the testimony of others who have experienced it or something very like it, then it is not possible to choose death rationally. Nor is any degree of knowledge of what one desires to escape by death helpful, since rational choice between two alternatives requires knowledge of both. The issue is not whether pain (say) is bad, but whether a certain degree of pain is worse than death. It might seem at least that progressively more intense misery gives progressively stronger reasons for killing oneself, but the situation is rather like this. If one is heating a metal whose melting point one does not know at all, one knows that the more heat one applies, the closer one gets to melting the metal. But it does not follow that it is possible to know—before the metal actually starts melting—that one has even approached the melting point.

It is necessary, however, seriously to consider the contention that there are experiences—being flayed and kept alive by ingenious means afterwards for instance—in preference to which it is clearly rational to choose death. At this point in the argument it is necessary to separate the claim that such a choice would be rationally required (that it would not be rational to decide to continue to live under such circumstances) from the claim that it is rationally permitted (that it might be rational both to decide to live and to decide to die). As far as the first of these possibilities is concerned, I do not see how someone could be considered irrational if he decides to show what a human being is capable of enduring. As for the second, while it is true that suicide under such circumstances has a powerful appeal, so does suicide in many other circumstances as well, such as when one will otherwise be exposed to disgrace and dishonor of an extreme sort, or when one is convinced that one's unbearable emotional difficulties will never be resolved. Perhaps all these kinds of suicide are rational too (although contemporary defenders of the possibility of rational suicide do not commonly think so), but if so their rationality is not of the calculative sort. We are dealing, that is, not with a situation concerning which rational men will exhibit a range of estimates, but with a situation in which one man's estimate is as good as another, because what is being done is a comparison with an unknown quality.

I do not mean to imply that we can have no knowledge of what death is, that we cannot for instance teach a child the meaning of "death." But consider what we can do. We can show the child a corpse, but a corpse is not a dead person (that is, not in the required sense of something which is dead and a person, something one of *us*—except in a stretched sense—could be), but only what a person leaves behind when he dies. We can make the child a witness at a deathbed, but to do that is simply to show a living person becoming a corpse. We can tell the child that death is not seeing friends any more (and so on), but somehow he will have to learn how to take these negatives properly, since otherwise death will be confused with all one's friends' leaving town. Finally, we can tell him a myth, even a subdued one such as "death is everlasting sleep," or that death is the absence of life, much as nakedness is the absence of clothing. (In nakedness, of course, the person who existed clothed continues to exist unclothed.) And that such mythology is logically appropriate is part of what I shall call the opaqueness of death.

The opaqueness of death does not result from uncertainty as to our condition afterward, although what I am getting at is sometimes expressed in such terms. My point is rather that it is folly to think that one can housebreak death by representing it as annihilation. One might—considering that the opaqueness of death is a *logical* opaqueness—be tempted to compare the qualms I have expressed about rationally choosing death with skeptical qualms about our right to believe that the sun will rise tomorrow, which rest on the logical difference between inductive and deductive reasoning. To press this comparison would be a mistake, however, for two reasons. First, we routinely have to make choices based on inductive evidence, whereas we do not routinely choose to die or to go on living. Second, the myths cited indicate that the opaqueness of death is a real element in human motivation and self-understanding, an element that cannot be neglected even, or especially, if one considers these myths all to be false.

Human beings characteristically find themselves in profound imaginative and intellectual difficulty when they attempt to envisage the end of their existence. This difficulty is not lessened by the experience of sleep, since sleep, even when dreamless, presupposes the continuation of the self in being and the possibility of an awakening. (I say the possibility, since someone might die before he wakes, and Sleeping Beauty remains alive though asleep even if Prince Charming never arrives.) Nor is the difficulty lessened by interviewing those whose hearts have stopped and who have revived, since what one would learn about in that way is not death but apparent dying.

The difficulty does not lie, at least not centrally, in imagining a world without me, but rather in connecting this world with my (self-regarding) concerns. (Altruistic and disinterested concerns are not at issue at this particular point, since they do not bear on the question of why death can be an evil for the dead person himself. In any case, an altruistic suicide can be rational or irrational in a straightforward way: I might be rational in believing that my suicide will protect my comrades from the secret police, whereas if I lived I would talk and they would be captured and tortured to death, and I might be quite unrealistic in my calculation of the effect my self-immolation will have on public opinion.) Even my aversions, my desires not to experience certain things, do not connect easily with such a world, since there is for instance a logical gap between "freedom from pain" resulting from the nonexistence of the subject of pain and ordinary painless existence. To put the same point another way, if I am contemplating suicide, I am not trying to choose (not centrally, that is) "between future world-courses: the world-course which contains my demise, say, an hour from now, and several possible ones which contain my demise at a later point."[4] What I am contemplating is much more intimate than a world-course. It is my own (self-chosen) death, and such a choice presents itself inevitably as a leap in the dark.

But the decision to kill oneself—it might be argued—need not reflect a preference of death over life, but rather of one (shorter) life over another, or of one (speedier) death over another. The clearest cases of preferences of this sort are choices it would be odd to call suicide. I might take a remedy that makes my present life more tolerable, while somewhat shortening its length, or I might, being tied up and about to be hanged, decide to jump rather than wait to be pushed. Self-execution is in a class apart from ordinary suicide in any case, as any reader of the *Phaedo* might confirm, and it may be possible to speak of self-execution even in cases where the person convicted does what the executioner ought to do, and commutes, with his own hand, a painful and degrading death to one that is relatively painless. The distinction between choosing death rather than life and choosing one kind of life or death rather than another does not turn, in any case, on the nearness of the death in question. A remedy that makes present life more tolerable may shorten a life expectancy of forty years to thirty-five, or of a week to a day. And if a twenty-year-old should choose irrevocably to be killed at seventy, it would, I think, be fair to say that he had chosen death (at seventy) in preference to old age.

One can perhaps get a better grip on what is involved here by comparing the choice of death with other radical and irreversible choices. (Some first-time choices, e.g., to visit London, present no problem, since one knows that one can always cut one's losses if things do not turn out as desired.) In many of these choices one can be guided, in part at any rate, by the experience of those who have gone before, but this will not always work, since there had to be a first person to undergo a sex-change operation, take LSD, and so on. Choices of this sort are not necessarily irrational, but if rational . . . their rationality must be explained in terms of the general rationality of risk-taking (which is supported to a degree by experience). This notion does not seem to apply in the case of choosing death. The difference between these choices and that of death is a logical one. While it is logically possible (even if not possible in this particular case) to get an idea of what it is like to have taken LSD, from someone who has done so, death is of necessity that from which no one returns to give tidings.

One might, indeed, attempt to explain our fear of death in precisely these terms: fear of death is fear of the unknown. Of course this is a metaphor, since the opaqueness of death is logical rather than epistemological. But the unknown is attractive as well as fearful, and death has in fact, alongside its fearfulness, the attractiveness which is a feature of the limits of human experience. It does not seem possible, on these premises alone, to resolve the tension between death's fearfulness and its attractiveness.

NOTES

1. *Nicomachean Ethics* 1115a 25, tr. W.D. Ross, in Richard McKeon, ed., *The Basic Works of Aristotle* (New York: Random House, 1941), p. 975.
2. Lucretius, *De Rerum Natura*, III, 870 ff.
3. I'd like to discuss these, that is, without falling into the logical errors criticized by someone like Paul Edwards. See his article 'My Death,' in Paul Edwards, ed., *Encyclopedia of Philosophy* (New York, 1967), Vol. 5.
4. Richard B. Brandt, "The Rationality of Suicide," p. 117.

SUICIDE AND FALSE DESIRES

Robert M. Martin

Martin argues against paternalistic intervention in suicide. He claims that the usual rationale for paternalistic intervention in other kinds of situations is that we are trying to protect the person from future regrets, which would result from acting on present "false desires." But a person who kills himself cannot regret. Thus, even though the desire to kill oneself may be a hastily conceived or misguided one, there is no justification for interfering since the person will suffer no bad consequences from his misguided action.

Is killing himself ever one's real aim? We can't deny that (at least) most people want to go on living. But it is sometimes claimed that all, or at least many, who seem bent on killing themselves do not *really* want to die—that death is not *really* in their interests. These claims are often part of an attempt to justify the policy of forceful intervention to prevent suicide, on the grounds that this would be doing people the favour of saving them from the death they don't really want.

Two parts of this argument are questionable: the claim that suicide is always or usually a *false desire* in some sense; and the implied premise that we are justified in interfering when someone is acting against his true interests or desires. I think there are *certain* cases when we might be justified in interfering in some mild ways when someone is about to act against his real interests or desires, though I won't go into the difficult question of exactly when this sort of paternalistic intervention is permissible. I shall argue that claims that suicide is always or usually a false desire are unfounded, and that we are not justified in interfering in even those cases in which the desire for death is a false one.

One sort of argument for intervention on the grounds that suicide isn't really desired is based on the claim that suicidal people are always or usually mentally ill, or at least pathologically disturbed or irrational. One does not want to make these claims trivial because they are definitionally true, by defining irrationality or mental illness to include suicidal desires or behaviours; for this argument to be any good, there have to be independent grounds for these claims. Professional opinion varies here. Some argue that being suicidal is not a symptom of mental illness at all.[1] Others want to distinguish people who are irrationally suicidal from those whose suicidal impulses spring from a "realistic assessment of life situations."[2] Still others claim that rational suicide is an extreme rarity, and that most suicidal individuals "are suffering from clinically recognizable psychiatric illnesses."[3] The debate is a complicated one, often involving questionable psychological theories, assertions about matters of fact one wishes were supported by more empirical observation, and the interesting problem that notions like *health* and *rationality* and their opposites skip around among descriptive, theoretical, and rather arbitrarily evaluative uses. Going further into these questions is beyond the scope of this paper, but I'll note the following: It is the suicidal desires of the *sane* I'm interested in here, and almost everyone admits that it's possible for sane people to have these desires. Nevertheless, it's not at all obvious that mentally ill or irrational people ought, in general, to be prevented from acting on their desires, or that they should be paternalistically forced to act in accord with what we think their desires ought to be. Furthermore, even if there *are* occasions when ill or irrational people ought, for their own good, to be prevented from doing what they think they want to, there are special considerations (which I'll raise later) which make it inappropriate to treat suicidal desires in particular this way.

An argument for intervention in suicide of the sane is based on the claim that suicides are always (or often) ambivalent, and thus don't really want death:

Individuals who are intent on killing themselves still wish very much to be rescued or to have their deaths prevented.

> Suicide prevention consists essentially in recognizing that the potential victim is "in balance" between his wishes to live and his wishes to die, then throwing one's efforts on the side of life.[4]

It is not clear why this author speaks of the contrary wishes of the suicidal individual as "in balance" while assuming that he is about to kill himself; one would imagine that the individual about to act this way has desires to die that have *outweighed* the contrary ones (especially if he is *"intent"* on killing himself). Perhaps what is really meant here is that suicides are "ambivalent" in the sense that although on balance they wish to die, still strong residual doubts and contrary feelings remain. But why is this supposed to justify intervention? We all continue to harbour doubts whenever we make up our minds about any difficult choice; but this hardly means that we don't *really* want to do what we've decided, or that someone else is then justified in stopping us.

There are, however, four legitimate senses in which we may be said to have false desires — to think we want what we really don't, or to desire something that's not really in our interests:

Sense 1: Someone sincerely says she wants to become famous; after she does succeed at this, however, she discovers that fame doesn't have the charms she thought it would, and has its own agonies. She says, "I thought I wanted to be famous, but I really didn't." This is a case of incomplete or mistaken information about the object desired.

Sense 2: Someone believes falsely that a tidal wave will flood his home town. He sells his house at a great loss, and quits his good job. Although he understood fully the nature and implications of his desired actions (selling and quitting), he discovers that those actions were not what he really wanted to do —that they were not really in his interests—when he finds out that there will be no tidal wave. Here there is false or incomplete information about circumstances.

Sense 3: Someone thinks that the only way to get good grades at school is to bribe her instructors, but later finds out that a bit of studying instead would have resulted in better grades at less cost. Her wanting to bribe her instructors wasn't in accord with her real interests because of false or incomplete information about alternatives.

Sense 4: Someone has a bad day at the office, and suddenly and uncharacteristically decides the business world is not for him. Later he regrets having thrown his career away; he feels that his earlier dissatisfaction, while it was real enough at the time, was false in the sense that it was fleeting and not representative of his enduring personality.

Now, desire to kill oneself may be false desire in any of these four senses. Someone may want to kill himself because (sense 1) he falsely believes he will go to a land of everlasting bliss after death; or because (sense 2) he falsely believes he is suffering from a terminal and debilitating disease; or because (sense 3) he isn't aware that there are forms of therapy which can cure his growing depressions; or because (sense 4) he feels a serious but atypical and fleeting suicidal urge. We can say of all these people that they don't *really* want to die, or that death is not congruent with their *real* values or interests.

Clearly, there have been suicides because of false desires like these, though I wouldn't want to guess what proportion of suicidal desires are false. George Murphy claims that the percentage of suicidal desires that are false in sense 4 is large:

> We can confidently predict recovery from [the suicidal] urge in the great majority of cases, when other symptoms of depression lift. The desire to terminate one's life is usually transient. The "right" to suicide is a "right" desired only temporarily.[5]

Louise Horowitz, in an article which otherwise strongly opposes interference with suicide, argues that

> one can distinguish between suicides which are appropriate and those which are the result of misinterpretations or failures to see the alternative courses of action. . . . We . . . have the right in the interest of rationality to point out alternative courses of action which we believe [the suicidal person] may have overlooked. But the individual contemplating suicide is not obliged to defend his decision, only to discuss it in order to avoid making a mistake.[6]

It seems to me that it is *sometimes* appropriate to interfere with the carrying out of false nonsuicide desires in the mild ways Horowitz indicates, especially when the person involved is a friend, has asked our advice, and the like. But I shall argue that intervention is *never* appropriate when the false desire is for suicide, because suicide desires are importantly different from others.

When (if ever) do we feel justified in intervening to prevent someone's actions? I should think that the justification for this could be that what the person was about to do was not *for his own good* (I ignore the other valid reason: when others would be harmed). Now, something is incompatible with the agent's own good when it conflicts either with his current interests and desires or when it will conflict with future interests and desires. The examples of nonsuicidal false desire, previously mentioned, are cases in which a current desire has consequences that will conflict with the agent's future interests and desires. (I am assuming here that something counts as harm for an individual only if it or its consequences conflict with some value or desire of that individual himself.) Intervention is (perhaps sometimes) justified, because it would spare the agent future grief.

But suppose that someone never is in position to suffer conflict with his real desires as a result of acting on false desires. Suppose, for example, that the woman who wanted to be famous (case 1, above) had felt satisfied with her life as she worked toward fame, but died before she became famous enough to find out that it was not what she thought it would be. What justification would there have been for preventing her from acting on her false desire? None, because she never did suffer conflict with her real values and desires as a result of her actions. Had she lived, she would have regretted her efforts to become famous; but her life, as actually lived, was satisfying to her and congruent with all her felt wishes and values.

Now let us examine the false desire for suicide. Suicide results in death, of course, and we normally count death as a harm. But we do because we value our life. However, if someone wants to die, death does not count as a harm *for him.* But what if the desire for death is a false desire? When we intervene in what would otherwise be a successful suicide, we *never* save the agent from a future state incompatible with any of his desires or values, from any grief or regret as a consequence of his actions. The man who believes that death will bring him to paradise will not be disappointed—not because he will go to paradise, but because there won't be any *him* left after his death to be disappointed. The person who kills himself because of the false belief that he has a terminal disease won't regret his decision. The man who killed himself unaware that therapy could have helped his depression won't be worse off than had we intervened, because after his death he won't be *any* way; and because before death he desired death and got it. And the man who had the fleeting desire for death won't suffer when he returns to more stable and characteristic contrary desires, because he won't return.

The point here is that suicide is the act of putting one's self out of existence—an obvious point, but one that seems to have been widely ignored in the discussion of the subject. We can't then make the usual sorts of judgment about acts and their consequences for the agent, because death is the only consequence for him, and after that there is no more agent. A false desire for death is, after all, a desire for death; suicide achieves that desire, and the agent does not live to suffer the normal consequences of acting on false desires.

It is this argument I referred to above when talking about insane or irrational suicidal desires. They are *desires,* after all, and thus have a *prima facie* claim for satisfaction; and if no agent will suffer bad consequences, why is it benevolent to interfere?

For these reasons I think that although false desires may sometimes justify intervention, in the case of suicide they never do. I do think, but for reasons I shall not argue here, that considerations related to our duties to others may show suicide to be sometimes immoral, and when these duties are so strong as to override an agent's valid claim to do what he wants to do, we are justified in interfering in suicide. But when such considerations are not relevant (and I think occasions when they are relevant are rare), we must not interfere in suicide.[7]

NOTES

1. Thomas S. Szasz, "The Ethics of Suicide," p. 185.
2. Jerome A. Motto, "The Right to Suicide: A Psychiatrist's View," p. 212.
3. George E. Murphy, "Suicide and the Right to Die," Editorial,

American Journal of Psychiatry 130 (No. 4, April 1973), p. 472.

4. Edwin S. Shneidman, "Preventing Suicide," *American Journal of Nursing* 65 (No. 5, 1965), p. 10.

5. Murphy, "Suicide and the Right to Die." p. 472.

6. Louise Horowitz, "The Morality of Suicide," *Journal of Critical Analysis* III (No. 4, January 1972), pp. 164–5.

7. The author expresses gratitude to his colleague, Dr. Susan Sherwin, and to the editors of this book, for helpful suggestions on preliminary drafts of this article.

SUICIDE AS INSTRUMENT AND EXPRESSION

David Wood

Wood criticizes as obsolete the concept of "natural death," and attempts to discredit the view that suicide is wrong because it preempts natural death. He then distinguishes instrumental *suicide (which aims at particular causal consequences) from* expressive *suicide (which seeks to convey a meaning), and examines the circumstances under which suicides of either type may be irrational.*

David Wood received his first degree in philosophy from the University of Manchester, and did his graduate work at Oxford. Since 1971 he has taught philosophy at the University of Warwick. He has published articles on moral philosophy and on contemporary French philosophy, in which he specializes. He is currently writing a book on time.

To choose suicide is not to choose to die. Being mortal, we have no choice about dying. What the suicide chooses is how, when, and where he will die, and perhaps to what end and with what meaning. We must learn to understand suicide against the background of the *alternatives* to suicide. These include, among others, accidental death, murder, and euthanasia. But the main contender may seem to be what we call natural death—dying "when one's time is up"—and many objections to suicide rest on a belief in the timeliness, appropriateness, rightness, and guaranteed dignity of natural death. I shall argue that the concept of natural death is muddled, and that many of the values it embodies are realized more effectively by suicide.

In John Steinbeck's *Grapes of Wrath*, the family at the center of the novel, who are driving a truck to California, discover that Granma, lost in a rear corner of the truck, has died. After many expressions of grief, the process of rationalization begins. Al says, "Well, she was ol'. Guess her time was up. Ever'body got to die. . . . Well ain't they?"

The fact of the matter is that Granma was sick and should not have been traveling through the heat of the desert in a truck. But that is not seen as any impediment to claiming that "her time was up." It is clear that the concept of natural death (or of one's time being up) is a convenient fiction in such cases, playing a central role in an accounting procedure by which an avoidable death is rationalized by those who remain.

Two social changes lead us to reexamine this notion of natural death. On the one hand we have a greatly increased knowledge of the effect of life-styles, habits, pleasures, and so on on one's life span; the partial truths contained in the many ways one is advised to become and stay healthier are all symptoms of a considerably increased personal health autonomy. On the other hand the huge strides in medicine have not only facilitated the cure of many diseases, but have also made possible ways of prolonging the lives of people who would previously have died earlier. These two developments knit oddly together, because they seem to represent conflicting values: self-help, and reliance on high technology. But they share an important feature: they make what was once thought "natural" dependent in part on human decision. More and more, people effectively have to say, "If that's the price (either financially or emotionally) of a year or two more, I'd rather not pay it." And both these developments can and do induce anxiety. The knowledge and the options they open up are often genuinely *unwelcome*, both because they pose choices we would rather not have to make (e.g., whether to opt for some hazardous, painful operation rather than die certainly and soon in comfort), and, more importantly, because the anxiety appears focused on the disappearance of any guaranteed *sense* to natural death, of dying "when one's time is up."

The notion of natural death makes reference to an intelligible, usually moral order of things. In this teleological picture, everything is for the best; everything has its reason, its place, and its time, in accord with "fate" or "destiny." It is a very old picture, a comforting one, but cognitively primitive. And the changes I have documented—increasing control over one's health and increasing technical means of forestalling death—attack this teleological framework. For they offer a perfectly intelligible sense in which we can say that a person would have died before now, if he had not done something to prevent it (e.g., stopped smoking, taken his insulin, or undergone a kidney transplant). The point at which decisions over life spans are made is no longer exclusively, if at all, a transcendent one. And as this framework is attacked at its roots and as a whole, we cannot continue to suppose that *some* deaths are natural and some are not, for in this teleological world picture either all deaths are natural or none are.

But it is this very concept of a natural death that has often been thought to give the time of death a seal of rightness that suicide lacks. Suicide, in this picture, expresses a capricious will, while natural death conforms to a divine will, an overarching world purpose, or some other principle of intelligible order. If we do value the *rightness* of the time at which we die, the moribund status of the concept of natural death opens the way for suicide to take its place as the best substitute. One might indeed make a tragic mistake, but there is no reason to suppose that nature is infallible either. And we can reduce the incidence of misguided suicide if we think hard about what a rational suicide would look like.

TWO TYPES OF RATIONAL SUICIDE: INSTRUMENTAL AND EXPRESSIVE

The best way of approaching this question is to think of suicide as an act. (There are of course many suicides of negligence and drawn-out suicides in which its quality as an act in any simple sense may be obscured; for present purposes we will have to ignore these complications.) We can immediately make a distinction between two kinds of acts: those that aim at bringing about some result, and those that are not primarily to be understood in terms of their efficacy. Some acts can be understood in cause/ effect terms, and other acts (like many speech-acts, for example) can be thought of in terms of *meaning*. We call the first group *instrumental* and the second group *expressive*. Since this way of distinguishing different acts is especially relevant to the way in which such acts can be *rational,* let us distinguish between instrumental and expressive suicides. We will see that this distinction is not exclusive.

By *instrumental suicide* I mean suicide intended to bring about some effect by the act. There are two important varieties of instrumental suicide:

1. *Suicide in which the result aimed at is an empirical consequence of the fact of one's death (purely instrumental).* This is by far the best endowed category, including both suicides which have effects on others, such as sparing one's family the excessive costs of terminal illness, and those which have effects on oneself, such as avoiding pain and suffering, humiliation, indignity, or scandal.

2. *Suicide in which the result arrived at is a consequence of the act of killing oneself, treated as an act (expressively instrumental).* The consequences of purely instrumental suicide would all have been achieved if instead one had died naturally at the same time. But there is a special range of consequences brought about by the fact that the suicide takes his own life. Here the *meaning* of one's act has an effect. I include here some martyrdom, some deliberate self-sacrifice (such as the self-immolation of Buddhist monks), and suicide as an act of revenge. The aim of dying is that one's act of dying by suicide will have an effect on others.

By *expressive suicide* I mean suicide intended to convey a meaning logically related to the act itself. Again there are two important varieties:

1. *Suicide which is exhausted by its meaning (purely expressive).* The only effect this type of expressive suicide seeks is to be understood: it may be a gesture of disgust, contempt, or perhaps an affirmation of belief in some better world beyond. It is widely accepted that many "attempted" suicides are really acts of com-

munication—cries for help, which can be unintendedly and tragically fatal—but true, deliberate suicide can equally be infused with a communicative intent.

2. *Suicide in which the result arrived at is a consequence of one's expressive act (expressively instrumental).* This second type of expressive suicide we have already dealt with as a form of instrumental suicide. In such a case it is not merely intended that the meaning of one's act be understood, but also that the meaning should have a further effect, such as inspiring action. The point of dealing with this type of suicide under both headings is that different considerations as to its rationality apply to it depending on the aspect under which it is being considered.

THE ASSESSMENT OF RATIONALITY: PROBLEMS AND PROVISOS

Instrumental suicides have seemed obviously capable of being rational, and yet two key questions must be asked. The first is whether the sums are right—whether one's act will bring about the end in mind. The second is whether one really does want that end. These questions have been extensively discussed in the literature, and we shall only sketch them here.

The adaptation of means to ends, the first question about the rationality of instrumental suicide, is not a matter of simple arithmetic. There is first the problem of having to make predictions in many areas not subject to simple scientific laws, where the absence of clear probabilities makes decisions very difficult. The second problem is that one cannot informedly predict one's own future reactions to the external circumstances one has managed to predict. Even if there were a consistent body of science devoted to the psychology of aging, or terminal illness, or any other condition which might occasion suicide, such disciplines would be of limited use to a particular individual.

It is true that these two basic problems of choice in instrumental suicide apply equally well to any future one chooses, so they do not constitute an obstacle to the rationality of suicide in particular. However, we must not lose sight of these problems. Despite the fact that the successful suicide loses all interest in the question of correction, he may be just as concerned, in advance, with making the right decision. And the very finality of suicide makes the indeterminacy of the future even more important than in most other acts.

A third problem concerning the rationality of instrumental suicide arises in the more complex area of the genuineness of one's desires. The normal principle that allows rationality to operate in the midst of errors of fact and judgment rests on the correctability of these errors by the same rational being. But as suicide rules out such correction, it is important that one really want the end one aims at by suicide.

We often do things we later regret because we did not think them through at the time. Sometimes what we do not think through is whether we really do value the principle at stake more than some other principle that is also, though less obviously, involved. I may lie to keep someone out of jail and later discover that no one believes what I say any longer. My general credibility is sacrificed for someone's freedom, and I might well not have done this had I thought it all through first. If so, such an act fails the test of rationality.

The rationality of instrumental actions depends also on the accuracy and trustworthiness of the empirical beliefs underlying an action. It is easy to suppose that the question of the rationality of one's acts is simply a logical one, and that all one need do is see whether the act would be a practical deduction from the beliefs and values taken as premises. But this is not so. It is irrational to make important decisions on the basis of sincere but weakly supported beliefs, even if it may not be irrational to make unimportant decisions on those same beliefs. If one judges from its appearance that the ice is thick enough, it might well not be irrational to cross a shallow puddle in the road; and yet it would be highly reckless to use the same evidence as a basis for crossing a deep lake. We cannot say that committing suicide on the basis of one's beliefs is rational, if to hold those beliefs is not. Making important decisions on the basis of weakly supported beliefs is irrational. And this is quite as true of the values and attitudes one holds as the beliefs one has in matters of fact.

We do not end up with any hard and fast way of deciding whether an instrumental suicide aimed at promoting a certain end is rational. What I do claim is that the simple fact that the person *believes* he will attain a certain end, or believes that he values the end highly, is not a sufficient condition for rationality. Furthermore, we take it to be a condition of a rational suicide that there are good reasons for thinking it to be the only or best means of realizing the end in question. It would be irrational to kill oneself to promote an end when writing a letter of protest would be equally effective. It is irrational, that is, if the suicide is treated instrumentally. But it does not follow that it is irrational per se, as we shall see.

The second main category of rational suicide we have called *expressive*. Two sorts of consideration bear on the rationality of such expressive acts: first, whether one really feels, means, or believes what one is expressing by one's act, and second, whether the act is appropriate or adequate to express those attitudes or beliefs.

Thus it would be irrational to kill oneself for what would otherwise be a good reason if that was just a thought that had crossed one's mind at breakfast, and had thus not had its adequacy explored. Second, the act must be adequate to the meaning supposed to be conveyed by it. There is no doubting the momentous nature of suicide, and even though there are no firm conventions as to what suicide can and cannot express, there are certainly meanings one would think inappropriate. Inappropriateness can take many forms: an old newspaper clipping reminds me of an arsonist who claimed to a judge that he set fire to a barn to show that Einstein was wrong. No doubt a longer story could be told, but one's first reaction is irrelevance. Finally, suicide could be relevant but still inappropriate: the action might for example be too extreme. It would be irrational to throw oneself in front of a car to publicize the evils of the internal combustion engine, since one's sanity might rather be questioned (though there is some relevance in choosing to die under a car rather than, say, horses' hooves).

The question of sanity and communication raises a difficult problem. If we accept that there are no logically private meanings, can it be rational to mean something by one's suicide that no one is likely ever to discover or understand? Ought one in principle always be able to write an informative suicide note to go with the body (perhaps like Shaw's prefaces to his plays)?

One might kill oneself intending that one's suicide embody a meaning that one nonetheless knows no one else is likely to understand. The claim that such a death could not be rational rests on a number of weak assumptions: first, that if an act is rational it ought to be publicly decidable that it is so, and second, that after the suicide is dead, his act will have no meaning and thus be irrational, unless he has succeeded in conveying that meaning to someone else. But the principle of public decidability—that if there is no one around who can recognize the meaning of an act, then it has no meaning—is either false or uninteresting. It is false if one takes the "has" tenselessly, because it did once have a meaning to the prospective suicide himself. If all that is meant is that no one *any longer* recognizes this, then it is quite true but rather less interesting; there are doubtless many acts performed by extinct and exotic primitive people—indeed, our own ancestors—that no one alive today would understand. But that does not confer retrospective irrationality—just cultural distance. The mere empirical absence of a public meaning to a suicide is no obstacle to the rationality of an expressive suicide, unless of course communication was specifically intended by the person in question. The disconcerting conclusion here is that a suicide can be rational not only without anyone knowing it, but without anyone understanding it at all, and that goes for suicides both in prospect and in retrospect. Meaning is logically but not on every contingent occasion linked to communication.

For instance, it is instructive to analyze our feelings of repugnance at the Jonestown "suicides" at the People's Temple in Guyana, in November 1978. It is easy to suppose that the object of one's repugnance is the mere fact of mass suicide. But it is more plausibly related to the mixture of coercion and indoctrination involved. If it were reported that the members of a recently discovered primitive tribe had collectively committed suicide to avoid what they realized was the inevitable destruction of their way of life, we would not feel repugnance so much as sorrow, misery, and shame. Such a collective act *could* clearly satisfy our criteria of expressive rationality.

To be quite clear about this, we are not claiming that an act of suicide could be rational if what it expressed could not in principle be understood by anyone else, but rather that it is quite possible that no one who in fact could understand it will turn up. We may never know what the meaning of the Jonestown suicides was, if indeed any of them had a *meaning* at all; but a suicide can still have a meaning even if the individual *knows* that no one who might understand it is likely to chance along. I would suggest as an example the suicide (by jumping) of an architect who pioneered high-rise apartments, realizing too late, and with considerable remorse, that the results of his life's work were to have substantially diminished the quality of human life. Even if there were no one around to understand his regrets, his suicide could be rationally grounded.

Thus, although the pitfalls are many, both instrumental and expressive suicide can sometimes be rational. In the case of instrumental suicide, whether one is aiming to avoid some unpleasant future or to bring about some effect by one's death, one must be aware of the difficulties of prediction of both future facts and one's attitude to them, and of the effects of one's suicide. And in expressive suicide, in which a meaning is intended, the act can suffer from lack of genuineness of feeling and from the irrelevance or inappropriateness of suicide as an expression of that feeling. All are grounds for deeming a particular case of suicide to be irrational. Nevertheless, some cases of suicide escape these difficulties and must be recognized as rational.

However, this has certain practical consequences. Once the possibility of suicide being a rational act is admitted—whether instrumental or expressive, and even, as we have claimed, when the reasons for it are not in fact publicly intelligible—then the mere desire to kill oneself cannot by itself be used as a convincing sign of mental illness or justification for involuntary institutionalization or treatment. Independent diagnostic grounds are necessary; and these may not be of the order of "unwillingness to be treated," "tends to go off on his own," and the like. On the other hand if we suppose that some people's desire for suicide can be changed by sunshine and fresh air, by relaxation therapy, dietary supplements, or a chance to talk, whether or not one labels them mentally ill, it is madness to leave such people to their own suicidal devices. While we respect a reasoned decision, we should not always counsel noninterference. In most cases simple prevention or delaying of a particular act of suicide is not inconsistent with respect for a person's autonomy in choosing suicide as either an instrumental or an expressive act.

The fact that a suicide is *rational* does not necessarily mean that it is reasoned. A rational suicide is one for which there are good reasons (subjective or objective), and a reasoned suicide is one performed after considering these good reasons. The considerations we have offered as to how a suicide may misfire from the point of view of its rationality suggest that a fully rational suicide is most likely to be a reasoned suicide, performed after reflection. I do not claim that reflection offers any guarantees, nor that it is impossible to die rationally without making one's reasons conscious, but that the chances are slimmer. If one is concerned that one's suicide be a rational choice, then reflection and perhaps discussion with others is the answer. It might be thought anachronistic to emphasize reflection rather than discussion. But discussion of one's suicide with friends has the danger of involving them too deeply and increasing their burden if one does kill oneself. Most professionals concerned with suicide count a successful suicide as a professional failure. And it may not be easy to arouse the interest of a stranger in one's plans to die. Yet I do think that an individual, carefully and honestly reflecting on his own aims and the meaning of his life, can arrive at a rational decision to bring that life to an end.

Even when suicide is a reasoned and rational act, it need not be the *only* rational thing to do, let alone the right thing. A chess move, for example, may be one of a number of rationally defensible alternatives. There is a big difference between *a* rational choice and *the* rational choice. The question of the rationality of suicide seems for too long to have been saddled with the demand that it justify death. But we do not have to show that death is a good or rational or desirable thing, or a condition for our lives being intelligible. The certainty of our mortality is a given, an *a priori* fact, and with the decline of the notion of natural death, suicide presents itself as a possible rational choice. There are no objections from the side of reason to choosing the meaning or circumstances of one's death or to converting an event that one must suffer into an act that one performs. The analysis of the conditions for a rational suicide—and the pitfalls to be avoided—is one more step not toward a defeated and decadent society, but a more vigorous and enlightened age.

THE ART OF
SUICIDE

Joyce Carol Oates

Oates argues that some people kill themselves because they have been seduced into believing suicide is a creative or artistic act, by metaphors which misrepresent dying as a kind of creating or death as beautiful and as something to be revered, rather than as the "mere, brute, blunt, flat, distinctly unseductive deadness" which it really is. She cites the writings—and suicides—of certain literary figures to substantiate her thesis.

An extraordinarily prolific writer of short fiction, novels, and poetry, Joyce Carol Oates' best known works include A Garden of Earthly Delights, Expensive People, Them, The Wheel of Love, Love and Its Derangements, Wonderland, Marriages and Infidelities, Angel Fire, Do with Me What You Will, Where Are You Going, Where Have You Been?, The Assassins, Crossing the Border, The Seduction, The Triumph of the Spider Monkey, Women Whose Lives Are Food, Men Whose Lives Are Money, *and* Son of the Morning. *She has taught at the University of Detroit and the University of Windsor, and is now Writer-in-Residence at Princeton University.*

In the morning of life the son tears himself loose from the mother, from the domestic hearth, to rise through battle to his destined heights. Always he imagines his worst enemy in

front of him, yet he carries the enemy within himself—a
deadly longing for the abyss, a longing to drown in his own
source, to be sucked down to the realm of the Mothers. His
life is a constant struggle against extinction, a violent yet
fleeting deliverance from ever-lurking night. This death is
no external enemy, it is his own inner longing for the
stillness and profound peace of all-knowing non-existence,
for all-seeing sleep in the ocean of coming-to-be and passing
away. . . .

C. G. Jung, *Symbols of Transformation*

Not only the artist, that most deliberate of persons, but all human
beings employ metaphor: the conscious or unconscious creation of
concrete, literal terms that seek to express the abstract, the not-at-
hand, the ineffable. Is the suicide an artist? Is Death-by-Suicide an
art form, the employment of a metaphor so vast, so final, that it
obliterates and sweeps into silence all opposition? But there are
many suicides, there are many deaths, some highly conscious and
others groping, perplexed, perhaps murderous, hardly conscious
at all: a succumbing to the gravitational pull of which Jung speaks
in the quotation above, which he envisions in terms of the hero
and his quest, which takes him away from the "realm of the
Mothers"—but only for a while, until his life's-energy runs its
course, and he is drawn down into what Jung calls, in metaphorical language that is beautiful, even seductive, the "profound peace
of all-knowing non-existence." Yet if we were to push aside
metaphor, if we were no longer even to speak in a reverential tone
of Death, but instead of Deadness—mere, brute, blunt, flat,
distinctly unseductive Deadness—how artistic a venture is it, how
meaningfully can it engage our deepest attention?

My thesis is a simple one: apart from circumstances which
insist upon self-destruction as the inevitable next move, the
necessary next move that will preserve one's dignity, the act of
suicide itself is a consequence of the employment of false metaphors. It is a consequence of the atrophying of the creative
imagination: the failure of the imagination, not to be confused
with gestures of freedom, or rebellion, or originality, or transcendence. To so desperately confuse the terms of our finite contract
as to invent a liberating Death when it is really brute, inarticulate
Deadness that awaits—the "artist" of suicide is a groping, blunder-

ing, failed artist, and his art-work a mockery of genuine achievement.

The "artistic" suicide—in contrast to the suicide who acts in order to hasten an inevitable end, perhaps even to alleviate terrible pain—is always mesmerized by the imaginative act of self-destruction, *as if it were a kind of creation.* It is a supreme gesture of the will, an insistence upon one's absolute freedom; that it is "contrary to nature," a dramatic violation of the life-force, makes the gesture all the more unique. One can determine one's self, one's identity, by choosing to put an end to that identity—which is to say, an end to finitude itself. The suicide who deliberates over his act, who very likely has centered much of his life around the possibility of the act, rejects our human condition of finitude (all that we are not, as well as all that we are); his self-destruction is a disavowal, in a sense, of what it means to *be* human. But does the suicide who is transfixed by metaphor suffer a serious derangement of perception, so that he contemplates the serene, transcendental, Platonic "all-knowing non-existence" while what awaits him is merely a biological death—that is, deadness?

In Sylvia Plath's famous poem "Lady Lazarus" the young woman poet boasts of her most recent suicide attempt in language that, though carefully restrained by the rigorous formal discipline of the poem, strikes us as very close to hysteria. She is a "smiling woman," only thirty; and like the cat she has nine times to die. (Though in fact Plath's next attempt, an attempt said not to have been altogether serious, was to be her last.) She is clearly proud of herself, though self-mocking as well, and her angry contempt for the voyeurs crowding around is beautifully expressed:

> What a million filaments.
> The peanut-crunching crowd
> Shoves in to see
>
> Them unwind me hand and foot—
> The big strip tease.
> Gentlemen, ladies
>
> These are my hands
> My knees
> I may be skin and bone,

Nevertheless I am the same, identical woman.

Dying
Is an art, like everything else.
I do it exceptionally well.

I do it so it feels like hell.
I do it so it feels real.
I guess you could say I've a call.

In this poem and in numerous others from the collections *Ariel* and *Winter Trees* the poet creates vivid images of self-loathing, frequently projected onto other people or onto nature, and consequently onto life itself. It is Sylvia Plath whom Sylvia Plath despises, and by confusing her personality with the deepest layer of being, her own soul, she makes self-destruction inevitable. It is not *life* that has become contaminated, and requires a radical exorcism; it is the temporal personality, the smiling thirty-year-old woman trapped in a failing marriage and overburdened with the responsibilities of motherhood, in one of the coldest winters in England's recorded history. Unable to strike out at her ostensible enemies (her husband Ted Hughes, who had left her for another woman; her father, long dead, who had "betrayed" her by dying when she was a small child) Plath strikes out at the enemy within, and murders herself in her final shrill poems before she actually turns on the gas oven and commits suicide. If her death, and even many of her poems, strike us as adolescent gestures it is perhaps because she demonstrated so little self-knowledge; her anguish was sheer emotion, never translated into coherent images. Quite apart from the surreal figures of speech Plath employs with such frenzied power, her work exhibits a curious deficiency of imagination, most evident in the autobiographical novel *The Bell Jar,* in which the suicidal narrator speaks of her consciousness as trapped inside a bell-jar, forced to breathe again and again the same stale air.

"There is but one truly serious philosophical question," Camus has said in a statement now famous, "and that is suicide." Camus exaggerates, certainly, and it is doubtful whether, strictly speaking, suicide is a "philosophical" problem at all. It may be social, moral, even economic, even political—especially political;

but is it "philosophical"? Marcus Aurelius noted in his typically prudent manner: "In all that you do or say or think, recollect that at any time the power of withdrawal from life is in your hands," and Nietzsche said, perhaps less sombrely, "The thought of suicide is a strong consolation; one can get through many a bad night with it." But these are *problems,* these are *thoughts;* that they are so clearly conceptualized suggests their detachment from the kind of anguish, raw and undifferentiated, that drove Sylvia Plath to her premature death. The poet Anne Sexton liked to claim that suicides were a special people. "Talking death" for suicides is "life." In Sexton's third collection of poems, *Live or Die,* she included a poem characterized by remarkable restraint and dignity, one of the most intelligent (and despairing) works of what is loosely called the "confessional mode." Is suicide a philosophical problem? Is it intellectual, abstract, cerebral? Hardly:

> Since you ask, most days I cannot remember.
> I walk in my clothing, unmarked by that voyage.
> Then the almost unnameable lust returns.
>
> Even then I have nothing against life.
> I know well the grass blades you mention,
> the furniture you have placed under the sun.
>
> But suicides have a special language.
> Like carpenters they want to know *which tools.*
> They never ask *why build.*

In Sexton the gravitational pull toward death seems to preclude, or exclude, such imaginative speculations as those of Camus; *that* death is desirable is never questioned.

Of course there are the famous suicides, the noble suicides, who do not appear to have been acting blindly, out of a confused emotional state: there is Socrates who acquiesced courteously, who did not choose to flee his execution; there is Cato; Petronius; Jesus of Nazareth. In literature there are, famously, Shakespeare's Othello, who *rises* to his death, and Shakespeare's Antony and Cleopatra, both of whom outwit their conquerors by dying, the latter an "easy" death, the former an awkward, ghastly Roman death, poorly executed. Macbeth's ferocious struggle with Macduff is a suicidal gesture, and a perfect one, as is Hamlet's final combat with the enemy most like himself in age and spirit. The Hamlet-like Stavrogin of Dostoyevsky's monumental *The Possessed* worries that he may lack the "magnanimity" to kill himself, and to rid the world of such a loathsome creature as he; but he acquires the necessary strength and manages to hang himself, a symbolic gesture tied up clearly with Dostoyevsky's instinct for the logic of self-destruction as a consequence of modern man's "freedom" (i.e., alienation) from his nation.

Is the subjective act, then, nursed and groomed and made to bring forth its own sort of sickly fruit, really a public, political act? "Many die too late, and a few die too early," Nietzsche says boldly. "The doctrine still sounds strange: *Die at the right time!*" Nietzsche does not address himself to the less-than-noble; he is speaking, perhaps, not to individuals at all but to trans-individual values that, once healthy, are now fallen into decay, and must be hastened to their inevitable historical end. If until recent times death has been a taboo subject in our culture, suicide has been nothing short of an obscenity: a sudden raucous jeering shout in a genteel gathering. The suicide does not play the game, does not observe the rules; he leaves the party too soon, and leaves the other guests painfully uncomfortable. The world which has struck them as tolerable, or even enjoyable, is, perhaps to a more discerning temperament, simply impossible: like Dostoyevsky's Ivan Karamazov, he respectfully returns his ticket to his creator. The private gesture becomes violently and unmistakably public, which accounts for the harsh measures taken to punish suicides — or the bodies of suicides — over the centuries.

It is possible to reject society's extreme judgment, I think, without taking up an unqualified cause for the "freedom" of suicide, particularly if one makes sharp distinctions between kinds of suicides — the altruistic, the pathological, and the metaphorical. It is in metaphorical self-murder that what is murdered is an aspect of the self, and what is attained is a fictitious "transcendence" of physical circumstance.

But can one freely choose a condition, a state of being, that has never been experienced except in the imagination and, even there, *only in metaphor?* The wish "I want to die" might be a confused statement masking any number of unarticulated wishes: "I want to punish you, and you, and you"; "I want to punish the loathsome creature that appears to be myself"; "I want to be taken up by my Creator, and returned to the bliss of my first home"; "I want to alter my life because it is so disappointing, or painful, or boring"; "I want to silence the voices that are always shouting instructions"; "I want—I know not what." Rationally one cannot "choose" Death because Death is an unknown experience, and perhaps it isn't even an "experience"—perhaps it is simply nothing; and one cannot imagine nothing. The brain simply cannot fathom it, however glibly its thought-clusters may verbalize *non-existence, negation of being, Death,* and other non-referential terms. There is a curious heckling logic to the suicide's case, but his initial premise may be totally unfounded. *I want to die* may in fact be an empty statement expressing merely an emotion: *I am terribly unhappy at the present time.*

Still, people commit suicide because it is their deepest, most secret wish, and if the wish is too secret to be consciously admitted it will manifest itself in any number of metaphorical ways. We can list some of them—alcoholism, accidents, self-induced malnutrition, wretched life-choices, a cultivation of melancholy. The world is there, the world *is*, not awaiting our interpretations but unresisting when we compose them, and it may be that the mere semblance of the world's acquiescence to our metaphor-making leads us deeper and deeper into illusion. Because passion, even misdirected and self-pitying and claustrophobic, is always appealing, and has the power to drown out quieter, more reasonable voices, we will always be confronted by the fascination an intelligent public will feel for the most skillfully articulated of death-wishes. Listen:

> Life, friends, is boring. We must not say so.
> After all, the sky flashes, the great sea yearns,
> we ourselves flash and yearn,
> and moreover my mother told me as a boy
> (repeatingly) 'Ever to confess you're bored
> means you have no
>
> Inner Resources.' I conclude now I have no
> inner resources, because I am heavy bored.
> Peoples bore me,
> literature bores me, especially great literature,
> Henry bores me, with his plights & gripes
> as bad as achilles,

who loves people and valiant art, which bores me.
And the tranquil hills, & gin, look like a drag
and somehow a dog
has taken itself & its tail considerably away
into mountains or sea or sky, leaving
behind: me, wag.

(John Berryman, *Dream Songs*, #14)

Manipulated Suicide

M. Pabst Battin

Social acceptance of the notion of rational suicide, Battin argues, opens the way for both individual and societal manipulation of individuals into choosing to end their lives when they would not otherwise have done so. Battin describes the two principal mechanisms by which such manipulation can occur, and suggests that contemporary society already gives very considerable evidence of change in these directions, such that increases in certain kinds of suicides can be expected to occur. However, she argues, if we accept the notion of rational suicide, we cannot object to the manipulated suicides which do occur.

Peggy Battin is assistant professor of philosophy at the University of Utah. She is the author of articles on several topics in classical philosophy and aesthetics, and a book Suicide, *forthcoming in the Prentice-Hall series, "Moral Problems in Medicine." She also writes fiction, and her short stories have appeared in various magazines and collections, including Martha Foley's* The Best American Short Stories of 1976.

Resuscitating an issue once quite widely explored by the Greeks, many contemporary bioethicists are now reexamining the notion of *rational* suicide, and are suggesting that death can, in some unfortunate cases (for instance, painful terminal illness), be a choice that is as reasonable, or more reasonable, than remaining alive. This is often accompanied by a call for more than merely intellectual assent and a demand for its recognition in religion,

169

custom, medicine, psychiatry, and law. Indeed, a relaxation of traditional impermissive attitudes about suicide is already—albeit slowly—beginning to take place.

Reservations about the notion of rational suicide may be based on the dangers of erroneous choice: the risk that acceptance of rational suicide might on some occasions encourage impulsive or irrational suicide among those whose choices are not reasoned or clear. However, this risk, it may be argued, is countered by the moral imperative of allowing individuals to exercise what is clearly their right to die. On this view, the moral issue in suicide centers on a weighing of the interests of two groups: the "irrational" suicides, who are now thwarted in their attempts, but in the absence of social, legal, and psychological barriers to suicide might succeed at something they do not really want, and the "rational" suicides, who, by these same barriers, are dissuaded from that to which they have a right.

The benefits which most advocates of rational suicide have in mind seem to be based on a scenario something like this. Consider the cancer victim who suffers his illness in a society (like ours) which rejects suicide on religious, legal, social, and psychological grounds: he is, in effect, forced to endure the disease until it kills him, watching it rob his family of financial security and emotional health, rather than perform an act which he and his family are led to believe would make him a coward, a sociopath, a deviant, a lunatic, and an apostate. "Hang on a little longer," he and they urge each other, for to do otherwise would on all counts be wrong.

But the same individual, suffering the same disease in a society that offers no barriers to self-administered death in the face of terminal illness, will be very much more able to choose suicide, since if he does he, and his family, may take him to be acting decently and rationally, to be making a socially responsible choice, and to be doing what is sane, moral, and devout. To make such choices possible, and to give them social support, it is held, would be a great gain for human welfare, by allowing us to forgo suffering for ourselves and ruin for others when they can in no other way be avoided. As David Hume once put this point:

> . . . both prudence and courage should engage us to rid ourselves at once of existence when it becomes a burden. This is the only way that we can then be useful to society, by setting an example which, if imitated, would preserve to

every one his chance for happiness in life, and would effectually free him from all danger or misery.[1]

But this is not the only outcome we might expect from the adoption of the notion of rational suicide. For, as I shall try to show, I think this notion—seemingly paradoxically—first gives rise to the possibililty of large-scale manipulation of suicide, and the maneuvering of persons into choosing suicide when they would not otherwise have done so. This is the other, darker side of the future coin.

I

Let us try to describe manipulation into suicide by sorting out its cases; I think we can distinguish two principal mechanisms at work.

1. *Circumstantial manipulation.* The rationality or irrationality of a given choice of suicide is in part a function of the individual's circumstances: his health, his living conditions, the degree of comfort or discomfort his daily life involves, his political environment, his opportunities for enjoyable or fulfilling activities and work, and so forth. Thus, when a person's circumstances change, so does the rationality or irrationality of his committing suicide: what may have been an unsound choice becomes, in the face of permanently worsened circumstances (say, a confirmed diagnosis of painful and incurable deteriorative illness) a reasonable one. But it is just this feature of suicide—that its rationality may change with changing circumstances—that makes one form of manipulation possible. What the manipulator does is alter his victim's immediate and/or long-range circumstances in such a way that the victim himself chooses death as preferable to continued life.

Manipulation of this sort may happen in a glaring way, as for instance in sustained torture; where blatant circumstantial manipulation of this sort is intended to result in suicide, we call it coercion, and count it as a form of murder. No doubt much more frequent, however, is the small, not very visible, often even inadvertent kind of manipulation that occurs in domestic situations, where what the manipulator does is to "arrange things" so that suicide becomes—given the other alternatives—the reasonable, even attractive choice for his victim.[2] For instance, negligent family members may fail to change the bed sheets of an incontinent bedridden patient, and in other ways provide poor or hostile nursing care; abusive parents may so thoroughly restrict and distort the circumstances of an adolescent child that suicide seems the only sensible way out. Perhaps only because it is so often invisible, we do not always recognize this kind of "domestic" manipulation as coercion and thus do not always call it murder.

Of course, suicide will not be the rational choice in such circumstances if these circumstances are likely to change or if they can be altered in some way. Where adverse circumstances are the result of coercion or manipulation by some other person or group, the obvious *rational* response would be to resist or attack the perpetrator in an effort to stop the manipulation and improve the circumstances. Thus, the incontinent bedridden patient's rational move is to complain to friends or authorities that his bed sheets are unchanged and that the care he is given is cruel; the beleaguered adolescent's may be to fight back or to run away.

In some cases, however, resistance may not be possible: the victim may be unable to elude his torturers, and suicide may *in fact* be the only way of escape. Perhaps such cases are rare. But if we recognize the notion of rational suicide, we must also recognize that in such cases, suicide may be the only rational choice for the victim, whether he is coerced and whether his circumstances have been deliberately worsened or not. Where the victim can identify the perpetrator and retaliate in some effective way, to do so is clearly the more rational choice, but manipulation is not always easy to detect, and even when it is, its perpetrators are not always easy to stop.

2. Ideological manipulation. The rationality of suicide is also in part a function of one's beliefs and values, and these, like circumstances, can also change. Suicide can be said to be irrational not only if it is chosen in a hasty, unthinking way, or on the basis of inadequate information, but also if it violates one's fundamental beliefs and values. For instance, suicide can be said to be an irrational choice for someone who believes that it will bring unwanted, eternal damnation, or for someone who believes that active, this-world caring for another is his primary goal.

But, of course, suicide may also be in accord with one's most fundamental beliefs and values. For instance, Stoic thinkers held slavery to be a condition so degrading that death was to be preferred to it, and those who took their lives to avoid slavery

(Cato, for instance) regarded themselves and were regarded by others as having made a fully rational choice.[3] These fundamental beliefs, of course, vary from one society and era to another: though loss of virginity and chastity was a basis for rational suicide in early medieval times,[4] the contemporary rape victim does not typically consider sexual assault reason to kill herself, even though it may cause very severe emotional distress. Nor does contemporary Western society countenance suicide in bereavement, for honor, or to avoid poverty, insanity, or disgrace, although all these have been recognized in various cultures at earlier times.[5]

Once we see that the beliefs and values on which the rationality of suicide in part depends can vary from one individual or historical era to another, we also recognize that such ideology can change. Ideological change may occur as part of the natural evolution of a culture; however, such changes can also be engineered. The contemporary world is already well familiar with deliberate attitude and values manipulation, from the gentle impress of advertising to the intensive programming and conditioning associated with various religious and political groups. If our attitudes and values in other areas can be deliberately changed, it is not at all unreasonable to think that our conceptions of the conditions under which suicide would be the rational choice can be changed too.

II

If we look at contemporary society, we can already see considerable evidence of change in areas relevant to the practice of rational suicide. To detect such change, of course, is not to find evidence of deliberate manipulation; but it is to show the kinds of change in association with which we might expect manipulation— deliberate or otherwise—to occur. These changes are all of a sort in which someone might be brought to choose suicide who would not otherwise have done so.

In the first place, we may note various kinds of circumstantial change relevant to the practice of rational suicide. Some are changes that might work to decrease the incidence of suicide: the development of more effective methods of pain relief, for instance, or institutions like Hospice.[6] But others tend on the whole to worsen the conditions of certain individuals or groups: here one might cite our increasing tendency to confine elderly persons in nursing homes, the increasing expense of such institutional care, the loss of social roles for the elderly, and the increasingly difficult financial circumstances of those living on marginal or fixed incomes. One might also mention increasing loss of autonomy in the seriously ill, as "heroic" practices in medicine become increasingly mechanized; new abilities to maintain seriously injured or birth-defective persons in marginal states, and so forth. Gerontologists and patients'-rights advocates have been pointing to the inhumane consequences of such circumstantial changes for some time, and such observations are hardly new; what is new, however, is alertness to their role with respect to rational suicide. Increasingly poor conditions, in a society which is coming to accept a notion of rational suicide, may mean an increasing likelihood that suicide will be the individual's choice.

Second, we can also diagnose in contemporary society several significant ideological changes. For instance, we may notice a profusion of recent literary accounts favorable to suicide and assisted suicide in terminal-illness cases—real-life stories of one partner assisting the other in obtaining and taking a lethal drug to avoid the ravages of cancer.[7] We observe increasingly frequent court decisions favoring patients' rights to refuse medical treatment, even when refusal will mean death.[8] We notice public accounts of suicides conceived of and conducted as rational: the Henry and Elizabeth Van Dusen, Wallace Proctor, and Jo Roman cases, to mention a few.[9] And we observe that some religious groups have begun to devote attention to the issue of whether suicide may be, in certain kinds of terminal circumstances, an act of religous conscience, even though Western Christianity has in general not allowed it since Augustine, for the past fifteen hundred years.[10] Almost all these cases involve suicide in the face of painful terminal illness, and that illness is very often cancer. If we were to diagnose our own ideological changes with regard to suicide, we would probably say that they involve a very recent move—by no means universal, but already clearly and widely evident—from the recently predominant view that there is *no* good reason for suicide (and hence that all suicide is irrational or insane) to the view that there is after all one adequate reason for suicide: extreme and irremediable pain in terminal illness.

The transition may not seem to be a very large one. But we have no reason to think it is complete, and we may perhaps predict the direction in which it will continue by noticing the kinds of reasons which are typically given to justify killing and non-prolongation of life in several closely associated phenomena: euthanasia, abortion, infanticide of defective newborns, and non-initiation or withdrawal of treatment in chronic or terminal-illness cases. Extreme pain is one such reason. So is extreme physical dependence, sometimes called degradation; this is often cited as a reason for discontinuing long-term tube feeding or maintenance on life-support systems, nonresuscitation, and hospital "no-code" procedures.[11] Financial burdens are now also sometimes mentioned, even by the Catholic Church: the expense of a protracted chronic or terminal illness may count among the reasons to withhold heroic treatment, even when the patient will die instead.[12] Expense is also often a consideration in decisions to withhold or terminate *ordinary* treatment, especially in the elderly and in defective newborns.[13] Still another consideration coming to the fore in current life-vs.-death decisions is that of impact on the immediate family: one now hears as a justification for passive and active euthanasia, abortion, infanticide, and withdrawal of treatment in the chronically or terminally ill the claim that this will "spare the family" the agony of watching someone die a protracted and painful death or enter a seriously deficient life. Considerations regarding scarce medical resources are also sometimes heard, together with those involving the care burden placed on medical personnel and family members by someone suffering a lengthy, difficult illness or with a severe birth defect. Finally, we now also recognize religious reasons for voluntary death when life could be continued: the Jehovah's Witnesses blood-transfusion cases appear to establish the right of an individual to relinquish his life in order to protect his basic religious beliefs, at least where this does not infringe on the rights of others.[14]

Except for pain, none of these considerations is now generally recognized as a reason for *suicide*. But they are already recognized as reasons which may justify the killing of others and the nonprolongation of one's own life, and it is highly plausible to expect that they will soon be recognized as relevant in suicide decisions too.

The kinds of alterations in the ideology and circumstances of rational suicide we have diagnosed as now in progress all involve medical and quasi-medical situations. They would begin to allow what we might call euthanatic suicide, or a choice of death in preference to prolonged and painful death. As the circumstantial changes mentioned earlier—increasing displacement of the elderly and increasing loss of autonomy for the ill—operate to make the conditions of those who are faced with dying increasingly difficult, there is reason to think the attractiveness of euthanatic suicide as an alternative will increase. But there are no *a priori* checks on the breadth of such extensions of the concept of rational suicide and no reason why future extensions must be limited to euthanatic medical situations. As we've said, such conditions as dishonor, slavery, and loss of chastity have been considered suicide-warranting conditions in Western culture in the past; widowhood and public dishonor have assumed such roles in the East, and it seems merely naive to assume that these conditions, or others we now find equally implausible reasons for suicide, could not come to be regarded so in the future. This is particularly obvious if we keep in mind the possibility of circumstantial manipulation and of both inadvertent and deliberate ideological engineering. The motivation for such manipulation and engineering, in a society confronted with scarcities and fearful of an increasingly large "nonproductive" population, may be very strong. Old age, insanity, poverty, and criminality have also been regarded as grounds for rational suicide in the past; given a society afraid of demands from increasingly large geriatric, ghetto, and institutional populations, we can see how interest in producing circumstantial and ideological changes, in order to encourage such people to choose the "reasonable" way out, might be very strong.

Not all manipulation into suicide need be malevolent or self-interested on the part of the manipulator. Manipulation into suicide can also be paternalistic, where one pleads with a victim to "consider yourself" and end a life the paternalist perceives as hopelessly burdensome.[15] And, of course, such pressures may be both paternalistic and other-interested at once: one imagines a counselor advising an old or ill person to spare both himself and his family the agony of an extended decline,[16] even though this person would not have considered or attempted suicide on his own and would have been willing to suffer the physical distress. Can he resist such pressures? Not, perhaps, in a climate in which suicide is "the rational thing to do" in circumstances such as these. To resist, indeed, might earn him the epithets now applied to the individual who does choose suicide: coward, sociopath, deviant, lunatic, apostate. He has, after all, refused to do what is rational and what is believed to be not only in his own intersts but in those of people he loves.

It is important to understand that such choices of suicide can be manipulated only under a prevailing notion of *rational* suicide. Manipulation of this sort does not involve driving one's victims into insanity or torturing them into irrationality; rather, it consists in providing a basis for the making of a *reasonable* decision about the ending of one's life and in providing the criteria upon which that decision is to be made. The choice remains crucially and essentially voluntary, and the decision between alternatives free. Furthermore, in a suicide-permissive society, the choice of suicide would be protected by law, religion, and custom and would be recognized as evidence of sound mental health. But the circumstances of the choice have been restructured so that choosing now involves weighing not only one's own interests but those of others. Where, on balance, the costs of death will be less for oneself and for others than the costs of remaining alive, suicide will be the rational—and socially favored—choice. Indeed, perhaps the choice is not so free after all.

As we've said, there is no reason to think that such questions must remain confined to medical situations or what we might call euthanatic suicide. Not only do these considerations apply to nonterminal- as well as terminal-illness cases (consider, for instance, the pain, dependence, expense, impact on the family, and use of scarce medical resources in connection with nonterminal conditions like renal failure, quadriplegia, or severe arthritis), but they will also apply to conditions where there is no *illness* as such at all: retardation, genetic deficiency, abnormal personality, and old age. One can even imagine that continuing ideological redefinition might invite us to regard life as not worth living and the interests of others as critical in a much wider variety of nonmedical situations: chronic unemployment, widowhood, poverty, social isolation, criminal conviction, and so forth. Such claims may seem hysterical. But all these conditions have been promoted as suicide-warranting at some time in the past, and they are all also very often associated with social dependence. After Hitler, we are, I trust, beyond extermination of unwanted or dependent groups. But we may not be beyond encouraging *as rational* the self-elimination of those whom we perceive to constitute a burden to themselves and to others, and I think that this is where the risk in manipulated suicide lies.

III

But there is a problem. Manipulated suicide is morally repugnant, and we recognize that families, social groups, and societies ought to encourage· loving care for their ill or disadvantaged members instead. But suicide may be both manipulated *and* rational, and herein lies the philosophical problem. Once we grant that it may be rational for an individual to choose death rather than to live in circumstances which for him are unacceptably or intolerably painful, physically or emotionally, or which are destructive of his most deeply held values, then we cannot object to his choice of death—even though he may be choosing to die because his circumstances have been deliberately or inadvertently worsened, because he has been brought to see his life as worthless, or because he believes he has an obligation to benefit his family by doing so. Certainly we can object to the manipulation of a person's circumstances or the distortion of his ideology. And we can attempt to point out to the victim what has happened. But we cannot object to his choice of suicide, if that remains his choice. To insist that we could not allow suicide which results from manipulation would be to insist that the victim remain alive in what to him have become intolerable circumstances or with his values destroyed; this would be to inflict a double misery—precisely what the notion of rational suicide is intended to prevent. Yet we must see that the very concept which allows this person escape is what first makes possible manipulation of these kinds, since it is the very notion of *rational* suicide which stipulates that under certain conditions one may reasonably seek to end one's life.

If we refuse to adopt the notion of rational suicide, we fail to honor the moral imperative of allowing individuals in intolerable and irremediable circumstances their fundamental right to die. If we do adopt it, we fail to honor a moral imperative of a different kind: protecting vulnerable individuals from manipulation into choices they otherwise might not make. Perhaps this second imperative is not so strong as the first, and a rational person may be willing to accept the possibility of manipulation which is engendered by the notion of rational suicide, in exchange for the social freedom to control one's own dying as one wishes—even knowing that he may eventually also succumb to that risk, and be "encouraged" to choose death sooner than might otherwise have been the case. Most of us, after all, will grow ill or old or both, and so become candidates for manipulation of this kind. But the alternative—to maintain or reestablish rigid suicide prohibitions— is not attractive either, and is particularly cruel to precisely those people for whom death is or may become the rational choice—that is, those persons in the most unfortunate circumstances of us all. I myself believe that on moral grounds we must accept, not reject, the notion of rational suicide. But I think we must do so with a clear-sighted view of the moral quicksand into which this notion threatens to lead us; perhaps then we may discover a path around.

N O T E S

1. David Hume, "On Suicide," in *The Philosophical Works of David Hume*, Vol. IV (Edinburgh: Printed for Adam Black and William Tait, 1826), p. 567. Hume's essay, in modernized spelling, is to be found in a number of contemporary collections, including Raziel Abelson and Marie-Louise Friquegnon, eds., *Ethics for Modern Life* (New York: St. Martin's Press, 1975); in an abridged version, Samuel Gorovitz, ed., *Moral Problems in Medicine* (Englewood Cliffs, N.J.: Prentice-Hall, 1976); and abridged but with a commentary in Tom L. Beauchamp and Seymour Perlin, *Ethical Issues in Death and Dying* (Englewood Cliffs, N.J.: Prentice-Hall, 1978).
2. It is Virgil Aldrich who suggests the use of the phrase "arrange things" in connection with manipulation into suicide. It is well to notice, however, that terms like "arrange things" and "manipulation" suggest conscious intentionality on the part of the "arranger" or "manipulator," though conscious intentionality need not always be a feature in these cases.
3. See e.g., Seneca, *Letters* 70, 77, and 78 on preferring death to slavery, and Plutarch's *Lives of the Noble Greeks and Romans* on the death of Cato the Younger. This view is not confined to

Stoicism; see Josephus, *The Jewish War,* VII 320-419, on the mass suicide of the 960 defenders of Masada.

4. See e.g., St. Ambrose, *On Virgins,* and St. Eusebius, *Ecclesiastical History,* Chapter 12, for accounts of Christian women who committed suicide rather than be violated by the Romans. Support for this view ends, however, with St. Augustine's repudiation of suicide as an alternative to sexual defilement, *City of God,* Book I, Chapters 16–28.

5. See H. Romilly Fedden, *Suicide: A Social and Historical Study* (London: Peter Davies Ltd., 1938), for an account of suicides for bereavement, insanity, dishonor, poverty, and disgrace in Western and non-Western cultures. Note also that bereavement suicides are familiar to us in the Hindu practice of *suttee,* and honor suicides in the Japanese practices of *seppuku* or *harakiri* and in *junshi.* See also the group of articles on suicide in various cultures in the *Encyclopaedia of Religion and Ethics,* ed. James Hastings (New York: Charles Scribner's Sons, 1925), Vol. XII.

6. Hospice, founded and directed by Cicely Saunders, is a movement devoted to the development of institutions for providing palliative but medically nonaggressive care for terminal-illness patients. Central to the extraordinary contribution of this movement is its development of methods of prophylactic pain control, according to which analgesics are administered on a scheduled basis in advance of experienced pain, rather than on demand after pain recurs; perhaps equally significant is its attention to the emotional needs of the patient's family. Hospice is not, however, a panacea, and is not designed to approach many of the sorts of social and physical problems which confront the chronically ill, the elderly, the seriously disabled, and others for whom suicide might be seen as a rational choice. An account of the theory and methodology of Hospice can be found in a number of the publications of Cicely Saunders, including "The Treatment of Intractable Pain in Terminal Cancer," *Proceedings of the Royal Society of Medicine* 56 (1963), p. 195, and "Terminal Care in Medical Oncology," in K. D. Bagshawe, ed., *Medical Oncology* (Oxford: Blackwell, 1975), pp. 563-76. A careful assessment of potentials for abuse of the Hospice system may be found in John F. Potter, M.D., "A Challenge for the Hospice Movement," *The New England Journal of Medicine* 302, No. 1 (Jan. 3, 1980), pp. 53-5.

7. Jessamyn West, *The Woman Said Yes* (New York; Harcourt Brace Jovanovich, 1976); Lael Tucker Wertenbacker, *Death of a Man* (Boston: Beacon Press, 1974); Derek Humphrey with Ann Wickett, *Jean's Way* (New York: Quartet Books, 1978).
8. See accounts of a number of these cases, including *In re Yetter, Saikewicz*, and *Perlmutter*, in Alan Sullivan's "A Constitutional Right to Suicide," this volume, p. 229.
9. For an account of the deaths of Henry P. Van Dusen, former president of Union Theological Seminary, and his wife Elizabeth, leaders in American theological life, see *The New York Times*, Feb. 26, 1975, p. 1. The Van Dusens left a note explaining the motivation for their suicide (he had had a disabling stroke five years before, and she had serious arthritis; he was 77 and she 80), and saying "we still feel this is the best way and the right way to go."

   An account of the suicide of Wallace Proctor, a retired dermatologist with Parkinson's disease, is reported in *The New York Times*, Dec. 11, 1977; that of Jo Roman, an artist with cancer who ended her life in a much-publicized gathering of intimates, is reported in *The New York Times*, June 17, 1979.
10. See, e.g., a pastoral letter of the Presbytery of New York City, March 9, 1976, which concludes that "it is clear that for some Christians, as a last resort in the gravest of situations, suicide may be an act of their Christian conscience."
11. Decisions which support the assertions made here are difficult to document in detail. However, the court in the Karen Ann Quinlan case observes:

> . . . it is perfectly apparent from the testimony we have quoted . . . , and indeed so clear as almost to be judicially noticeable, that humane decisions against resuscitative or maintenance therapy are frequently a recognized *de facto* response in the medical world to the irreversible, terminal, pain-ridden patient, especially with familial consent. And these cases, of course, are far short of "brain death." (*Matter of Quinlan* 355A.2d 647 at 667)

12. The text of Pope Pius XII's 1958 statement on medical resuscitation, "The Prolongation of Life," is available in Stanley Joel Reiser, Arthur J. Dyck, and William J. Curran, eds., *Ethics in Medicine* (Cambridge, Mass.: MIT Press, 1977), pp. 501–4. The physician is not obligated to use "extraordin-

ary means" (including, e.g., respirators) to sustain the biological life of someone who is "virtually dead." Considerations to be made in individual cases include whether an attempt at resuscitation is "such a burden for the family that one cannot in all conscience impose it upon them," and is usually interpreted to include both financial and emotional burdens.

13. Again, though particular decisions on such bases are difficult to document, see the symposia "Spina Bifida" and "Infants and Ethics" (in *The Hastings Center Report*, 7 [No. 4, August 1977] and 8 [No. 1, February 1978], respectively) and many other articles in this and other bioethics and medico-legal journals for a sense of the kinds of considerations which are made with respect to life-vs.-death choices.

14. *Erickson v. Dilgard* (252 N.Y.S.2d 705) held that an adult patient had the right to refuse a blood transfusion even if medical opinion was to the effect that the patient's decision not to accept blood was tantamount to the taking of the patient's own life; *Application of President and Directors of Georgetown College* (331 F.2d 1000 [1964]) authorized an unwanted transfusion to a patient who objected on religious grounds, but apparently because she was the mother of a 7-month-old child.

15. Diogenes Laertius relates that when Antisthenes was mortally ill, Diogenes brought him a dagger, offering it to Antisthenes to release himself from his pains. Antisthenes declined, saying he wanted release from his pains, not from his life; Diogenes Laertius observes "it was thought that he showed some weakness in bearing his malady through love of life." (*Lives of Eminent Philosophers*, VI, 18–19, on Antisthenes, tr. R. D. Hicks, [Cambridge, Mass.: Harvard University Press, 1965], Vol. ii, p. 21.) Tales of paternalistic assistance in suicide are common in Stoic Greece and Rome.

16. In Thomas More's *Utopia*, the state priests and magistrates come to a person suffering from painful incurable illness and "urge him to make the decision not to nourish such a painful disease any longer. He is now unequal to all the duties of life, a burden to himself and to others . . ." (Book II: "Their Care of the Sick and Euthanasia," tr. H.V.S. Ogden [Northbrook, Ill: AHM Publishing Corp., 1949], p. 57).

Suicide and Psychiatry

THE ETHICS OF SUICIDE

Thomas S. Szasz

Szasz attacks what he takes to be the prevailing medical commonplace that suicide is a manifestation of mental illness. He argues that suicide is a product of choice by an agent, not a symptom of a disease beyond the control of the individual, and that such a choice must be respected by psychiatrists, police, and others who might attempt to intervene in suicide. He recognizes that suicide is "medical heresy," but argues that the paternalistic prevention of suicide—whether by fraud or force—results in a "far-reaching infantilization and dehumanization of the suicidal person."

A psychiatrist and prolific writer on human behavior, law, and ethics, Thomas Szasz is well known for his thoroughgoing critique of the psychiatric establishment in such works as The Myth of Mental Illness *(1961),* Law, Liberty, and Psychiatry *(1963), and* The Manufacture of Madness: A Comprehensive Study of the Inquisition and the Mental Health Movement *(1970). He is professor of psychiatry at the Upstate Medical Center of the State University of New York, located in Syracuse.*

In 1967, an editorial in *The Journal of the American Medical Association* declared that "The contemporary physician sees suicide as a manifestation of emotional illness. Rarely does he view it in a context other than that of psychiatry."[1] It was thus implied, the emphasis being the stronger for not being articulated, that to view suicide in this way is at once scientifically accurate and morally uplifting. I submit that it is neither; that, instead, this perspective on suicide is both erroneous and evil: erroneous because it treats an act as if it were a happening; and evil, because it serves to legitimize psychiatric force and fraud by justifying it as medical care and treatment.

Before going further, I should like to distinguish three fundamentally different concepts and categories that are combined and confused in most discussions of suicide. They are: 1. Suicide proper, or so-called successful suicide; 2. Attempted, threatened, or so-called unsuccessful suicide; and 3. The attribution by someone (typically a psychiatrist) to someone else (now called a "patient") of serious (that is, probably successful) suicidal intent. The first two concepts refer to acts by an actually or ostensibly suicidal person; the third refers to the claim of an ostensibly normal person about someone else's suicide-proneness.

I believe that, generally speaking, the person who commits suicide intends to die; whereas the one who threatens suicide or makes an unsuccessful attempt at it intends to improve his life, not to terminate it. (The person who makes claims about someone else's suicidal intent does so usually in order to justify his efforts to control that person.)

Put differently, successful suicide is generally an expression of an individual's desire for greater autonomy—in particular, for self-control over his own death; whereas unsuccessful suicide is generally an expression of an individual's desire for more control over others—in particular, for compelling persons close to him to comply with his wishes. Although in some cases there may be legitimate doubt about which of these conditions obtains, in the majority of instances where people speak of "suicide" or "attempted suicide," the act falls clearly into one or the other group.

In short, I believe that successful and unsuccessful suicide constitute radically different acts and categories, and hence cannot be discussed together. Accordingly, I have limited the scope of this essay to suicide proper, with occasional references to attributions of suicidal intent. (The ascription of suicidal intent is, of course, a very different sort of thing from either successful or unsuccessful suicide. Since psychiatrists use it as if it designated a potentially or probably fatal "condition," it is sometimes necessary to consider this concept together with the phenomenon of suicide proper.)

*   *   *

It is difficult to find "responsible" medical or psychiatric authority today that does not regard suicide as a medical, and specifically as a mental health, problem.

For example, Ilza Veith, the noted medical historian, writing in *Modern Medicine*[2], asserts that ". . . the act [of suicide] clearly represents an illness. . . ."

Bernard R. Shochet, a psychiatrist at the University of Maryland, offers a precise description of the kind of illness it is. "Depression," he writes, "is a serious systemic disease, with both physiological and psychological concomitants, and suicide is a part of this syndrome." And he articulates the intervention he feels is implicit in this view: "If the patient's safety is in doubt, psychiatric hospitalization should be insisted on."[3]

Harvey M. Schein and Alan A. Stone, both psychiatrists at the Harvard Medical School, are even more explicit about the psychiatric coercion justified, in their judgment, by the threat of suicide. "Once the patient's suicidal thoughts are shared," they write, "the therapist must take pains to make clear to the patient that he, the therapist, considers suicide to be a maladaptive action, irreversibly counter to the patient's sane interests and goals; that he, the therapist, will do *everything* [emphasis mine, T.S.] he can to prevent it; and that the potential for such an action arises from the patient's illness. It is equally essential that the therapist believe in the professional stance; if he does not he should not be treating the patient within the delicate human framework of psychotherapy."[4]

Schein and Stone do not explain why the patient's confiding in his therapist to the extent of communicating his suicidal thoughts to him should *ipso facto* deprive the patient from being the arbiter of his own best interests. The thrust of their argument is prescriptive rather than logical. They seek to justify depriving the patient of a basic human freedom—the freedom to grant or withhold consent for treatment: "The therapist must insist that patient and physician—*together* [italics in the original]—communicate the suicidal potential to important figures in the environment, both professional and family. . . . Suicidal intent must not be part of therapeutic confidentiality." And further on they write: "Obviously this kind of patient must be hospitalized. . . . The therapist must be prepared to step in with hospitalization, with security measures, and with medication. . . ."

Schein and Stone thus suggest that the "suicidal" patient should have the right to choose his therapist; and that he should have the right to agree with his therapist and follow the latter's therapeutic recommendation (say, for hospitalization). At the same time, they insist that if "suicidal" patient and therapist disagree on therapy, then the patient should *not* have the right to disengage himself from the first therapist and choose a second— say, one who would consider suicidal intent a part of therapeutic confidentiality.

Many other psychiatric authorities could be cited to illustrate the current unanimity on this view of suicide.

Lawyers and jurists have eagerly accepted the psychiatric perspective on suicide, as they have on nearly everything else. An article in the *American Bar Association Journal*[5] by R. E. Schulman, who is both a lawyer and a psychologist, is illustrative.

Schulman begins with the premise that "No one in contemporary Western society would suggest that people be allowed to commit suicide as they please without some attempt to intervene or prevent such suicides. Even if a person does not value his own life, Western society does value everyone's life."

But I should like to suggest, as others have suggested before me, precisely what Schulman claims no one would suggest. Furthermore, if Schulman chooses to believe that Western society—which includes the United States with its history of slavery, Germany with its history of National Socialism, and Russia with its history of Communism—really "values everyone's life," so be it. But to accept this assertion as true is to fly in the face of the most obvious and brutal facts of history.

When a person decides to take his life, and when a physician decides to frustrate him in this action, the question arises: Why should the physician do so?

Conventional psychiatric wisdom answers: Because the suicidal person (now called "patient" for proper emphasis) suffers from a mental illness whose symptom is his desire to kill himself; it is the physician's duty to diagnose and treat illness: *ergo*, he must prevent the "patient" from killing himself and, at the same time, must "treat" the underlying "disease" that "causes" the "patient" to wish doing away with himself. This looks like an ordinary medical diagnosis and intervention. But it is not. What is missing? Everything. This hypothetical, suicidal "patient" is not ill; he has no demonstrable bodily disorder (or if he does, it does not "cause" his suicide); he does not assume the sick role; he does not seek medical help. In short, the physician uses the rhetoric of illness and treatment to justify his forcible intervention in the life of a fellow human being—often in the face of explicit opposition from his so-called "patient."

I do not doubt that attempted or successful suicide may be exceedingly *disturbing* for persons related to, acquainted with, or caring for the ostensible "patient." But I reject the conclusion that the suicidal person is, *ipso facto*, disturbed, that being disturbed equals being *mentally ill*, and that being mentally ill *justifies* psychiatric hospitalization or treatment. I have developed my reasons for this elsewhere, and need not repeat them here.[6] For the sake of emphasis, however, let me state that I consider counseling, persuasion, psychotherapy, or any other *voluntary measure*, especially for persons troubled by their own suicidal inclinations and seeking such help, unobjectionable, and indeed generally desirable, interventions. However, physicians and psychiatrists are usually not satisfied with limiting their help to such measures—and with good reason: from such assistance the individual may gain not only the desire to live, but also the strength to die.

But we still have not answered the question: Why should a physician frustrate an individual from killing himself? As we saw, some psychiatrists answer: Because the physician values the patient's life, at least when the patient is suicidal, more highly than does the patient himself. Let us examine this claim. Why should the physician, often a complete stranger to the suicidal patient, value the patient's life more highly than does the patient himself? He does not do so in medical practice. Why then should he do so in psychiatric practice, which he himself insists is a form of medical practice? Let us assume that a physician is confronted with an individual suffering from diabetes or heart failure who fails to take the drugs prescribed for his illness. We know that this often happens, and that when it does the patient may become disabled and die prematurely. Yet it would be absurd for a physician to consider, much less to attempt, taking over the conduct of such a patient's life, confining him in a hospital against his will in order to treat his disease. Indeed, any attempt to do so would bring the physician into conflict with both the civil and the criminal law. For, significantly, the law recognizes the medical patient's autonomy despite the fact that, unlike the suicidal individual, he suffers from a real disease; and despite the fact that, unlike the nonexistent disease of the suicidal individual, his illness is often easily controlled by simple and safe therapeutic procedures.

Nevertheless, the threat of alleged or real suicide, or so-called dangerousness to oneself, is everywhere considered a proper ground and justification for involuntary mental hospitalization and treatment. Why should this be so?

Let me suggest what I believe is likely to be the most important reason for the profound antisuicidal bias of the medical profession. Physicians are committed to saving lives. How, then, should they react to people who are committed to throwing away their lives? It is natural for people to dislike, indeed to hate, those who challenge their basic values. The physician thus reacts, perhaps "unconsciously" (in the sense that he does not articulate the problem in these terms), to the suicidal patient as if the patient had affronted, insulted, or attacked him: The physician strives valiantly, often at the cost of his own well-being, to save lives; and here comes a person who not only does not let the physician save him, but, *horribile dictu*, makes the physician an unwilling witness to that person's deliberate self-destruction. This is more than most physicians can take. Feeling assaulted in the very center of their spiritual identity, some take to flight, while others fight back.

Some non-psychiatric physicians will thus have nothing to do with suicidal patients. This explains why many people who end up killing themselves have a record of having consulted a physician, often on the very day of their suicide. I surmise that these persons go in search of help, only to discover that the physician wants nothing to do with them. And, in a sense, it is right that it should be so. I do not blame the doctors. Nor do I advocate teaching them suicide prevention—whatever that might be. I contend that because physicians have a relatively blind faith in their life-saving ideology—which, moreover, they often need to carry them through their daily work—they are the wrong people for listening and talking to individuals, intelligently and calmly, about suicide. So much for those physicians who, in the face of the existential attack which they feel the suicidal patient launches on them, run for *their* lives. Let us now look at those who stand and fight back.

Some physicians (and other mental health professionals) declare themselves not only ready and willing to help suicidal patients who seek assistance, but all persons who are or are alleged to be, suicidal. Since they, too, seem to perceive suicide as a threat, not just to the suicidal person's physical survival but to their own value system, they strike back and strike back hard. This explains why psychiatrists and suicidologists resort, apparently with a perfectly clear conscience, to the vilest methods: they must believe that their lofty ends justify the basest means. Hence the prevalent use of force and fraud in suicide prevention. The consequence of this kind of interaction between physician and "patient" is a struggle for power. The patient is at least honest about what he wants: to gain control over his life *and* death—by being the agent of his own demise. But the (suicide preventing) psychiatrist is completely dishonest about what he wants: he claims that he only wants to help his patient, while actually he wants to gain control over the patient's life in order to save himself from having to confront his doubts about the value of his own life. Suicide is medical heresy. Commitment and electro-shock are the appropriate psychiatric-inquisitorial remedies for it.

In the West, opposition to suicide, like opposition to contraception and abortion, rests on religious grounds. According to both the Jewish and Christian religions, God created man, and man can use himself only in the ways permitted by God. Preventing conception, aborting a pregnancy, or killing oneself are, in this imagery, all sins: each is a violation of the laws laid down by God, or by theological authorities claiming to speak in His name.

But modern man is a revolutionary. Like all revolutionaries, he likes to take away from those who have and to give to those who have not, especially himself. He has thus taken Man from God and given him to the State (with which he often identifies more than he knows). This is why the State gives and takes away so many of our rights, and why we consider this arrangement so "natural." (Hence the linguistic abomination of referring to the abolition of prohibitions, say against abortion or off-track betting, as the "legalizing" of these acts.)

But this arrangement leaves suicide in a peculiar moral and philosophical limbo. For if a man's life belongs to the State (as it formerly belonged to God), then surely suicide is the taking of a life that belongs not to the taker but to everyone else.

The dilemma of this simplistic transfer of body-ownership

from God to State derives from the fundamental difference between a religious and secular world view, especially when the former entails a vivid conception of a life after death, whereas the latter does not (or even emphatically repudiates it). More particularly, the dilemma derives from the problem of how to punish successful suicide? Traditionally, the Roman Catholic Church punished it by depriving the suicide of burial in consecrated ground. As far as I know, this practice is now so rare in the United States as to be practically nonexistent. Suicides are given a Catholic burial, as they are routinely considered having taken their lives while insane.

The modern State, with psychiatry as its secular-religious ally, has no comparable sanction to offer. Could this be one of the reasons why it punishes so severely—so very much more severely than did the Church—the *unsuccessful* suicide? For I consider the psychiatric stigmatization of people as "suicidal risks" and their incarceration in psychiatric institutions a form of punishment, and a very severe one at that. Indeed, although I cannot support this claim with statistics, I believe that accepted psychiatric methods of suicide prevention often aggravate rather than ameliorate the suicidal person's problems. As one reads of the tragic encounters with psychiatry of people like James Forrestal, Marilyn Monroe, or Ernest Hemingway, one gains the impression that they felt demeaned and deeply hurt by the psychiatric indignities inflicted on them, and that, as a result of these experiences, they were even more desperately driven to suicide. In short, I am suggesting that coerced psychiatric interventions may increase, rather than diminish, the suicidal person's desire for self-destruction.

But there is another aspect of the moral and philosophical dimensions of suicide that must be mentioned here. I refer to the growing influence of the resurgent idea of self-determination, especially the conviction that men have certain inalienable rights. Some men have thus come to believe (or perhaps only to believe that they believe) that they have a right to life, liberty, and property. This makes for some interesting complications for the modern legal and psychiatric stand on suicide.

This individualistic position on suicide might be put thus: A man's life belongs to himself. Hence, he has a right to take his own life, that is, to commit suicide. To be sure, this view recognizes that a man may also have a moral responsibility to his family and others, and that, by killing himself, he reneges on these responsibilities. But these are moral wrongs that society, in its corporate capacity as the State, cannot properly punish. Hence the State must eschew attempts to regulate such behavior by means of formal sanctions, such as criminal or mental hygiene laws.

The analogy between life and other types of property means that a person can dispose of it even if in so doing he injures himself and his family. A man may give away, or gamble away, his money. But, significantly, he cannot—our linguistic conventions do not allow it—be said to *steal from himself.* The concept of theft requires at least two parties: one who steals and another from whom is stolen. There is no such thing as "self-theft." The term "suicide" blurs this very distinction. The etymology of this term implies that suicide is a type of homicide, one in which criminal and victim are one and the same person. Indeed, when a person wants to condemn suicide he calls it "self-murder." Schulman, for example, writes: "Surely, self-murder falls within the province of the law."

History does repeat itself. Until recently, psychiatrists castigated as sick and persecuted those who engaged in self-abuse (that is, masturbation);[7] now they castigate as sick and persecute those who engage in self-murder (that is, suicide).

The suicidologist has a literally schizophrenic view of the suicidal person: He sees him as two persons in one, each at war with the other. One-half of the patient wants to die; the other half wants to live. The former, says the suicidologist, is wrong; the latter is right. And he proceeds to protect the latter by restraining the former. However, since these two people are, like Siamese twins, one, he can restrain the suicidal half only by restraining the whole person.

The absurdity of this medical-psychiatric position on suicide does not end here. It ends in extolling mental health and physical survival over every other value, particularly individual liberty.

In regarding the desire to live as a legitimate human aspiration, but not the desire to die, the suicidologist stands Patrick Henry's famous exclamation, "Give me liberty, or give me death!" on its head. In effect, he says: "*Give him* commitment, *give him* electroshock, *give him* lobotomy, *give him* life-long slavery, but *do not let him choose* death!" By so radically invalidating another person's (not his own!) wish to die, the suicide-preventer redefines the aspiration of the Other as not an aspiration at all: The wish to die thus becomes something an irrational, mentally diseased being displays, or something that happens to a lower form of life. The result is a far-reaching infantilization and dehumanization of the suicidal person.

For example, Phillip Solomon writes in the *Journal of the American Medical Association*[8], that "We [physicians] must protect the patient from his own [suicidal] wishes." While to Edwin Shneidman, "Suicide prevention is like fire prevention. . . ."[9] Solomon thus reduces the would-be suicide to the level of an unruly child, while Shneidman reduces him to the level of a tree! In short, the suicidologist uses his professional stance to illegitimize and punish the wish to die.

There is, of course, nothing new about any of this. Do-gooders have always opposed personal autonomy or self-determination. In "Amok," written in 1931, Stefan Zweig put these words into the mouth of his protagonist: "Ah, yes, 'It's one's duty to help.' That's your favorite maxim, isn't it? . . . Thank you for your good intentions, but I'd rather be left to myself. . . . So I won't trouble you to call, if you don't mind. Among the 'rights of man' there is a right which no one can take away, the right to croak when and where and how one pleases, without a 'helping hand'."[10]

But this is not the way the scientific psychiatrist and suicidologist sees the problem. He might agree (I suppose) that, in the abstract, man has the right Zweig claimed for him. But, in practice, suicide (so he says) is the result of insanity, madness, mental illness. Furthermore, it makes no sense to say that one has a right to be mentally ill, especially if the illness is one that, like typhoid fever, threatens the health of other people as well. In short, the suicidologist's job is to try to convince people that wanting to die is a disease.

This is how Ari Kiev, director of the Cornell Program in Social Psychiatry and its suicide prevention clinic, does it: "We say [to the patient], look, you have a disease, just like the Hong Kong flu. Maybe you've got the Hong Kong depression. First, you've got to realize you are emotionally ill. . . . Most of the patients have never admitted to themselves that they are sick. . . ."[11]

This pseudo-medical perspective is then used to justify psychiatric deception and coercion of the crudest sort.

Here is how, according to the *Wall Street Journal*, the Los Angeles Suicide Prevention Center operates. A man calls and says he is about to shoot himself. The worker asks for his address. The man refuses to give it. "'If I pull it [the trigger] now I'll be dead,' he [the caller] said in a muffled voice. 'And that's what I want.' Silently but urgently, Mrs. Whitbook [the worker] has signalled a co-worker to begin tracing the call. And now she worked to keep the man talking. . . . An agonizing 40 minutes passed. Then she heard the voice of a policeman come on the phone to say the man was safe."[12]

But surely, if this man was able to call the Suicide Prevention Center, he could have, had he wanted to, called for a policeman himself. But he did not. He was thus deceived by the Center in the "service" he got.

I understand that this kind of deception is standard practice in suicide prevention centers, though it is often denied that it is. A report about the Nassau County Suicide Prevention Service corroborates the impression that when the would-be suicide does not cooperate with the suicide-prevention authorities, he is confined involuntarily. "When a caller is obviously suicidal," we are told, "a Meadowbrook ambulance is sent out immediately to pick him up."[13]

One more example of the sort of thing that goes on in the name of suicide prevention should suffice. It is a routine story from a Syracuse newspaper. The gist of it is all in one sentence: "A 28-year-old Minoa [a Syracuse suburb] man was arrested last night on a charge of violation of the Mental Hygiene Law, after police authorities said they spent two hours looking for him in the Minoa woods."[14] But this man has harmed no one; his only "offense" was that someone claimed he might harm himself. Why, then, should the police look for, much less arrest, him? Why not wait until he returns? Or why not look, offer help, but avoid arrest and coerced psychiatry?

These are rhetorical questions. For our answers to them depend on and reflect our concepts of what it means to be a human being.

I submit, then, that the crucial contradiction about suicide viewed as an illness whose treatment is a medical responsibility is that suicide is an action but is treated as if it were a happening. As I showed elsewhere, this contradiction lies at the heart of all so-called mental illnesses or psychiatric problems.[15] However, it poses a particularly acute dilemma for suicide, because suicide is the only fatal "mental illness."

Before concluding, I should like to restate briefly my views on the differences between diseases and desires, and show that by persisting in treating desires as diseases, we only end up treating man as a slave.

Let us take, as our paradigm case of illness, a skier who takes a bad spill and fractures an ankle. This fracture is something that has happened to him. He has not intended it to happen. (To be sure, he may have intended it; but that is another case.) Once it has happened, he will seek medical help and will cooperate with medical efforts to mend his broken bones. In short, the person and his fractured ankle are, as it were, two separate entities, the former acting on the latter.

Let us now consider the case of the suicidal person. Such a person may also look upon his own suicidal inclinations as an undesired, almost alien, impulse and seek help to combat it. If so, the ensuing arrangement between him and his psychiatrist is readily assimilated to the standard medical model of treatment: the patient actively seeks and cooperates with professional efforts to remedy his "condition."

But as we have seen this is not the only way, nor perhaps the most important way, that the game of suicide prevention is played. It is accepted medical and psychiatric practice to treat persons for their suicidal desires against their will. And what exactly does this mean? Something quite different from that to which it is often analogized, namely the involuntary (or non-voluntary) treatment of a bodily illness. For a fractured ankle can be set whether or not a patient consents to its being set. That is because setting a fracture is a *mechanical act on the body*. But a threatened suicide cannot be prevented whether or not the "patient" consents to its being prevented. That is because, suicide being the result of human desire and action, suicide prevention is a *political act on the person*. In other words, since suicide is an exercise and expression of human freedom, it can be prevented only by curtailing human freedom. This is why deprivation of liberty becomes, in institutional psychiatry, a form of treatment.

In the final analysis, the would-be suicide is like the would-be emigrant: both want to leave where they are and move elsewhere. The suicide wants to leave life and embrace death. The emigrant wants to leave his homeland and settle in another country.

Let us take this analogy seriously. It is much more faithful to the facts than is the analogy between suicide and illness. A crucial characteristic that distinguishes open from closed societies is that people are free to leave the former but not the latter. The medical profession's stance toward suicide is thus like the Communists' toward emigration: the doctors insist that the would-be suicide survive, just as the Russians insist that the would-be emigrant stay home.

Whether those who so curtail other people's liberties act with complete sincerity, or with utter cynicism, hardly matters. What matters is what happens: the abridgement of individual liberty, justified, in the case of suicide prevention, by psychiatric rhetoric; and, in the case of emigration prevention, by political rhetoric.

In language and logic we are the prisoners of our premises, just as in politics and law we are the prisoners of our rulers. Hence we had better pick them well. For if suicide is an illness because it terminates in death, and if the prevention of death by any means necessary is the physician's therapeutic mandate, then the proper remedy for suicide is indeed liberticide.

N O T E S

1. "Changing Concepts of Suicide," *Journal of the American Medical Association*, Vol. 199, No. 10 (March 6, 1967), p. 162.
2. "Reflections on the Medical History of Suicide," *Modern Medicine*, August 11, 1969, p. 116.
3. "Recognizing the Suicidal Patient," *Modern Medicine*, May 18, 1970.
4. "Psychotherapy Designed to Detect and Treat Suicidal Potential," *American Journal of Psychiatry*, Vol. 125 (March 1969), pp. 1247–51.
5. "Suicide and Suicide Prevention: A Legal Analysis," *American, Bar Association Journal*, Vol. 54 (September 1968), pp. 855–62.
6. T.S. Szasz, *Law, Liberty and Psychiatry* (New York: Macmillan 1963); T. S. Szasz, *Ideology and Insanity* (Garden City, N.Y.: Anchor Books, 1970), especially chapters 9 and 12.
7. T. S. Szasz, *The Manufacture of Madness* (1970), chapter 11.
8. "The Burden of Responsibility in Suicide and Homicide," *Journal of the American Medical Association*, Vol. 199, No. 5 (Jan. 30, 1967), pp. 321–4.

9. "Preventing Suicide," *American Journal of Nursing*, Vol. 65, No. 5 (May 1965), p. 112.
10. "Amok," in *The Royal Game* (New York: Viking, 1944), p. 137.
11. *The New York Times*, February 9, 1969, p. 96.
12. March 6, 1969, p. 1.
13. *Medical World News*, July 28, 1967, p. 17.
14. Syracuse *Post Standard*, September 29, 1969, p. 10.
15. T. S. Szasz, *The Myth of Mental Illness* (New York: Harper & Row, 1961).

CHOOSING THE TIME TO DIE

Eliot Slater

Although many writers defend a right to rational suicide, Slater adopts a much more extreme view and argues that this right should extend to those who are incurably mentally ill, since they may need it the most. He points out that mental illness often involves extreme suffering, and asks whether the impulsive psychopath, who has opted for death, may not really be doing "his best, both for himself and everyone else."

Eliot Slater is one of Britain's leading specialists in the study and treatment of mental illness. Awarded the title of Commander of the Order of the British Empire in 1966, he is a founding member of the World Federation of Neurology, a Distinguished Fellow of the American Psychiatric Association, and is vice-president of Britain's Voluntary Euthanasia Society. Dr. Slater's publications have been collected in Man, Mind, and Heredity: Selected Papers of Eliot Slater on Psychiatry and Genetics, *edited by James Shields and Irving I. Gottesman (Johns Hopkins Press, 1971), and he has published a book of poems entitled* The Ebbless Sea. *Dr. Slater's other researches include an interest in Shakespeare, and he has been vice-president of the Shakespearean Authorship Society.*

Considering that we all of us have to die one day, it is truly remarkable that we should not wish to choose for ourselves the most suitable and convenient time to do so, but instead put that moment off for as long as possible, no matter what the penalties. Both the patient on the one hand and his medical attendant on the other agree about this, though from different points of view. Even when the continuance of life has become almost wholly disagreeable, the sufferer would rather die tomorrow than today. The relics of an obsolescent Christian tradition, the fear of the unknown, the fear of the process of dying, even the fear of an afterlife, have led this way in the past. But things are changing, and thoughtful people are beginning to take a very different attitude. To them the fears of dying and of death have become less dreadful than the fear of what doctors can and will do to them in an intensive care unit; and what may be their ultimate end when, mindless and incontinent, their vegetable life is still being maintained in a geriatric ward. Those who have contemplated this prospect have not hesitated to express a preference for a short and easy passage, conducted with the decency and dignity which is possible when one is in one's right senses, and sees and assents to one's fate. The death of Socrates is the ideal on which they would wish to model their leave-taking.

Doctors have come to the present consensus along a different road. We believe that it is our duty to save life, wherever possible, even when, as it may seem, this is against the express wish of those who have opted for death. It has been shown very convincingly that in perhaps as many as six out of every seven cases, the attempted suicide is calling for help with his problems of this life, rather than wanting above all things to die. The seventh case we confine, if we can, to the range of the pathological. Such is the strength of the normal wish to survive that when this urge fails there must be illness. If a man really does not wish to live, then we think he must be insane, and unfit therefore to decide his own fate. It becomes our duty to save him willy nilly, first to save his life and then to cure his melancholy.

This simpleminded view was perhaps a fair one in times gone by; but even now there are cases in which it is dangerously irrelevant, and more and more it calls for reconsideration. We must become sensitive to the predicament of those human beings who come to a settled and firm conviction that they want no more of this life and would prefer to end it. This is especially the case when such a decision has been reached on sound principles, when all a man's most obvious obligations to himself, his family and to society have been discharged, and full consideration has been given to the feelings of others. If a man then proposes to die, it is an impertinence on the part of his medical attendant to offer to intervene.

Yet what can the sufferer do to attain his end? There exists for him no automated Euthanasia Institute; and he cannot call on his doctor or his family or his friends to murder him. He has only the recourse of suicide; but if he tries to emulate Socrates he is only too likely to find the cup of hemlock dashed from his lips. The passing of the Suicide Act of 1961 has brought new hope to such a man. Killing oneself is no longer an unlawful act, and a man has a right to do anything with his own person that is not unlawful. In the Euthanasia Society we have considered the problem of the would-be suicide who finds himself threatened on all sides by those who would frustrate his wishes. In such circumstances it is up to him to declare his intentions, and give good warning of what he proposes to do. Those who might interfere should be told in plain terms that they have no right to do so. The Society's Legal adviser offers the following form of notice:

TO WHOM IT MAY CONCERN
I have decided, for reasons of health and age, to exercise my lawful right to bring my life to its end, and I hope that my last wish will be treated with proper respect.

I absolutely forbid anyone to lay hands on me or interfere with me in any way while I remain alive (except for the purpose of removing organs for transplantation when my death is certain) and I warn anyone who is minded to disregard this notice that treating or even touching a person against his will is in law both a criminal and civil offence. I hereby instruct my personal representatives to initiate proceedings against any person who attempts unsuccessfully to resuscitate me, and if the attempt is successful I shall take action myself.

I am of sound and contented mind, and having now made my peace with life and death in my own way I ask to be allowed to die in my own time.
                                        Signed
                                        Dated

So much for the situation of the man who wishes to end his life on grounds whose validity would be recognized by all not warned back by their religious convictions. But what of the man whose grounds are not reasonable in this sense? Does he not have the same personal right as a last recourse? And who are we to say his reasons are not cogent if they are cogent to him? Speaking personally, I would maintain that the right to die transcends the claims of family or society. A man's life is his own, and if we say it is not, we are saying that he is a slave and not a free man. Slavery is still slavery, even when it is near and dear ones who are the slavemasters.

What—to take the argument to its logical extreme—are the humane considerations we should bear in mind in treating the irretrievably psychotic patient who has repeatedly shown his determination to die? An account of such a patient has been given by Watkins, Gilbert and Bass in the *American Journal of Psychiatry*. . . . This man made eight separate and desperate attempts at suicide by slashing himself, jumping from a height and running with his head full tilt against a wall. The authors refer to other such patients, and comment that as supervision and control are increased, more and more ingenious methods of evading them are used, such as aspirating torn up paper tissues and tearing the blood vessels with the fingers. They say, "It is only by constant alertness on the part of the staff that the determined patient may be prevented from killing himself." What this means is that the invasion of his privacy must be complete. The patient must be stripped down to the state in which there is absolutely nothing of him, not one of his bodily or mental functions, which can be his to call his own. I ask you, what right do we have to debase and degrade both the patient and his custodians to this level? What harm would be done if, by the accident of a blind eye, the patient did make away with himself?

In preventing suicide, we are only attacking a symptom. We are doing the patient no service, perhaps a disservice, if we cannot influence permanently for the better the state of mind that led him to his attempt. What is the value of saving the life, say, even of a suicidal recurrent depressive, if it is only to force him to face again, in a few weeks or months, the same predicament? How can we be sure that the impulsive psychopath, who has opted for death, is not really doing his best, both for himself and everyone else?

Nor should we forget the welfare of society. If a chronically sick man dies, he ceases to be a burden on himself, on his family, on the health services and on the community. If we can do nothing to get a patient better, but do our best to retard the process of dying—extend it perhaps over months and years—we are adding to the totality of ill health and incapacity. To take an obvious example, transplant surgery, in providing a spare set for people who have run through one pair of kidneys, one liver or heart, increases the number of people in the community who at any one time are suffering from diseases of the kidneys, liver and heart. There is, of course, absolutely no limit to the burdens we can go on piling up, by trying to keep badly damaged individuals alive. Improving techniques and increasing effort in such directions make the very words "Health Service" a misnomer.

Professional optimism must not blinker us from reality. There are processes that lead through physical or mental illness, through accumulating incapacities or senescence, to conditions which doctors cannot mitigate, but can only try to render tolerable. A stage is reached at last, which to psychiatrists needs no description, to which death would certainly be preferable, but one which could have easily been avoided. How, then, has the patient been allowed to get so far? Has there been no mistake along the way? No failure of courage? Surely, in nearly all these cases there was a turning point, when the doctors knew that there was nothing effective to be done, when the patient could have seen, could have been shown, the road ahead, and could have decided how much further he wanted to go?

These difficult problems derive in part from the confusion of our standards of value. Since death is inevitable, it is pathetic that in facing it we should be full of fear. The fact that we can look forward with certainty to an end at some time should be a source of consolation and serenity. Death is not the least enviable of all states, and is to be preferred to living and suffering misery and degradation. Long illness is only to be endured if there is hope of eventual recovery; it should not be endured when there is no such hope.

In combating death, when we are not able to combat the causes that are leading to death, we are fighting against nature instead of using natural forces to help us. We are beginning to realize, in a hundred different fields, that we cannot do this without paying a price: whether or not the ultimate end is attained and is worthwhile, along the way there will have been immense efforts spent to no avail, and the disagreeable surprises of unexpected and unwanted consequences.

Death is the natural cure of all incurable suffering. Those of our patients who would welcome such a cure must be met with respect and understanding. Should we not look forward to a future when we exercise more than our present control both of our exits and our entrances? Would it not be a noble world in which no child would be born that was not a wanted child, and those who died, died of their own volition? The biological role of death is not only inescapable, but of inestimable value. We must appreciate the part that death plays in the promotion of health. Death is an equal partner with birth in the renewal of life, for human societies, for human kind, and indeed for the entire world of living things.

SUICIDE PREVENTION AND THE VALUE OF HUMAN LIFE

Erwin Ringel

Ringel vigorously opposes libertarian attitudes toward suicide, including those which would allow "planned death" to the terminally ill, and argues that they reflect a tendency to devalue human life. The impact of such tendencies is strongest on such groups as psychopaths, addicts, the elderly, criminals, and those who are victims of religious, racial, and political oppression. Arguing that every human life is important, Ringel sees it as the purpose of suicide prevention to revalue human life, by extending the help which psychiatry and crisis intervention now make possible, to all human beings.

Erwin Ringel, M.D., a psychiatrist and president of the Austrian Adlerian Society, is well known as a pioneer of suicide prevention. He founded the suicide-prevention service of Vienna in 1948; in 1960 he founded the International Association for Suicide Prevention, and is now its honorary president.

From time to time voices are heard accusing those who prevent suicide of inhumanity. One of man's fundamental rights, they say, is to put an end to his own life—that is, a right to suicide—and it is inhuman to want to take this right away from him. It is cruel, these voices say, to see men and women suffering abysmally, and in spite of this to encourage them to go on living. Eliot Slater, for instance, has claimed that it is inhuman to stand by and watch a patient's repeated attempts at suicide; he says that rather than repeatedly trying to save the patient, there is only one really humane solution: to give him the chance of an "honorable" death. I think Slater is right in just one point: to stand by and watch a series of suicide attempts without doing anything about them would indeed be inhuman.

It is an obvious human duty to grasp the hand which is extended in search of help. Anyone who has given serious scientific consideration to the problem of suicide knows that death—the state of not-being—is for the most part chosen under pathological circumstances or under the influence of diseased feelings. In fact, suicide cannot really be "chosen," since an intense, overwhelming inner compulsion renders any free "choice" null and void. The strongest human driving force is that of self-preservation. No one is ever, as Edwin Shneidman put it, 100 percent suicidal—no human being, no matter how determined he or she may seem to be to put an end to life, does not somewhere cherish the hope of being saved.

This is true even in the case of so-called planned death. In England some years ago, the Voluntary Euthanasia Bill of 1969 proposed that an individual suffering from a terminal illness should be able to decide the date of his own death: each individual would be encouraged to submit an application for painless death, said death to occur after a commission had met to examine and approve the application, provided the applicant continued to insist on this request. Fortunately, this proposal was turned down by an overwhelming majority. A physician who was a member of such a commission would, in carrying out such a function, be denying his true calling; he would be an accomplice, equally guilty, in the deadly outcome of such a request. Even nonmedical members of such a commission—people not bound by the Hippocratic Oath— would be faced with an insoluble task. Who can presume to judge with certainty and finality what any one man is likely to experience during the rest of his natural life—whether that life lasts for years, or days, or only hours? The future and the shape of that future remain for us all unforeseeable and unknowable, and we can only truly be humane if we do not try to exceed our limitations, or try to know the unknowable before the time is ripe. Let me remind you of what happened to Konrad Adenauer when he was arrested after the attempt on Hitler's life on July 20, 1944. He was taken to a concentration camp. The camp commander had him brought up to his office and said to him, "Herr Adenauer, there is one thing you simply must not do—and that is to commit suicide!" Adenauer was taken by surprise, and asked him what on earth had given him this idea. The camp commander, surprised in turn, said, "Look, you are an old man, you are a prisoner, the future holds nothing for you. Isn't it obvious that you must be thinking of suicide?" As you know, of course, that "old man," that "prisoner without a future," was many years later to transform the face of his country, and with it, the face of Europe. This story is not just an example, but a warning.

But there are others who are threatened by suicide as well, and we who hope to prevent suicide must extend our efforts to these. Before the majesty of the law—in this case the law governing suicide prevention—all men are truly equal. It is precisely the despised, those people upon whom society heaps contempt, who are in particular need of special prophylactic treatment, because it is they who are particularly endangered. The crucial principle of suicide prevention, after all, is that *each* individual life is important! The aim of suicide prevention is not so much to reduce the suicide rates, after all (we know how unreliable the figures are anyway), but to help people: to make it possible for each individual person to take the road of self-realization rather than that of failure, of which the final consequence is suicide. We cannot value different people in different ways; each human life is equally valuable. There are no supermen and no subhuman beings; there are only human beings to whom one feels "incorrigibly drawn," as Morgenstern put it, and to whom one offers one's hand.

Labels like "psychopath," "drunkard," and "addict" have become invectives, and automatically call forth contempt and antipathy. But the people who bear these labels are human beings, urgently in need of special and specialized help. We need to give them understanding and therapy, not prejudice and contempt. And we need to recognize these labels as labels for disease, so that we can provide treatment and hope for therapeutic success.

We must also set more value on older people. In almost all

countries in the world, the rates of suicide among persons over sixty are high and are steadily increasing. This may be no surprise: if we look at the behavior of many people toward the old and even toward the merely aging, we may begin to wonder just how sincere the wish of the community is to keep its older people alive. Unfortunately, we often hear the argument that people who commit suicide at a relatively advanced age would not have had very much longer to live. Worse, still, we hear the relatives of those who have died by suicide saying, comfortably, "Well, he didn't have much to expect of life anyway!" It is an impressive and important fact that in areas where the aged enjoy real esteem (as in certain Far Eastern countries), suicide among the old is actually a rare occurrence.

Suicide prevention must also have particular concern for people who have become criminals. Nobody has the right to differentiate between lives which are worth preserving and those which are not. The prisoner is isolated and his possibilities are restricted; when in addition attitudes towards prisoners are laden with contempt, this produces a suicidal climate, and sharply increases the prisoner's risk. Suicide prevention works to counteract this, and to show how important it is even for persons who have gone astray—the asocial elements—to maintain their human rights and their human dignity.

The slightest deviation from this principle—that *every* human life is important, and so *every* human life is to be saved—would not only undermine the entire idea of suicide prevention; it would be, as Grillparzer put it, "that first step from humanity to bestiality." We have of course seen tendencies to devalue human life again and again throughout history. Hegel talked of supermen, for whom "the litany of private virtues" such as modesty, humbleness, charity, and good-doing is not valid because, he argued, "such great figures must necessarily crush many an innocent flower and destroy many a thing along their way." Napoleon met the insistent demands of the Austrian chancellor Metternich to end a war costing innumerable human lives with the cynical reply, "A man like me doesn't care for the lives of a million people." But since the explorations of Sigmund Freud, we can no longer regard the rise of inhuman tyrants as accidental. We now know that "Führer personalities" achieve their power only because countless ordinary people project their own wishes, especially their own unconscious wish for self-punishment, onto these figures. A Hitler is no accident; we are all jointly responsible for the devaluation of human life carried out by some individuals. Our century has reached the climax of contempt for human life as such and for human beings in particular.

Let us not forget those people (and unfortunately, their names are legion in our times) who are persecuted for reasons of race, religion, or politics. The persecution of the Jews is the most conspicuous, perhaps, but certainly only one of many examples. Suicide prevention efforts must be particularly aware of the kinds of situations that arise under oppression of this sort, especially since the ruling powers tend to prohibit any kind of assistance for the endangered group. External factors can become so difficult under conditions of persecution that even people who do not, by and large, have tendencies toward suicide will nevertheless—as a last resort—kill themselves. For instance, during the period 1933–1945 the rate of Jewish suicide increased heavily under the pressure of Nazi persecution, although it is precisely the Jews who are normally not prone to suicide.

It is in these situations that suicide prevention can transcend itself into courageous humaneness. Life would not be worth living were one not able to observe, in situations like these, that miraculously there are always a few courageous individuals who may form into small groups or even larger communities to maintain and implement humane thinking. Among the persecuted, this may take the form of a compassionate turning toward one's fellow man. Jean-François Steiner, for instance, in his book about the uprising at Treblinka,[1] describes the way in which each inmate of the concentration camp was initially indifferent to the fate of the others. Gradually, though, it dawned upon them that each man's duty was to prevent the suicide of the others. In this, out of the mere aggregates of individuals or "series," as Sartre puts it, there arises the task of forming a human *community*. Here, as in other forms of human togetherness, we recognize this principle: only when the individual comes to feel responsible for the fate of the others, and for their remaining alive in the struggle against self-destruction, can the "series" become a group. After all, "no man is an island entire of itself; every man is a piece of the continent, a part of the main . . ."

Man is truly the only living creature who can choose to be, or not to be. But our endeavor must be to maintain and to keep this life, and all the implications and possibilities inherent in it, to the very last. Suicide prevention is the implementation of human responsibility toward one's fellow human beings. Thus, it is by no means inhuman to reject—decisively—any demand for suicide or for the planned termination of life.

Over and over again, those who support the idea of voluntary euthanasia present to us the picture of a patient suffering from incurable cancer and unbearable pain; this, they claim, is a perfect example of a psychologically understandable, justified suicide. But I think this is wrong. First, such "understandable" cases form only a very small percentage of all suicides. For most suicides, the situation was in no way hopeless, and often not even critical. More people take their own lives because they wrongly believe themselves to be suffering from cancer, than do those who actually have cancer. Carcinophobia is a psychic disease; and it is the mental and spiritual condition of the person, not the cancer, which is the actual cause for the suicide. In the great majority of all cases, suicide is based on transient psychic illnesses which can today be cured. About a third of all suicides, for instance, can be traced to depression, or "melancholia"—yet it is now possible, with appropriate administration of antidepressants, to shorten the phases of depression considerably and to help the patient to regain normal psychic condition.

Second, we must remain aware of the concept of the "mental crisis," during which there is intense psychic conflict and often, as a direct result of this, a false assessment of the situation. The tragic story of Romeo and Juliet shows how such a misinterpretation can lead to suicide. What suicide prevention practices is "crisis intervention," for all is won if the time of crisis can be overcome. Of course, it is not enough to keep people who have attempted suicide alive by medical measures, for example, detoxification; they also require intense psychiatric treatment and postclinical care. When both methods are put into action simultaneously, it is very often possible—as declining relapse rates have shown—to prevent a recurrence of a suicide attempt. In the face of these facts, would it not be inhuman to deprive those in need and sorrow of such medical, psychological, and social aid as have in the past proved their value?

Fortunately, psychiatry has made vast progress in recent years, and enables us to offer this help more and more effectively. An increasing number of crisis-intervention clinics for giving practical aid have been set up. But it is not only the retaining of human life that is the objective; it is to help and guide the despairing to enable them to make their lives happier and more worthwhile. It is in this way that we work to restore value to human life. Suicide prevention and humane thought go hand in hand, and suicide prevention must necessarily mobilize all available humaneness if it is to triumph over a wavering ethical background.

There is possibly no better way to sum up all the humanitarian impulses released in the most various fields and levels of suicide prevention than in the admirable words of Pope John XXIII, "I want to be good always, and to all!" This quotation serves to remind us that suicide prevention has contributed to the attempt of the Christian churches to go back to the values of early Christianity. The innumerable counseling centers of the churches do not practice suicide prevention merely in order to prevent this deadly sin, but first and foremost in order to practice the Christian call: "Behold how they love one another!"

Perhaps we can see this most clearly in the happiness and gratefulness of patients who have survived a crisis. These are the feelings experienced by those patients who have been saved after an attempted suicide; perhaps these feelings could also be described as gratitude for the gift of a new life.

No one can dispute the right of man to end his life. But it is also the case that no one can dispute our right to help, in whatever way we can, those who are in spiritual need, and who are at risk of suicide. The right to prevent suicide only dims when therapy cannot succeed in restoring to a person the feeling that his life is worth living; thanks to improved therapeutic possibilities, however, this is only very, very seldom the case.

N O T E S

1. Jean-François Steiner, *Treblinka*. Preface by Simone de Beauvoir. Original French edition: Librairie Arthème Fayard, 1966; English translation by Helen Weaver, New York: Simon and Schuster, 1967.

THE RIGHT TO SUICIDE: A PSYCHIATRIST'S VIEW

Jerome A. Motto

Motto accepts the right to commit suicide. He acknowledges that limitations may be placed on that right in some kinds of psychiatric situations, but argues that the right must be respected if the individual has a realistic assessment of his life situation and if he displays little ambivalence about his decision. Motto then considers ways in which the stigma currently associated with suicide might be reduced and how this might facilitate clearer thinking by persons contemplating suicide.

Jerome A. Motto, M.D., professor of psychiatry at the University of California School of Medicine at San Francisco and associate director of its Psychiatric Consultation-Liaison Service, has been president of the American Association of Suicidology and secretary general of the International Association for Suicide Prevention. He has had special interests in depressive and suicidal states throughout his professional career.

To speak as a psychiatrist may suggest to some that psychiatrists have a certain way of looking at things. This would be a misconception, though a common one. I know of no professional group with more diverse approaches to those matters concerning it than the American psychiatric community. All physicians, however, including psychiatrists, share a tradition of commitment to both the preservation and the quality of human life. With this one reservation, I speak as a psychiatrist strictly in the singular sense.

The emergence of thoughts or impulses to bring an end to life is a phenomenon observed in persons experiencing severe pain, whether that pain stems from physical or emotional sources. Thus physicians, to whom persons are inclined to turn for relief from suffering, frequently encounter suicidal ideas and impulses in their patients. Those who look and listen do, at least.

From a psychiatric point of view, the question as to whether a person has the right to cope with the pain in his world by killing himself can be answered without hesitation. He does have that right. With a few geographical exceptions the same can be said from the legal and social point of view as well. It is only when philosophical or theological questions are raised that one can find room for argument about the right to suicide, as only in these areas can restrictions on behavior be institutionalized without requiring social or legal support.

The problem we struggle with is not whether the individual *has* the right to suicide; rather, we face a twofold dilemma stemming from the fact that he does have it. Firstly, what is the extent to which the exercise of that right should be subject to limitations? Secondly, when the right is exercised, how can we eliminate the social stigma now attached to it?

LIMITATIONS ON THE INDIVIDUAL'S RIGHT TO SUICIDE

Putting limitations on rights is certainly not a new idea, since essentially every right we exercise has its specified restrictions. It is generally taken for granted that certain limitations must be observed. In spite of this, it is inevitable that some will take the position that unless the right is unconditional it is not "really" granted.

I use two psychological criteria as grounds for limiting a person's exercise of his right to suicide: *(a)* the act must be based on a realistic assessment of his life situation, and *(b)* the degree of ambivalence regarding the act must be minimal. Both of these criteria clearly raise a host of new questions.

REALISTIC ASSESSMENT OF LIFE SITUATION

What is reality? Who determines whether a realistic assessment has been made? Every person's perception is reality to *him*, and the degree of pain experienced by one can never be fully appreciated by another, no matter how empathetic he is. Differences in capacity to *tolerate* pain add still another crucial yet unmeasurable element.

As formidable as this sounds, the psychiatrist is obliged to accept this task as his primary day-to-day professional responsibility, whether or not the issue of suicide is involved. With an acute awareness of how emotions can—like lenses—distort perceptions which in turn shape one's thoughts and actions, and with experience in understanding and dealing with this underlying substrate of emotion, he is constantly working with his patients on the process of differentiating between what is realistic and what is distorted. The former must be dealt with on a rational level; the latter must be explored and modified till the distortion is reduced at least to the point where it is not of handicapping severity. He is aware of the nature and extent of his own tendency to distort ("Physician, heal thyself"), and realizes that the entire issue is one of degree. Yet he must use his own perception of reality as a standard, shortcomings notwithstanding, realizing full well how much information must be carefully considered in view of the frailty of the human perceptual and reality-testing apparatus.

Some persons have a view of reality so different from mine that I do not hesitate to interfere with their right to suicide. Others' perceptions are so like mine that I cannot intercede. The big problem is that large group in between.

In the final analysis, then, when a decision has to be made, what a psychiatrist calls "realistic" is whatever looks realistic to *him*. At the moment of truth, that is all any person can offer. This inherent human limitation in itself is a reality that accounts for a great deal of inevitable chaos in the world; it is an article of faith that not to make such an effort would create even greater chaos. On a day-to-day operational level, one contemporary behavioral scientist expressed it this way: "No doubt the daily business of helping troubled individuals, including suicides, gives little time for the massive contemplative and investigative efforts which alone can lead to surer knowledge. And the helpers are not thereby to be disparaged. They cannot wait for the best answers conceivable. They must do only the best they can *now*."[1]

Thus if I am working with a person in psychotherapy, one limitation I would put on his right to suicide would be that his assessment of his life situation be realistic as *I* see it.

A related concept is that of "rational suicide," which has enjoyed a certain vogue since at least the seventeenth century, when the "Rationalist Era" saw sharp inroads being made into the domination of the church in determining ethical and social values.[2] According to one contemporary philosopher, "the degree of rationality of the [suicidal] act would depend on the degree of rationality of the philosophy which was guiding the person's deliberations."[3] Rationality is defined as a means of problem solving, using "methods such as logical, mathematical, or experimental procedures which have gained men's confidence as reliable tools for guiding instrumental actions." The rationality of one's philosophy is determined by the degree to which it is free of mysticism. Further, "A person who is considering how to act in an intensely conflicting situation cannot be regarded as making the most rational decision, unless he has been as critical as possible of the philosophy that is guiding his decision. If the philosophy is institutionalized as a political ideology or a religious creed, he must think critically about the institution in order to acquire maximum rationality of judgment. This principle is clear enough, even if in practice it is enormously difficult to fulfill."[4]

The idea of "rational suicide" is a related yet distinctly different issue from the "realistic assessment of one's life situation" referred to above. Making this assessment involves assembling and understanding all the facts clearly, while the idea of a "rational suicide" can only be entertained after this assessment is done and the question is "what to do" in the light of those facts.

The role of the psychiatrist and the thinking of the rationalist tend to merge, at one point, however. In the process of marshaling all the facts and exploring their meaning to the person, the psychiatrist must ensure that the patient does indeed critically examine not only his perception of reality but his own philosophy. This often entails making that philosophy explicit for the first time (without ever using the term "philosophy"), and clarifying how it has influenced his living experience. The implication is clear that modification of the person's view of his world, with corresponding changes in behavior, may lead to a more satisfying life.

The rationalist concedes that where one's philosophy is simply an "intellectual channeling of emotional forces," rational guidelines have severe limitations, since intense emotional conflicts cut off rational guidance. These circumstances would characterize "irrational" grounds for suicide and would identify those persons whose suicide should be prevented.

The argument for "rational suicide" tends to apply principally to two sets of circumstances: altruistic self-sacrifice for what is perceived as a noble cause; and the severe, advanced physical illness with no new therapeutic agents anticipated in the foreseeable future. This does not help us very much because these circumstances generate relatively little real controversy among behavioral scientists. The former situations are not usually recognized till after the act, and the latter at present are receiving a great deal of well-deserved attention from the point of view of anticipating (and sometimes hastening) the foreseeable demise in comfort and dignity.

Our most difficult problem is more with the person whose pain is emotional in origin and whose physical health is good, or at most constitutes a minor impairment. For these persons, the discussion above regarding "rational" and "irrational" distinctions seems rather alien to the clinical situation. This is primarily due to the rationalist's emphasis on intellectual processes, when it is so clear (at least to the psychiatrist) that it is feelings of worthiness of love, of relatedness, of belonging, that have the strongest stabilizing influence on the suicidal person.

I rarely hear a patient say, "I've never looked at it that way," yet no response is more frequently encountered than, "Yes, I understand, but I don't feel any differently." It is after a continuing therapeutic effort during which feelings of acceptance and worthiness are generated that emotional pain is reduced and suicidal manifestations become less intense. Either exploring the philosophy by which one lives or carefully assessing the realities of one's life can provide an excellent means of accomplishing this, but it is rarely the influence of the philosophy or the perception of the realities per se that brings it about. Rather, it is through the influence of the therapeutic relationship that the modified philosophy or perception develops, and can then be applied to the person's life situation.

MANIFESTATIONS OF AMBIVALENCE

The second criterion to be used as the basis for limiting a person's exercise of his right to suicide is minimal ambivalence about ending his life. I make the assumption that if a person has no ambivalence about suicide he will not be in my office, nor write to me about it, nor call me on the telephone. I interpret, rightly or wrongly, a person's calling my attention to his suicidal impulses as a request to intercede that I cannot ignore.

At times this call will inevitably be misread, and my assumption will lead me astray. However, such an error on my part can be corrected at a later time; meanwhile, I must be prepared to take responsibility for having prolonged what may be a truly unendurable existence. If the error is made in the other direction, no opportunity for correction may be possible.

This same principle regarding ambivalence applies to a suicide prevention center, minister, social agency, or a hospital emergency room. The response of the helping agency may be far from fulfilling the needs of the person involved, but in my view, the ambivalence expressed is a clear indication for it to limit the exercise of his right to suicide.

REDUCING THE STIGMA OF SUICIDE

The second horn of our dilemma about the right to suicide is the fact that the suicidal act is not considered respectable in our society. It can be maintained that granting a right but stigmatizing the exercise of that right is tantamount to not having granted it in the first place. In order to develop a realistic approach to this problem it is necessary to reduce the negative social implications attached to it.

The first step is to talk about it freely—with each other, with doctors, ministers, patients, and families. Just as with past taboos—TB, cancer, sex (especially homosexuality), drug addiction, abortion—it will gradually lose the emotional charge of the forbidden. The second step is the continued institutionalization of supportive and treatment services for suicidal persons, through local, state, and federal support.

News media should be responsible for reporting suicidal deaths with dignity and simplicity, without attempting either to cover up or sensationalize pertinent information. In an economically competitive field this would not be a reasonable expectation unless it were made part of an accepted ethical code.

Instruction regarding this problem should be provided as a matter of course in the education and training for all health care personnel, emergency services (police, firemen), behavioral sciences (psychology, sociology, anthropology), and those to whom troubled people most often turn, such as ministers, teachers, and counselors. In short, every person who completes the equivalent of a high school education would be provided with an orientation toward the problem of suicide, and those responsible for responding to others in stressful circumstances should be prepared to assist in providing— or at least locating—help when needed.

A question has been raised whether incorporating concern for suicide into our social institutions might depersonalize man to some extent. I would anticipate the contrary. The more our social institutions reflect awareness of and concern for man's inner life and provide means for improving it, the greater is the implied respect for that life— even if this takes the form of providing a dignified means of relinquishing it.

It seems inevitable to me that we must eventually establish procedures for the voluntary cessation of life, with the time, place, and manner largely controlled by the person concerned. It will necessarily involve a series of deliberate steps providing assurance that appropriate criteria are met, such as those proposed above, as we now observe specific criteria when a life is terminated by abortion or by capital punishment.

The critical word is "control." I would anticipate a decrease in the actual number of suicides when this procedure is established, due to the psychological power of this issue. If I know something is available to me and will remain available till I am moved to seize it, the chances of my seizing it now are thereby much reduced. It is only by holding off that I maintain the option of changing my mind. During this period of delay the opportunity for therapeutic effort—and the therapy of time itself—may be used to advantage.

Finally, we have to make sure we are not speaking only to the strong. It is too easy to formulate a way of dealing with a troublesome problem in such a manner, that if the person in question could approach it as we suggest, he would not be a person who would have the problem in the first place.

When we discuss—in the abstract—the right to suicide, we tend to gloss over the intricacies of words like "freedom," "quality of life," "choice," or even "help," to say nothing of "rational" and "realistic." Each of these concepts deserves a full inquiry in itself, though in practice we use them on the tacit assumption that general agreement exists as to their meaning.

Therefore it is we who, in trying to be of service to someone else, have the task of determining what is rational for us, and what our perception of reality is. And we must recognize that in the final analysis it will be not only the suicidal person but we who have exercised a choice, by doing what we do to resolve our feelings about this difficult human problem.

N O T E S

1. J. Diggory, "Suicide and Value." In H. Resnik, ed., *Suicidal Behaviors* (Boston: Little, Brown, 1968), p. 18.
2. S. C. Sprott, *The English Debate on Suicide—From Donne to Hume* (LaSalle, Ill.: Open Court, 1961).
3 S. Pepper, "Can a Philosophy Make One Philosophical?" In E. S. Shneidman, ed., *Essays in Self-Destruction* (New York: Science House, 1967), p. 121.
4. Ibid., p. 123.

Suicide,
Law, and
Rights

SUICIDE AND THE INALIENABLE RIGHT TO LIFE

Joel Feinberg

Feinberg takes as his starting point the Jeffersonian view, embodied in the U.S. Constitution, that the rights to life, liberty, and the pursuit of happiness are inalienable. *He asks whether this could mean that suicide is wrong because it involves "alienating" or relinquishing a right to life which is inalienable. He then provides three different interpretations of the original Jeffersonian dictum, and argues that the most plausible of these does not preclude voluntarily relinquishing one's right to life by committing suicide.*

Joel Feinberg, educated at the University of Michigan, has taught at Brown, Princeton, U.C.L.A, and the Rockefeller Universities, and is now professor of philosophy at the University of Arizona. He has been a Guggenheim Fellow and a National Endowment for the Humanities Senior Fellow, and is the author of Reason and Responsibility *(1965),* Moral Concepts *(1969),* Doing and Deserving *(1970), and* Social Philosophy *(1973), as well as numerous articles in philosophical journals.*

It is surprising that in this bicentennial period we have not yet heard an argument that seems to bolster the case of opponents of suicide and voluntary euthanasia. The argument derives from an interpretation of Thomas Jefferson's famous words that all men "are endowed with certain unalienable Rights, that among these are Life . . . ," and from similar passages in the writings of other founding fathers. To kill another person even with his consent or at his considered request, it might well be claimed, is to infringe his "Right to Life," a right the founders clearly held to be incapable of being waived or surrendered. Willfully to take one's own life or to permit another to take one's life, the argument continues, is in the relevant sense to *alienate* one's right to go on living; hence, suicide and voluntary euthanasia can both be viewed as efforts to alienate the inalienable, to give away what cannot properly be given away.

There is at least a superficial plausibility in this effort to invoke the authority of Jefferson as a basis for refusing legal sanction or denying moral legitimacy to such practices as suicide, aiding another's suicide, and voluntary euthanasia. The argument seems to present a dilemma for those of us who would defend a "right to die": either we must abandon our defense of what seem to us to be morally justifiable practices, or else we must reject the exalted eighteenth-century doctrine of inalienable rights, at least as it applies to the right to life. The former alternative seems inhumane and paternalistic, the latter seems virtually un-American. I have my doubts about the theory of inalienable rights in any case . . . but my primary intention in this essay is to find a way between two alternatives by reconciling a right to die with the inalienability of the right to live, properly interpreted.

✓ A RIGHT TO DIE? THREE VIEWS

How could a person have a right to terminate his own life (by his own hand or the hand of another) if his right to life is inalienable? . . . Most people in normal circumstances have a duty not to kill themselves that is derived from the rights of other people who rely or depend on them. . . . In these circumstances of interpersonal reliance, one's general right to life, even if it is discretionary and absolute in its own domain, is subject to "territorial" limitation. One's own personal autonomy ends where the rights of others begin, just as national sovereignty comes to a limit at the boundaries of another nation's territory. My life may be my property, but there are limits to the uses to which I can put anything I own, and I may not destroy what is mine if I thereby destroy or seriously harm what does not belong to me. So some suicides may violate the rights of *other* persons, though equally certainly some suicides do not.

But how could my suicide violate my *own* right to life? Is that right a claim against myself as well as against others? Do I treat myself unjustly if I deliberately end my life for what seem to me the best of reasons?[1] Am I my own victim in that case? Do I have a moral grievance against myself? Is suicide just another case of murder? Am I really two persons for the purposes of moral judgment, one an evil wrong-doer and the other the wronged victim of the first's evil deed? Can one of me be blamed or punished without blaming or punishing the other? Perhaps these questions make the head reel because they raise interestingly novel moral possibilities. On the other hand, their paradoxes may derive, as the predominant philosophical tradition maintains, from the conceptual violence they do to the integrity of the self and the way we understand the concept of a right . . .

THE PATERNALIST

According to the first possible view, the right to life is a nonwaivable, *mandatory right,* one which must be exercised. On this view there is no right to die but only a right to live. Since there is no morally permitted alternative to the one prescribed path, following it is a duty, like the duty of children to attend school and the duty of convicted felons to undergo punishment. But since continued life itself is a benefit in all circumstances whatever the person whose life it is may think about it, we may with propriety refer to it as a right. In this respect, too, the right to life is similar to the right to education and the right to punishment (as understood by Hegelians). The "right to life" is essentially a duty, but expressible in the language of rights because the derivative claims against others that they save or not kill one are *necessarily* beneficial—goods that one could not rationally forswear. The right therefore must always be "exercised" and can never be "waived." Anyone who could wish to waive it must simply be ignorant of what is good for him.

THE FOUNDING FATHERS

The second position differs sharply from the first in that it takes the right to life to be a discretionary, not a mandatory right. In this respect that right is exactly like the most treasured specimens in the "right to liberty" and "right to property" categories. Just as we have rights to come or go as we choose, to read or not read, to speak or not speak, to worship or not worship, to buy, sell, or sit tight, as we please, so we have a right, within the boundaries of our own autonomy, to live or die, as we choose. The right to die is simply the other side of the coin of the right to live. The basic right underlying each is the right to be one's own master, to dispose of one's own lot as one chooses, subject of course to the limits imposed by the like rights of others. Just as my right to live imposes a duty on others not to kill me, so my right to die, which it entails, imposes a duty on others not to prevent me from implementing my choice of death, except for the purpose of determining whether that choice is genuinely voluntary, hence truly mine. When I choose to die by my own hand, I insist upon my claim to the noninterference of others. And should I find myself unable to terminate my own life, I may *waive* my right to live in exercising my right to die, which is one and the same thing as releasing at least one other person from his duty not to kill me. In exercising my own choice in these matters, I am not renouncing, abjuring, forswearing, resigning, or relinquishing my right to life; quite the contrary, I am *acting* on that right by exercising it one way or the other. I cannot relinquish or effectively renounce the right, for that would be to alienate what is not properly alienable. To alienate the right would be to abandon my discretion; to waive the right is to exercise that discretion. The right itself, as opposed to that to which I have the right, is inalienable.

The state can properly prohibit some suicide, however, without annulling the discretionary right to life, just as the state may limit the right to property by levying taxes, or the right to liberty by requiring passports or imposing speed limits. To limit discretion in the public interest is not to cancel it or withdraw it. Ritual suicide among healthy young men, for instance, might be forbidden, not because our lives are not our own to risk (what is more risky than mountain climbing or car racing?), but rather because: (a) it cannot be in the public interest to permit wide-spread carnage, to deprive the population of a substantial portion of its most vital youthful members, and leave large numbers of dependent widows and orphans and heartbroken friends and relations; and (b) the "voluntariness" of the participation in a suicide ritual, like that of the private duel to death, must be suspect. These are reasons enough for a legal prohibition of some suicide practices, even in a community that recognizes an indefensible discretionary right to life (and death).

THE EXTREME ANTIPATERNALIST

The third position springs from a profound and understandable aversion to the smug paternalism of the first view. Like the second view, it interprets the right to life as a discretionary right which we may exercise as we please within the limits imposed by the like rights of others and the public interest. So far, I suspect, Paine, Adams, and Jefferson would be in solid agreement, since the natural rights emphasized in their rhetoric and later incorporated in our Constitution were, for the most part, protected options, and these writers made constant appeal to personal autonomy in their arguments about particular political issues. But this third view goes well beyond anything the fathers contemplated, since it holds that not only is life alienable; the discretionary right to life is alienable too. This view, of course, cannot be reconciled with the explicit affirmations of inalienability made in most of the leading documents of the revolutionary period, thus it cannot be attributed to the founding fathers. But it would be a mistake to dismiss it too quickly, for paternalism is a hard doctrine to compromise with, and it rejects paternalism *totally*. According to this third view, a free and autonomous person can renounce and relinquish any right, *provided only that his choice is fully informed, well considered, and uncoerced*, that is to say, *fully voluntary*. It may well be, as I have argued elsewhere, that there is no practicable and reliable way of discovering whether a choice to abjure a natural right is fully voluntary.[2] The evidence of voluntariness which we can acquire may never be sufficiently strong to override the natural presumption that no one in his right mind, fully informed, would sell himself into permanent poverty or slavery or sell his discretionary right to life. On that ground the state might always refuse to sanction requests from citizens that they be permitted to alienate the right to life. But that ground is quite consistent with the acknowledgment that even the natural right to life is alienable *in principle*, though not in fact. At least such a consistent antipaternalistic strategy would keep us from resorting, like Sam Adams, to the peculiar idea of a "gift" that cannot be declined, given away, or returned, and would enable us to avoid the even more peculiar notion that the right to life of an autonomous person is not properly his own at all, but rather the property of his creator.

Whatever judgment we make of the third position, however, will be consistent with the primary theses of this essay: that the inalienable right to life can be interpreted in such a way that it is not infringed by suicide or voluntary euthanasia, that that interpretation (the second position above) is coherent and reasonably plausible, and that it is very likely the account that best renders the actual intentions of Jefferson and the other founding fathers.

NOTES

1. St. Thomas Aquinas grants the point, on the authority of Aristotle, that nobody can commit an injustice to himself, even by committing suicide. The sinfulness of suicide, according to Aquinas, consists not in the fact that one violates one's own rights (which Aquinas finds incoherent) but rather in that (a) the suicide violates God's rights just as in killing a slave one violates the rights of the slave's master; (b) the suicide violates his community's rights by depriving it of one of its "parts"; (c) the suicide acts against the *charity* (not the justice) that a person should have toward himself. Aquinas therefore would agree that the suicide, sinful though he may be, does not violate his own "right to life." See *Summa Theologica*, 2a 2ae, Question 64, A5.
2. See the discussion in Joel Feinberg, "Legal Paternalism," *Canadian Journal of Philosophy* 1 (1971): 105–24.

A CONSTITUTIONAL RIGHT TO SUICIDE

Alan Sullivan

Sullivan argues for a constitutional right to suicide. He points out that U.S. law has never addressed this issue squarely. On the one hand, the Constitution protects the right of self-determination in many significant matters of personal choice, including choices involving the treatment of one's own body. On the other hand, the law also appears to recognize state interests in preventing suicide. Because the Supreme Court has never spelled out the principle determining which personal choices are protected from state inter- ference and which are not, the Court cannot be said to have taken a stand on the issue of suicide. Sullivan argues for a resolution of this tension in favor of a right to self-determination in the matter of suicide, subject to appropriate tests of competency.

Alan Sullivan is a partner in the law firm of Van Cott, Bagley, Cornwall & McCarthy, Salt Lake City, Utah, and has interests both in corporate and constitutional law.

This essay considers whether government can lawfully restrain competent people from committing suicide. Despite its importance, the courts have not treated this issue or its close variants in a thorough fashion. Judicial decisions on the subject usually weigh the state's interest in "preserving life" or in policing the "crime" of self-destruction against any of several constitutional rights of the individual involving principles of self-determination or religious belief. Yet modern courts have not explained the reasons for the government's interest in preventing self-destructive acts by competent people. And the courts have only recently begun to identify with care the scope of a person's right to a death of his own choosing.

Over the last decade suicide has received a good deal of publicized consideration as a responsible alternative;[1] these discussions, however, have often focused on a "right to die" without offering a clear explanation of its origins or limits. Recent cases involving the rights of terminally ill or comatose patients have begun the task of defining this right,[2] but they have not addressed the issue of suicide persuasively. That issue, as I approach it here, is perhaps best framed in the following hypothetical problem:

A man whom we shall call Harris is a chronically ill patient living at a Veterans' Administration hospital. He is fifty-four years old; he has no family, and no one depends upon him for financial support. His illness (it does not matter for our purposes whether it is cancer or emphysema or tuberculosis) will probably kill him before old age but is not imminently terminal. In the meantime Harris's illness prevents him from earning a living and caring for himself. Harris is mentally competent, in the usual sense of the term. But because his illness has deprived him of the capacity to do what he considers worthwhile, Harris wants to end his life. He does not want to die in pain or alone, but would prefer to end his life at the hospital where the only people he knows would care for his remains. He does not ask that anyone administer the means of death to him, but only that those around him refrain from preventing him from doing so himself. However, the Veterans' Administration personnel who care for him have already intervened in one attempt at suicide, and they continue to watch him closely.

Does Harris have a constitutional basis to enjoin these agents of the federal government from taking steps to prevent his suicide?

This hypothetical question is not posed because Harris's predicament is necessarily common or because Harris's intentions are heroic or foolish. Rather, it is intended to probe—as extreme cases often do—the limits of an individual's right of self-determination protected under the concept of "privacy" developed by the Supreme Court in decisions since *Griswold v. Connecticut*.[3] These authorities and others dealing more directly with suicide have generated difficult and important questions. Does the right to privacy attach only to those intimate relationships having a "claim to social protection,"[4] such as marriage and the family, as recent Supreme Court opinions imply? Or does the right protect from government interference the individual's choice to do with his body what he will, so long as that choice does not affect the rights of others? Does the government have an interest in preserving life from rational acts of self-destruction? Or is government's only justifiable interest in protecting the choice-making process?

These questions presuppose that sane persons commit suicide. Ever since the common law made crimes of suicide and attempted suicide,[5] intent has been a necessary element, and the element of intent implies the actor's sanity.[6] Although courts have said that suicide is morally wrong[7] and even that it constitutes a "grave public wrong,"[8] modern cases have consistently acknowledged that suicide may be the result of voluntary choice exercised when the suicide is in full command of his faculties.[9] Certainly a rational person may choose to die rather than prolong a hopelessly painful life. As one philosopher has put it, "The fantasy that existence as such, regardless of its how and wherefore, is better than nonexistence is a quirk of metaphysical verbalization and not an inference from actual experience of actual people."[10]

This essay will examine the right-to-privacy cases since *Griswold* and will suggest that the Supreme Court has steadfastly refused to describe what privacy is. On a case-by-case basis, the Court has told us that the right to privacy protects certain choices and not others, but the Court has never explained the principle underlying the Constitution's protection.[11] Yet, it will be argued, the Court's decisions anchoring privacy to the guarantees of "liberty" in the Due Process Clauses of the Fifth and Fourteenth Amendments imply two important propositions:[12] (1) the right to privacy belongs to individuals and does not necessarily flow from relationships sanctioned by society; and (2) the right protects personal choices in areas historically screened from the state's interference. I will argue that the decision to live or die is just such a choice, and that government has no legitimate interest in preventing suicide by competent persons where the lives of others are not seriously affected. The paternalism of the state must instead be directed at protecting the person's right to choose free of coercion, mental instability, or ignorance.

✓ I. THE CONSTITUTIONAL FRAMEWORK

The Supreme Court has applied two different tests to determine whether government may lawfully interfere with a person's conduct. The first, which is often applied to questions involving economic liberty, is whether the state has a "rational basis" for its restraint upon the individual's conduct.[13] Only if the state's regulation is so unrelated to legitimate state interests as to be arbitrary will the individual's conduct be protected by the guarantees of personal liberty in the Fifth and Fourteenth amendments.[14] The Supreme Court's rulings under the "rational basis" test demonstrate that courts generally accept at face value the state's conclusion that its proscription rests upon a legitimate governmental interest.

When, however, a challenger to state action demonstrates that his conduct entails the exercise of a "fundamental" personal right, the rational basis test and its presumption of validity give way to a stricter judicial scrutiny of the state's regulation. In such "strict scrutiny" cases, the state must prove that its regulation or practice advances some "compelling" state interest.[15] The state must also prove that its challenged infringement constitutes the least restrictive means available to sustain its compelling purpose.[16]

The key to invoking this "strict scrutiny" analysis is the individual's allegation that the state's practice infringes his "fundamental right." As a general matter, fundamental rights are those explicitly guaranteed by the Bill of Rights. But the Supreme Court has recognized another class of fundamental right whose source lies outside specific guarantees of the Constitution, such as the rights to marital and sexual privacy,[17] the right of a woman to exercise control over her body,[18] the right to travel freely from one place to another,[19] and the right to learn certain subjects in school.[20] In a variety of formulations, the Supreme Court has held these rights to be "fundamental" because they are entailed in or assumed by explicit constitutional guarantees of individual liberty.

In arriving at this conclusion with respect to particular rights, the Court has assessed the importance of the individual's conduct in light of the legal and social history underlying the right infringed by the state.[21] Analysis of this sort, however, inevitably entails uncertainty for litigants and courts alike. The Supreme Court has been unwilling to map the entire range of conduct protected by the right to privacy; its tactic in privacy cases has been to limit its rulings to the facts before it and to caution against extension of privacy to new areas of conduct. Thus in *Paris Adult Theatres I v. Slaton,* the Court noted that "for us to say that our Constitution incorporates the proposition that conduct involving consenting adults only is always beyond state regulation is a step we are unwilling to take."[22]

Despite the Court's cautionary approach it is clear that once a person's conduct is deemed to be protected by the right to privacy, the state must demonstrate a compelling interest before it may lawfully interfere with the conduct.[23] In recent cases dealing with the individual's right to refuse lifesaving medical treatment, courts have required government to prove a compelling interest that justifies treatment.[24] These cases have invoked the "strict scrutiny test" in the name of the individual's right to privacy. Two of the difficult questions they raise are whether a right to refuse lifesaving treatment squares with the Supreme Court's rulings on privacy, and whether the same right extends to an individual's choice to commit suicide.

II. Privacy and Self-Destructive Conduct

Although the Court has occasionally made it appear that the word "privacy" is a unitary concept, in fact any of a number of distinct rights may lie behind a claim of privacy protection. The two most frequently used meanings for privacy are (1) what has been called "the right to selective disclosure,"[25] or the right to control dissemination of otherwise confidential information, and (2) personal autonomy, or the individual's right to make certain personal choices concerning his destiny free from government interference. It is, of course, the development of the second of these meanings that concerns us in relation to suicide.

In *Griswold v. Connecticut,*[26] the Supreme Court held unconstitutional a state criminal statute that prohibited the use of contraceptives. In so holding the Court acknowledged the existence of a fundamental 'right protecting the marriage relation from government intrusion. Although this right finds no explicit support in the Constitution, it is entailed, said the Court, in a combination of the First Amendment's "right of association," the Third Amendment's prohibition against quartering of soldiers "in any house," the Fourth Amendment's right to be free of unreasonable searches and seizures, and the Fifth Amendment, which in the words of the Court, "enables the citizen to create a zone of privacy which government may not force him to surrender to his detriment." [27]

In *Eisenstadt v. Baird*,[28] the Court extended the privacy right to choices outside the marriage relation and struck down a statute proscribing distribution of contraceptives to unmarried persons. The Court held:

> If under *Griswold* the distribution of contraceptives to married persons cannot be prohibited, a ban on distribution to unmarried persons would be equally unpermissible. It is true that in *Griswold* the right of privacy in question inhered in the marital relationship. Yet the marital couple is not an independent entity with a mind and heart of its own, but an association of two individuals each with a separate intellectual and emotional makeup. If the right to privacy means anything, it is the right of the *individual,* married or single, to be free from unwarranted governmental intrusion into matters so fundamentally affecting a person as the decision whether to bear or beget a child.[29]

Since *Eisenstadt* the federal courts have repeatedly struck down statutes proscribing or limiting the rights of both married and unmarried persons to sexual self-determination.[30] These cases are founded upon a right to sexual privacy quite apart from the marriage-centered privacy of *Griswold*.

In an apparently separate vein the Supreme Court has upheld a right of privacy centered upon the home. In *Stanley v. Georgia*,[31] the Supreme Court held unconstitutional a statute proscribing the private possession of obscene material. Although the Court's decision was nominally based upon First Amendment notions of freedom of belief and access to information,[32] the Court also considered the constitutional protection to be accorded the home:

> If the First Amendment means anything, it means that a State has no business telling a man, sitting alone in his house, what books he may read or what films he may watch. Our whole constitutional heritage rebels at the thought of giving government the power to control men's minds.[33]

In this connection the Court quoted from Brandeis's celebrated dissent in *Olmstead v. United States*,[34] to the effect that the framers of the Constitution "conferred, as against the Government, the right to be let alone—the most comprehensive of rights and the most valued by civilized man."[35] Just as importantly, the *Stanley* court cited *Griswold* in support of "the right to be let alone."[36]

Roe v. Wade,[37] one of the Supreme Court's abortion cases, is a watershed in the history of privacy protection. The Court held that, until a human fetus becomes a "person" within the Fourteenth Amendment's due process protection of life, the state may not constitutionally interfere with the mother's choice to abort. Essential to the Court's ruling was its conclusion that "the right of personal privacy includes the abortion decision."[38] The Court's decision in this respect is of special importance to us because, for the first time, although with some reluctance, the Court implicitly acknowledged that a person's control of her body, irrespective of any relation in which she may be engaged, is a fundamental right under the Constitution.

The *Roe* Court began its consideration of the privacy issue with a lesson in constitutional method. The Court noted that various of its decisions have found the roots of privacy in the First Amendment, in the Fourth and Fifth Amendments, in the penumbras of the Bill of Rights, or in the "concepts of liberty guaranteed by the first section of the Fourteenth Amendment."[39] But the Court then seems to have abandoned all other approaches in favor of the last: "[O]nly personal rights that can be deemed 'fundamental' or 'implicit in the concept of ordered liberty' . . . are included in this guarantee of personal privacy."[40] Since *Roe* the Supreme Court has reaffirmed its adherence to this general test in determining the reach of privacy protection.[41]

Roe next considered whether the right to privacy protects the abortion decision from government interference. The right, said the Court, "has some extension to activities relating to marriage . . . procreation . . . contraception . . . family relationships . . . and child rearing and education."[42] Without defining exactly what each of these "activities" has in common with the others, the Court concluded that the same "right" protecting their free pursuit "is broad enough to encompass a woman's decision whether or not to terminate her pregnancy."[43] Buttressing its conclusion, the Court analyzed the impact of laws against abortion upon the personal lives of women: physical harm from delivery, a "distressful life and future" from unwanted children, distress to the mother's family, and the stigma of unwed motherhood.[44] This catalogue is particularly important because it implies, as *Eisenstadt* stated explicitly, that the right of privacy guarantees the individual's choice to control his body so as to avoid personal harm or distress. The woman's right to abortion should therefore not depend on societal values protecting procreation and family life; rather the right acknowledged in *Roe* should be directed at the protection of physical autonomy in the individual, not at fostering the family, marriage, or any such relation.

Thus the Court's conclusions in *Roe* seem to imply that family life, procreation, and marriage are worthy of privacy protection because official assaults upon their integrity threaten the individual's most intimate choice-making, and not because these relations have some special claim to protection beyond the individual rights of persons who join in them. But the Court muddied the waters in *Roe* by stating:

> [I]t is not clear to us that the claim . . . that one has an unlimited right to do with one's body as one pleases bears a close relationship to the right of privacy previously articulated in the Court's decisions. The Court has refused to recognize an unlimited right of this kind in the past.[45]

The Court has reaffirmed this confusing insistence upon tying the privacy right to "matters of procreation, marriage and family life," in two cases since *Roe*.[46] In doing so the Court has arbitrarily restricted the right of privacy to those associational and domestic values protected by the First, Third and Fourth Amendments; it has restricted the right to privacy in a way that ignores the historically comprehensive reach of the due process clause's guarantee of personal liberty.

To see this, let us recall that the Fourteenth Amendment's guarantees are rooted in a tradition protecting the individual from unwarranted governmental restraint; this tradition only incidentally relates to societal norms protecting the family, marriage, or the home. In his dissent in *Poe v. Ullman*,[47] Justice Harlan noted that Connecticut's statute proscribing the use of contraceptives was "not an intrusion into the home so much as on the life which characteristically has its place in the home." He concluded that "if the physical curtilage of the home is protected, it is surely as a result of solicitude to protect the privacies of the life within."[48] In precisely the same sense the Court stated in *Eisenstadt* as noted earlier that "[i]f the right of privacy means anything, it is the right of the *individual,* married or single, to be free from unwarranted governmental intrusion into matters . . . fundamentally affecting a person. . . ."[49]

The words "life, liberty and property" in the Fourteenth Amendment were borrowed from the English common law and the thirty-ninth article of the Magna Carta.[50] According to this tradition, personal liberty meant no more and no less than "the power of locomotion, of changing situation, or moving one's person to whatever place one's inclination may direct, without imprisonment or restraint, unless by due course of law."[51] In a variety of contexts courts in this country have extended the notion of personal liberty to physical autonomy—the individual's freedom from unconsented interference with choices concerning his body.

> The attitude of the courts has not, in general, been one of paternalism. Where no public interest is contravened, they have left the individual to work out his own destiny, and are not concerned with protecting him from his own folly. . . .[52]

The tort law doctrine of informed consent begins with "the premise of thorough-going self-determination."[53] As Cardozo held in his famous opinion in *Schloendorff v. Society of New York Hospital,* "Every human being of adult years and sound mind has a right to determine what shall be done with his own body. . . ."[54] The Fourteenth Amendment's guarantee of personal liberty bears an obvious and important relation to the doctrine of self-determination underlying informed consent. Both, insofar as the courts have been concerned, are based upon the individual's "fundamental" right to do with his body what he wishes,[55] so long as neither the rights of others nor the public interest is threatened in the process.[56] The Supreme Court's insistence upon restricting privacy—the range of personal choices protected from government interference—to matters of family, home, and procreation ignores the traditional value that the law has attached to self-determination.

Recent decisions of the Supreme Court have made it clear that the autonomy protected by the right to privacy does not extend to all matters of intimate personal discretion— or even to all *important* decisions affecting the individual's destiny. For example, such important matters as choosing to live with several persons,[57] the choice of one's school companions,[58] and the choice of sexual partners and practices are not included in the right's protection.[59] Although, according to one commentator, "[t]here is no clear cut definition between these arguably excluded matters and the 'procreative rights' clearly covered by the right to privacy."[60] The line of demarcation apparently concerns whether such matters of choice are of traditional significance to the law.[61] It should go without saying that the decision of a rational person to continue living or to die is of such traditional significance. The host of recent cases upholding the right of comatose or dying patients to resist lifesaving or life-prolonging treatment have held as much. For example, in *Superintendent v. Saikewicz*,[62] the Massachusetts Supreme Court upheld the right of a sixty-seven-year-old leukemia patient to refuse life-prolonging treatment. The court acknowledged the state's "implicit recognition" that "a person has a strong interest in being free from nonconsensual invasion of his bodily integrity."[63] The court held that

> [o]f even broader import, but arising from the same regard for human dignity and self-determination, is the unwritten constitutional right of privacy. . . . As this constitutional guaranty reaches out to protect the freedom of a woman to terminate pregnancy under certain conditions [citing *Roe v. Wade, supra*], so it encompasses the right of a patient to

preserve his or her right to privacy against unwanted infringements of bodily integrity in appropriate circumstances.[64]

The difficult question posed by these decisions, however, is whether the legal position of a comatose or terminally ill patient who resists lifesaving treatment is the same as that of a rational person who wishes to commit suicide. One might argue that refusing treatment is not the same as choosing to die, although the end result may be the same; the willful, self-destructive intent of the potential suicide might be said to disqualify him from privacy protection respecting his decision to die. On the other hand, one might argue that the right to privacy protects *any* choice an individual may make, so long as that choice does not affect the rights of others. The cases have seldom, if ever, addressed this problem squarely; at least a case like that of our hypothetical Harris has never been reported. However, I would like to suggest a solution to this problem based on two important considerations.

First, the principle of self-determination embodied in the Fourteenth Amendment's guarantee of liberty is value-free in one sense: regardless of the folly that may be entailed in a purely personal decision, the law will protect the right to decide. As Chief Justice Burger (then a court of appeals judge) stated in a refusal-of-treatment case:

> Mr. Justice Brandeis, whose views have inspired much of the "right to be let alone" philosophy, said . . . "The makers of our Constitution . . . sought to protect Americans in their beliefs, their thoughts, their emotions and their sensations. They conferred, as against the Government, the right to be let alone—the most comprehensive of rights and the right most valued by civilized man." Nothing in this utterance suggests that Justice Brandeis thought an individual possessed these rights only as to *sensible* beliefs, *valid* thoughts, *reasonable* emotions, or *well-founded* sensations. I suggest he intended to include a great many foolish, unreasonable and even absurd ideas which do not conform, such as refusing medical treatment even at great risk.[65]

The Fourteenth Amendment's protection of the right to self-determination in significant matters of personal choice manifestly rests upon a belief in the primacy of personal responsibility. The law cannot consistently protect the right to decide, on the one hand, while permitting, on the other, official interference with choices that it deems to be foolish or morally blameworthy—unless, of course, important interests of others would be jeopardized by those choices. The law's acknowledgment of the right to decide entails acceptance of the consequences, whatever they may be, of choice.

Second, the choice of a person to take affirmative steps to end his life is not legally different from the choice of a person to order termination of artificial means used to prolong his life. Arguments that support a "right to die" in the second instance, but not in the first,[66] ignore the profoundly personal nature of the decision in both instances. In *In re Quinlan*,[67] the New Jersey Supreme Court upheld the right of a guardian to assert the right of a permanently comatose patient to require termination of the patient's life-support system. The court stated:

> [N]o external compelling interest in the State could compel Karen to endure the unendurable, only to vegetate a few measurable months with no realistic possibility of returning to any semblance of cognitive or sapient life. We perceive no thread of logic distinguishing between such a choice on Karen's part and a similar choice which, under the evidence in this case, could be made by a competent patient terminally ill, riddled by cancer and suffering great pain. . . .[68]

The *Quinlan* court, however, saw "a real distinction between the self-infliction of deadly harm and a self-determination against artificial life support or radical surgery, for instance, in the face of irreversible, painful and certain imminent death."[69] Accordingly the court held that the state's interest in preserving Karen Quinlan's life diminishes, and the individual's right to privacy grows, "as the degree of bodily invasion [via medical intervention] increases and the prognosis dims."[70]

The distinction in *Quinlan* between affirmative acts of self-destruction and the act of a terminally ill or comatose patient to refuse further medical intervention really rests upon the question of competence.[71] The court's implicit assumption is that, under certain circumstances, refusal of life-sustaining treatment is reasonable and therefore the result of competent choice; but the "self-infliction of deadly harm" is never reasonable. Surely under a variety of circumstances life may be unendurable to a reasonable person, even though he does not face the prospect of immediate and painful death. The burden of such circumstances to a fully conscious person may, indeed, be more difficult than the prospect of permanent coma. But more importantly, this aspect of the *Quinlan* decision intrudes upon the very choice that the right to privacy protects. The law of privacy does not protect the individual's right to make reasonable choices, but *all* choices so long as they concern matters of intimate importance to the individual. Once a competent person has decided not to live, the law should protect him from government interference in the consequences. A distinction between affirmative and passive methods of death has no relevance to the scope of the actor's freedom from unwarranted restraint.

Other authorities have suggested that the decision of a terminally ill or injured patient to refuse lifesaving treatment stems from the patient's belief that treatment will be harmful, despite medical advice to the contrary. Such patients, it has been argued, desire to live and not—like the potential suicide—to die, and their decision should be protected.[72] Thus in *Erickson v. Dilgard*,[73] a patient suffering intestinal bleeding refused a blood transfusion, which his doctors deemed necessary to his recovery. The court upheld his right to refuse. In doing so the court addressed the state's argument that the patient's refusal amounted to suicide:

> The County argues that it is in violation of the Penal Law to take one's own life and that as a practical matter the patient's decision not to accept blood is just about the taking of his own life. The court [does not] agree . . . because it is always a question of judgment whether the medical decision is correct. . . . [I]t is the individual who is subject to the medical decision who has the final say. . . .[74]

Certainly in cases like *Erickson* a terminally ill patient may refuse lifesaving treatment in the desperate hope that his life will be somehow saved by his refusal. And certainly such cases are different from suicide, where the actor wishes to die. But *Erickson* ignores the crucial factor common to both the refusing patient and the suicide: in both instances a person has made a decision the

242 Alan Sullivan

result of which, according to the best evidence available, will be his death; the legal question entailed in both instances is whether, in light of that probable consequence, the individual will be permitted to decide. One might well contend that a patient *in extremis* or a patient having an irrational fear of surgery should not be permitted the choice to refuse treatment;[75] difficult questions of competence, the patient's expressed desire to live, and the press of time would argue for substituting the will of the court for that of the patient. By the same token, and if the will of the patient is decisive, the suicide decision of a person who has rationally reflected upon his predicament should have a manifestly stronger claim to protection. The argument that the suicide's decision is not protected because he wants to die simply ignores the possibility of the suicide's competence; such an argument misdirects the paternalism of the state's police power.

IV. The State's Interest

If, as many cases posit, the state has an interest in preventing suicide, that interest has never been persuasively articulated. As demonstrated earlier, modern courts and commentators have frequently conceded that a terminally ill patient has the right to end his life, but they distinguish his predicament from suicide; with respect to suicide, it is said, the state has a compelling interest in intervening. This interest is usually articulated as the duty to "preserve life" or to protect the "sanctity of life."[76] The reasons for the state's interest in preserving the lives of persons who wish to die are seldom explained in detail. The New Jersey court's terse formulation in *State v. Congdon* is not unusual:

> [T]he basis of the State's police power is the protection of its citizens. This protection must be granted irrespective of the fact that certain individuals may not wish to be saved or protected.[77]

In perhaps the most expansive recent explanation of the state's duty to preserve life against suicide, law professor Robert M. Byrn has cast in modern terms the four "objections to suicide" that, under the common law, justified the state's opposition.[78] First, Byrn asserts, suicide is "unnatural" (and therefore undeserving of the law's protection) because of "the apparent contradiction inherent in a claim of right to destroy the life from which all rights flow."[79] Second, suicide "devalues human life, *qua* human, because it constitutes aggression against life"; since life is "unalienable, one may not be allowed to cause . . . his own destruction."[80] Third, the care of human life and happiness is the only legitimate function of government; as a result, the life of every human being is "under the protection of the law, and cannot be lawfully taken by himself . . . except by legal authority."[81] Fourth, "to the extent that killing invites imitation," suicide might "encourage" others to the same act.[82]

Lurking in all but the last of these justifications for government intervention are the related presuppositions (1) that the state must enforce the commands of God or of the community's conscience, and (2) that the people are subservient to the state, as a child to his parent and as a subject to his king. Perhaps because both of these notions have never had much currency in this country, Professor Byrn's justifications for government prevention of suicide fail to persuade. Government in this country has always been looked upon as subservient to the people and as the protector of the individual's right to choose his own morality.[83] Americans, moreover, have generally valued their individualism and their personal independence to the exclusion of any compelling allegiance to a protective state or to posterity.[84] In short, arguments that suicide is "unnatural" or that it transgresses some ideal of life or deprives the state of its rightful function proceed from a governmental ideal with which we are not familiar in this country.

Professor Byrn's last justification—that one suicide might encourage other suicides and ought, for that reason, to be proscribed—rests upon psychological assumptions about the suicidal character that are beyond the scope of this essay. Those assumptions were also beyond the scope of Professor Byrn's paper, for he offered no authority for the proposition that "active self-destruction may serve as an 'evil example' to other susceptible members of society."[85] But perhaps this argument is best put to rest by conceding that people who are mentally ill or who are otherwise susceptible to the suggestion of suicide should be prevented from committing suicide. Few would dispute that government has the duty to protect psychologically imbalanced people from irrational acts of self-destruction. Government is entitled to require that the right of privacy, like any other right involving serious consequences, be exercised only by competent people.[86]

The problem of competence suggests the direction in which the state's paternalism should be directed. It also raises the most serious practical impediment to judicial recognition of the right to die at a chosen time and in a chosen way: do courts have the ability to discern whether a person is competent to choose to die?

In a culture that places freedom of choice among the most important of all protected values, the state has no plausible interest in preventing suicide by competent people. Rather, the state's "compelling interest" is in protecting choice, in insuring that persons making critical decisions within the ambit of the right to privacy are not coerced, are mentally competent, and are sufficiently informed to decide for themselves. The state should intervene to prevent suicide where the individual lacks the capacity or the competence to make a choice in the matter. The state should not intervene merely because the incipient suicide's decision appears foolish or because it is regarded as morally wrong.

The Supreme Court recently formulated a rule—instructive for our purposes—relating to the right of pregnant minors to choose to have abortions. In *Bellotti v. Baird*,[87] the Court held that if a state decides to require a girl to obtain parental consent to any abortion, it must also provide an alternative, nonparental forum from which authorization may come:

> A pregnant minor is entitled in such a proceeding to show either: (1) that she is mature enough and well enough informed to make her abortion decision, in consultation with her physician, independently of her parents' wishes; or (2) that even if she is not able to make this decision independently, the desired abortion would be in her best interests.[88]

The "alternative proceeding" mandated by the Court protects the minor's right to choose by insuring that (1) her choice is not induced by parental coercion, and (2) either she is competent to choose or else the abortion is in her best interests. The paramount value operating in *Bellotti* is the liberty to choose free of coercion, incapacity, and ignorance.

The problem of competence in the case of people who wish to end their own lives is more difficult, in part because the stakes are higher. A mistake in this choice cannot be corrected and will probably result in a viable life being needlessly wasted. Judges have been known to shrink from direct confrontation with the issue of competence where voluntary death is imminent—to err, if at all, "on the side of life." [89] But two related ideas suggest one way in which courts could approach the problem of competence in such cases.

First, competence should be defined by courts in a way that does not deprive the potential suicide of the right to choose. It must be defined with a view to securing for the subject the right to choose to die despite the wishes of doctors, friends, psychologists, and judges. [90] The test of competence should inquire whether the subject has the mental capacity to comprehend his predicament and to evaluate the alternatives. Furthermore, competence should be presumed; the presumption should be rebutted only by convincing evidence of coercion, mental instability, or ignorance. [91]

Second, although competence must be presumed, the weight accorded that presumption must vary from case to case. The courts must look not only to the testimony of persons who know the subject, but they must also pay attention to his objective circumstances: his age, his illness, and his prospects. As the subject's prognosis dims, the presumption of his competence must be entitled to greater weight. Insofar as the subject is shown to have viable alternatives to suicide, however, his presumed competence must be examined with greater care. Few would question the competence of a person's decision to die if he is old and suffers from a painful, incurable illness. But if a person is young and healthy and wishes to end his life, his competence must be scrutinized more closely. This is not to say that courts should substitute their own choice for that of the person who wishes to die. Rather, courts should apply a flexible standard of competence to avoid the tragic results of insanity or ignorance. The court's objective in both instances should be to protect the right to choose by insuring the subject's ability to choose.

N O T E S

1. See e.g.: "A Survivor's Notes," *Newsweek* (April 30, 1979), p. 17; Doris Portwood, *Commonsense Suicide* (New York: Dodd,

Mead, 1978); Thomas Szasz, "Our Despotic Laws Destroy the Right to Self-Control," *Psychology Today* (Dec. 1974), p. 19; Helen Epstein, "A Sin or a Right?" *New York Times Magazine* (Sept. 8, 1974), p. 91. See also R. M. Veatch, *Death, Dying, and the Biological Revolution* (New Haven: Yale University Press, 1976), pp. 116-203; D. C. Maguire, *Death by Choice* (New York: Schocken Books, 1975); M. D. Heifetz and C. Mangel, *The Right to Die* (New York: Putnam, 1975), pp. 73-98; and R. H. Williams, "Propagation, Modification, and Termination of Life," in R. H. Williams, ed., *To Live and To Die* (New York: Springer-Verlag, 1973), pp. 89-97.

2. See e.g., *Satz v. Perlmutter,* 362 So.2d 160 (Fla.App. 1978); *Superintendent v. Saikewicz,* 370 N.E.2d 417 (Mass. 1977); *In re Quinlan,* 70 N.J. 10, 355 A.2d 647 (1976); *John F. Kennedy Memorial Hospital v. Heston,* 58 N.J. 576, 279 A.2d 670, 673 (1971).

3. 381 U.S. 479 (1965).

4. *Poe v. Ullman,* 367 U.S. 497, 553 (1961) (Harlan, J., dissenting).

5. Blackstone contended that the suicide was guilty of a double offense:

> one spiritual, in invading the prerogative of the Almighty, and rushing into his immediate presence uncalled for; the other temporal, against the king, who hath an interest in the preservation of all his subjects; the law has therefore ranked this among the highest crimes, making it a peculiar species of felony, a felony committed on one's self. . . . A *felo de se* therefore is he that deliberately puts an end to his own existence, or commits any unlawful malicious act, the consequence of which is his own death. . . . The party must be of years of discretion, and in his senses, else it is no crime.

IV *Chitty's Blackstone* 19 (19th London ed.), quoted in *State v. Willis,* 255 N.C. 473, 121 S.E.2d 854, 855 (1961). At common law attempted suicide was a misdemeanor punishable by fine and imprisonment. *State v. Willis, supra,* 121 S.E.2d at 857.

6. See e.g., *State v. Willis, supra,* note 5, 121 S.E.2d at 858; *Stiles v. Clifton Springs Sanatorium Co.,* 74 F. Supp. 907, 909 (W.D.N.Y. 1947); *Connecticut Mutual Life Ins. Co. v. Groom,* 86 Pa. 92, 97

(1878). *Contra, Maycock v. Martin,* 157 Conn. 156, 245 A.2d 574, *cert. den.* 393 U.S. 1111 (1969).

7. See e.g., *Wykoff v. Mutual Life Ins. Co.,* 173 Or. 592, 147 P.2d 227, 229 (1944).

8. *Stiles v. Clifton Springs Sanatorium Co., supra,* note 6, 74 F.Supp. at 909.

9. *Tate v. Canonica,* 5 Cal.Rptr. 28, 40 (Cal.App. 1960). See also W. L. Prosser, *Handbook of The Law of Torts* §44, 4th ed. (St. Paul: West Publishing Co., 1971), pp. 282–3.

10. H. M. Kallen, "An Ethic Freedom: A Philosopher's View," 31 *N.Y.U.L.Rev.* 1164, 1168 (1956).

11. Writing shortly after *Griswold,* Thomas Emerson predicted that the Court would "proceed slowly, developing the right to privacy on a case-by-case basis." Emerson, "Nine Justices in Search of a Doctrine," 64 *Mich.L.Rev.* 219, 233 (1965). The Supreme Court's choice to develop the doctrine gradually and cautiously is apparent in *Loving v. Virginia,* 388 U.S. 1 (1967); *Roe v. Wade,* 410 U.S. 113 (1973); *Paris Adult Theatre I v. Slaton,* 413 U.S. 49 (1973); *Paul v. Davis,* 424 U.S. 693 (1976); and *Kelley v. Johnson,* 425 U.S. 238 (1976). See also Note, "Roe and Paris: Does Privacy Have a Principle?" 26 *Stan.L.Rev.* 1161 (1974).

12. *Roe v. Wade, supra,* note 11, 410 U.S. at 153; *Paul v. Davis, supra,* note 11, 424 U.S. at 713.

13. *Williamson v. Lee Optical, Inc.,* 348 U.S. 483, 488 (1955).

14. *Kelley v. Johnson, supra,* note 11, 425 U.S. at 249.

15. See e.g., *Roe v. Wade, supra,* note 11, 410 U.S. at 156; *Kramer v. Union Free School District,* 395 U.S. 621, 627 (1969); *Shapiro v. Thompson,* 394 U.S. 618, 634 (1969).

16. *Shelton v. Tucker,* 364 U.S. 479, 488 (1960).

17. *Griswold v. Connecticut, supra,* note 3; *Eisenstadt v. Baird,* 405 U.S. 438 (1971).

18. *Bellotti v. Baird,* 47 U.S.L.W. 4969 (July 2, 1979); *Planned Parenthood v. Danforth,* 428 U.S. 52 (1976); *Roe v. Wade, supra,* note 11.

19. *Shapiro v. Thompson,* 394 U.S. 618 (1969); *Kent v. Dulles,* 357 U.S. 116 (1958).

20. *Pierce v. Society of Sisters,* 268 U.S. 510 (1925); *Meyer v. Nebraska,* 262 U.S. 390 (1923).

21. See e.g., *Roe v. Wade, supra,* note 11, 410 U.S. at 154-5; *Eisenstadt v. Baird, supra,* note 17, 405 U.S. at 453.

22. 413 U.S. 49, 68 (1973).
23. *Roe v. Wade, supra,* note 11, 410 U.S. at 156.
24. *Satz v. Perlmutter, supra,* note 2; *In re Quinlan, supra,* note 2; *In re Osborne,* 294 A.2d 372 (D.C.App. 1972); *Winters v. Miller,* 446 F.2d 65 (2d Cir. 1971). See also *John F. Kennedy Memorial Hospital v. Heston, supra,* note 2.
25. Note, "Does Privacy Have a Principle?" supra, note 11, 26 *Stan.L.Rev.* at 1163. See also *California Bankers Ass'n v. Schultz,* 416 U.S. 21 (1974).
26. 381 U.S. 479 (1965).
27. *Id.* at 484.
28. 405 U.S. 438 (1971).
29. *Id.* at 453.
30. *Bellotti v. Baird, supra,* note 18; *Planned Parenthood v. Danforth, supra,* note 18; *Poe v. Gerstein,* 517 F.2d 787 (5th Cir. 1975); *Doe v. Rampton,* 366 F.Supp. 189 (D.Utah 1973).
31. 394 U.S. 557 (1969).
32. *Id.* at 564.
33. *Id.* at 565.
34. 277 U.S. 438, 478 (1928).
35. 394 U.S. at 564.
36. *Id.*
37. 410 U.S. 113 (1973).
38. *Id.* at 154.
39. *Id.* at 152.
40. *Id.* See also 410 U.S. at 153:

> This right of privacy, whether it be founded in the Fourteenth Amendment's concept of personal liberty and the restrictions upon state action, as we feel it is, or . . . in the Ninth Amendment's reservation of rights to the people, is broad enough to encompass a woman's decision whether or not to terminate her pregnancy.

41. See *Paul v. Davis, supra,* note 11, 424 U.S. at 713.
42. 410 U.S. at 152–3.
43. *Id.* at 153.
44. *Id.* at 154.
45. *Id.*
46. *Kelley v. Johnson, supra,* note 11, 425 U.S. at 244; *Paul v. Davis, supra,* note 11, 424 U.S. at 713.

47. 367 U.S. 497, 551 (1961).
48. *Id.*
49. 405 U.S. 438, 453 (1971).
50. In his dissenting opinion in the *Slaughter-House Cases*, 16 Wall. 36, 114–5 (1872), Justice Bradley stated:

> The people of this country brought with them to its shores the rights of Englishmen; the rights which had been wrested from English sovereigns at various periods of the nation's history. One of these fundamental rights was expressed in these words, found in Magna Carta: "No freeman shall be taken or imprisoned, or be disseized of his freehold or liberties or free customs, or be outlawed or exiled, or any otherwise destroyed; nor will we pass upon him or condemn him but by lawful judgment of his peers or by the law of the land." English constitutional writers expound this article as rendering life, liberty, and property inviolable, except by due process of law. This is the very right which the plaintiffs in error claim in this case. Another of these rights was that of *habeas corpus*, or the right of having an invasion of personal liberty judicially examined into, at once, by a competent judicial magistrate. Blackstone classifies these fundamental rights under three heads, as the absolute rights of individuals, to wit: the right of personal security, the right of personal liberty, and the right of private property.

See also *Poe v. Ullman, supra*, note 4, 367 U.S. at 541.
51. The quoted words are attributed to Blackstone, in Shattuck, "The True Meaning of the Term 'Liberty' in Those Clauses in the Federal and State Constitutions Which Protect 'Life, Liberty and Property,'"[20] 4 *Harv. L. Rev.* 365, 377 (1891).
52. Prosser, *supra*, note 5, at 101.
53. *Natanson v. Kline*, 186 Kan. 393, 350 P.2d 1093, 1104 (1960); *Canterbury v. Spence*, 464 F.2d 772, 780 (D.C.Cir. 1972). See also *Union P. R. Co. v. Botsford*, 141 U.S. 250, 251 (1891).
54. 211 N.Y. 125, 105 N.E. 92, 93 (1914).
55. In *Superintendent v. Saikewicz*, 360 N.E.2d 417, 424 (Mass. 1977), the court observed that the law of Massachusetts has long recognized the individual's interest in being free from

nonconsensual invasion of his bodily integrity, and that the doctrine of informed consent is one "means by which the law has developed . . . consistent with the protection of this interest." The court then noted that "arising from the same regard for human dignity and self-determination is the unwritten constitutional right of privacy." *Id.*

56. In *Jacobsen v. Massachusetts*, 197 U.S. 11 (1905), the Supreme Court upheld the state's right to require unwilling persons to submit to vaccinations on the ground that the state has an overriding interest in maintaining public health. In *Buck v. Bell*, 274 U.S. 200 (1927), the Court sustained attempts by penal authorities to force "congenital criminals" to be sterilized in protection of public safety. In the same vein, courts have denied the wishes of medical patients to refuse lifesaving treatment where orphans would survive. *Application of President and Directors of Georgetown College, Inc.*, 331 F.2d 1000 (D.C.Cir. 1964). This is not to say, however, that the right to privacy does not include the right of physical self-determination where neither the public interest nor the rights of others are involved.

57. *Village of Bell Terre v. Boraas*, 416 U.S. 1 (1974).

58. *Runyan v. McCrary*, 427 U.S. 160 (1976).

59. *Doe v. Commonwealth's Attorney*, 425 U.S. 901 (1976), *aff'ing mem.* 403 F.Supp. 1199 (E.D.Va. 1975).

60. Cantor, "Privacy and the Handling of Incompetent Dying Patients," 30 *Rutgers L. Rev.* 243, 247 (1977).

61. *Id.;* note, "Does Privacy Have a Principle?" *supra*, note 11, 26 *Stan. L. Rev* at 1180; *Poe v. Ullman*, *supra*, note 4, 367 U.S. at 522.

62. 370 N.E.2d 417 (Mass. 1977).

63. 370 N.E.2d at 424.

64. *Id., Accord: In re Quinlan*, 70 N.J. 10, 355 A.2d 647, 663 (1976); *In re Osborne*, *supra*, note 24, 794 A.2d at 376 (Yeagley, J., concurring); *Winters v. Miller*, *supra*, note 24, 446 F.2d at 70; *In re Brookes' Estate*, 32 Ill.2d 361, 205 N.E.2d 435, 442-43 (1965); *Erickson v. Dilgard*, 44 Misc.2d 27, 252 N.Y.S.2d 705 (Sup.Ct. 1962). *Contra: John F. Kennedy Memorial Hospital v. Heston*, *supra*, note 2, 279 A.2d 670; *Application of President and Directors of Georgetown College, Inc.*, 331 F.2d 1000 (D.C.Cir.), *cert. den.*, 377 U.S. 978 (1964).

65. *Application of President and Directors of Georgetown College, Inc.*,

supra, notes 56 and 64, 331 F.2d at 1016 (Burger, J., concurring).

66. See e.g., Peter J. Riga, "Compulsory Medical Treatment of Adults," 22 *Catholic Law*, 105, 133 (1976).

67. 70 N.J. 10, 355 A.2d 647 (1976).

68. 355 N.E.2d at 663.

69. *Id.* at 665.

70. *Id.* at 664.

71. In *John F. Kennedy Memorial Hospital v. Heston*, 58 N.J. 576, 279 A.2d 670 (1971), the New Jersey court considered the propriety of the order of a lower court requiring a blood transfusion of an unconsenting twenty-two-year-old single woman. The court treated the case as one of suicide.

> Complicating the subject of suicide is the difficulty of knowing whether a decision to die is firmly held. Psychiatrists may find that beneath it all a person bent on self-destruction is hoping to be rescued, and most who are rescued do not repeat the attempt, at least not at once. Then, too, there is the question whether in any event the person was and continues to be competent (a difficult concept in this area) to choose to die. And of course there is no opportunity for trial of these questions in advance of intervention by the State or a citizen.

279 A.2d at 673.

72. See R. M. Byrn, "Compulsory Lifesaving Treatment for the Competent Adult," 44 *Ford.L.Rev.* 1, 5 (1975).

73. 44 Misc.2d 27, 252 N.Y.S.2d 705 (Sup.Ct. 1972).

74. 44 Misc.2d at 28, 252 N.Y.S.2d at 706.

75. In *In re Yetter*, 62 Pa.D.&C.2d 619 (C.P., Northampton County Dist.Ct. 1973), a patient in a mental institution refused surgery to prevent the spread of a carcinoma in her breast. In support of her refusal she testified that she was afraid of surgery; with no factual basis she believed that, years earlier, her aunt had died from breast surgery. The court upheld the patient's right to decide "even though her decision might be considered unwise, foolish or ridiculous." 62 Pa.D.&C.2d at 623. Citing *Roe v. Wade*, 410 U.S. 113 (1973), and the right to privacy, the court ruled in favor of "giving the greatest possible protection to the individual in furtherance of his own

desires." *Id.* at 624. The court characterized the patient's decision to refuse treatment as "irrational but competent." *Id.*

76. See e.g., *Satz v. Perlmutter, supra,* note 2, 362 So.2d at 162-63; *In re Quinlan, supra,* note 2, 355 N.E.2d at 663; P. J. Riga, "Compulsory Medical Treatment of Adults," 22 *Catholic Law.,* 105, 133-37 (1976); R. M. Byrn, *supra,* note 72, 44 *Ford.L.Rev.* at 19–20.

77. 76 N.J. Super. 493, 185 A.2d 21, 32 (1962). See also *John F. Kennedy Memorial Hospital v. Heston, supra,* note 2, 279 A.2d at 672.

78. R. M. Byrn, *supra,* note 72, 44 *Ford.L.Rev.* at 19 *passim.* Professor Byrn translates the ruling of Justice Dyer in *Hales v. Petit,* 75 Eng.Rep. 387 (C.B. 1562), into terms recognizable to "a modern, right-oriented society." *Id.* at 20.

79. *Id.*

80. *Id.* at 20–21.

81. *Id.* at 21.

82. *Id.* at 22.

83. See e.g., *In re Osborne,* 294 A.2d 372 (D.C.App. 1972), in which a Jehovah's Witness refused a blood transfusion necessary to save his life. The court held that it would not intervene to appoint a guardian to consent to the transfusion. Concluding that the state had no compelling interest that justified overriding the patient's desire, the court said: "The notion that the individual exists for the good of the state is, of course, quite antithetical to our fundamental thesis that the role of the state is to ensure a maximum of individual freedom of choice and conduct." 294 A.2d at 376. See also *Erickson v. Dilgard,* 44 Misc.2d 27, 252 N.Y.S.2d 705, 706:

> "[T]he Court concludes that it is the individual who is the subject of a medical decision who has the final say and that this must necessarily be so in a system of government which gives the greatest possible protection to the individual in the furtherance of his desires."

84. Tocqueville said of nineteenth-century Americans: "The woof of time is every instant broken, and the track of generations effused. Those who went before are soon forgotten; of those who will come after, no one has any idea: the interest of man is confined to those in close propinquity to himself." 2 A. de

Tocqueville, *Democracy in America,* pp. 119–20 (Reeve Tr. 1974).

85. Byrn, *supra* note 72, 44 *Ford.L.Rev.* at 22.
86. See *Bellotti v. Baird, supra,* note 18, 47 U.S.L.W. at 4974.
87. 47 U.S.L.W. 4969 (July 2, 1979).
88. *Id.* at 4974.
89. *Application of President and Directors of Georgetown College, Inc., supra,* note 64, 331 F.2d at 1015.
90. See Note, "Informed Consent and the Dying Patient," 83 *Yale L.J.* 1632, 1652–53 (1974):

> The definition of competency . . . must be formulated consistently with the objective of informed consent—to secure for the patient the right to forego treatment even if the medical profession or society would feel the reasons to be irrational.

91. See *Grannum v. Berard,* 70 Wash.2d 304, 422 P.2d 812, 814 (1967):

> [T]he law will presume sanity rather than insanity, competency rather than incompetency; it will presume that every man is sane and fully competent until satisfactory proof to the contrary is presented. . . . [W]e have held that the standard of proof required to overcome this presumption, in civil cases, is that of clear, cogent and convincing evidence. [Citations omitted.]

ASSISTING SUICIDE: A PROBLEM FOR THE CRIMINAL LAW

Leslie Pickering Francis

Surveying the variety of ways in which the United States and other jurisdictions treat assisted suicide, Francis argues that the legal situation is chaotic and provides neither protection for the person who would help a friend end his life in the face of painful terminal illness, nor assurance of punishment for the person who would coerce another into taking his life. Francis points out the deficiencies of various legal approaches to the problem of assisting suicide and proposes a solution which will, she thinks, allow the law to differentiate between those cases of assisting suicide which we find sympathetic and those which we find morally repugnant.

Leslie Francis, educated at Wellesley College and the University of Michigan, is assistant professor of philosophy and a member of the Law Review at the University of Utah. Her principal research interests include philosophy of law and moral theory.

254

In the United States and Britain, those who aid others to commit suicide—by giving information, comfort, or encouragement; by providing a secluded place; or by making available the means— are rarely criminally prosecuted. Yet the law can and sometimes does reach out extremely harshly. Perhaps its harshest moment occurred in Michigan, in 1920, in a case widely cited today. Frank Roberts's wife was incurably ill and bedridden with multiple sclerosis. At her request, he mixed poison and left it by her bedside; she drank the poison, quite clearly knowing what she was doing. The Michigan Supreme Court affirmed Roberts's conviction of murder, reasoning that he had intended his wife to be able to take her life as she wished, and that she would have been unable to do so without his aid. In the words of the court:

> It is beyond my comprehension how a human being, of normal conditions at least, or apparent normal conditions, can commit such a crime as you have in this case, by placing poison within reach of your wife or giving it to your wife with the intention as you claim.[1]

People v. Roberts seems a severe injustice, yet the legal theory on which it was based persists. Some of this persistence can be explained by the common-law condemnation of suicide and by continued social ambivalence about the morality of suicide. However, assisting suicide presents an extremely difficult problem for the criminal law. Frank Roberts's action is one for which we may have sympathy, but there are unsympathetic cases of assisting suicide as well, such as "helping along" a burdensome, ill, elderly relative who does not really want to die.[2] Our reactions of sympathy roughly parallel the distinction between suicide-assistance cases we tend to regard as morally permissible or even praiseworthy, and cases in which "assisting" suicide seems morally wrong.[3] What we need is a legal policy which brings the unsympathetic, morally impermissible cases within the criminal law, while leaving the permissible, sympathetic cases unscathed. To promote the establishment of such a policy, I shall first argue that current legal approaches to assisting suicide are unsatisfactory. Then, in light of a reconsideration of the rationale for making assisting suicide criminal, I make some suggestions for a more defensible way to structure the crime of assisting suicide.

1. CURRENT LEGAL APPROACHES TO ASSISTING SUICIDE

In England and the United States today, jurisdictions take three noteworthy approaches to the criminality of assisting suicide. First, twenty-five states, including nine with recent penal code revisions, contain no separate statutory treatment of assisting suicide. Only a few of these states have passed on the question of whether assisting suicide falls within their criminal homicide statutes. Of those states which have, most, like Michigan, have argued that assisting suicide is murder. Only Texas has reasoned that once the decriminalization of suicide removed the basis for the common-law theory that assisting suicide was criminal because it was aiding a crime, the homicide statutes provided no other legal basis for making assisting suicide criminal.[4] In states which have not treated the question of whether assisting suicide falls within their homicide statutes, the law is simply uncertain, one must guess at the result, and the bulk of precedent indicates that the guess will be at one's peril if one is prosecuted. This approach is intolerably vague.

A second approach is to make assisting suicide a form of manslaughter, on a par with recklessly causing the death of another or causing the death of another under provocation, such as finding him or her in bed with one's spouse. Twelve states take this approach, and the British Suicide Act of 1961, applicable in England and Wales, provides that the survivor of a genuine suicide pact is guilty of manslaughter (rather than murder) if she or he administered the means of death to the other party to the pact.[5] Manslaughter is typically punishable by sentences ranging from one to ten years; New York provides the harshest manslaughter penalty, a mandatory two-year sentence. While this approach has the advantage of increased predictability, it does not provide a framework for reflecting separately about the special characteristics of suicide assistance.

The third approach is to treat assisting suicide as a separate statutory offense altogether. This approach has gained ground in recent years; it is now followed by the British Suicide Act (for all but the active survivors to suicide pacts); it is recommended by the Model Penal Code of the American Law Institute; and it has been adopted by thirteen states, in some cases under the influence of the Model Penal Code. The Model Penal Code proposal reflects the typical characteristics of current statutes:

> Section 210.5. Causing or Aiding Suicide
> (1) *Causing Suicide as Criminal Homicide.* A person may be convicted of criminal homicide for causing another to commit suicide only if he purposely causes such suicide by force, duress or deception.
> (2) *Aiding or Soliciting Suicide as an Independent Offense.* A person who purposely aids or solicits another to commit suicide is guilty of a felony of the second degree if his conduct causes such suicide or an attempted suicide, and otherwise of a misdemeanor.[6]

The Model Penal Code proposal is noteworthy both for the distinctions it draws and for the distinctions it fails to draw. Section 1 singles out purposefully forcing or tricking someone into suicide as a form of murder; Section 2 defines the special crime of assisting suicide. Seven states explicitly make forcing suicide a form of murder, and there is precedent in other states for treating it as murder; this distinction seems to me to be correct and will not be discussed further. Second, the Model Penal Code makes only "purposeful" suicide assistance criminal. By "purposeful" action, the Model Penal Code means action taken with the "conscious object to engage in conduct of that nature or to cause such a result";[7] thus the state must prove that the defendant "meant to" help the suicide, rather than merely knew of or recklessly failed to inquire about its likelihood. States which give separate statutory treatment to assisting suicide almost always limit the offense to intentional assistance, and although it is possible, it is unlikely that anyone would be prosecuted under general homicide statutes for knowingly, recklessly, or negligently helping a suicide.[8] Since the question of whether those who intentionally aid suicides should be punished is controversial enough, for present purposes I will assume that the criminal law should go no further.

A third distinction incorporated by the Model Penal Code is far more puzzling. Aid which "causes" a subsequent attempted suicide (i.e., aid "but for which" a suicide attempt would not have occurred) is treated much more severely than aid which bears no fruit. If a potential suicide uses the instrument his or her helper intentionally provides, the helper is guilty of a second-degree felony and therefore subject to a minimum sentence of from one to three years in prison, up to a maximum sentence of ten years, according to the Model Penal Code recommendations. If the potential suicide does not act, however, his or her erstwhile helper is guilty only of a misdemeanor and therefore subject at most to a sentence of a year in prison.[9] While this distinction might be a reflection of a lingering presumption that the criminal law should act only when harm occurs, the Model Penal Code does not in general mitigate penalties for fruitless criminal aid. One can be guilty of aiding a burglary (and thus subject to the penalty for burglary) even if no burglary occurs. The drafters state that in the case of suicide we can rely on the instinct for self-preservation to warrant making an exception in the case of "unsuccessful" suicide assistance.[10] They thus appear to recognize that suicide assistance is not dangerous in quite the same way other crimes are.

However, this reasoning is in curious contrast to the reasoning offered for the most striking distinction which the Model Penal Code fails to make: all cases of intentionally assisting suicide—both the sympathetic and the unsympathetic—are made criminal, on the grounds that suicide assistance is often proffered with mixed or unclear motivations.[11] The drafters appear to hold that more often than not suicide assisters, like ordinary criminals, do what they do for gain and therefore should be prevented or punished. The draftsmen go on to suggest that we rely on mitigating punishment to avoid injustice in especially sympathetic cases. But this suggestion does not insure that some sympathetic cases—like Frank Roberts's—will not suffer at the hands of the law; mitigation is discretionary and in any event does not wipe out the trauma of a criminal prosecution. While the drafters of the Model Penal Code may be correct in the guess that most of the cases of suicide assistance which are actually prosecuted involve some elements of selfishness, it by no means follows that most suicide assistance is selfish. What is worse, one might speculate that a general prohibition of suicide assistance is more likely to deter unselfish than selfish assistance, since the unselfish assister must risk a jail sentence without the prospect of personal gain.

This strategy of treating all cases of intentional suicide assistance as criminal is perhaps even more problematic in light of another distinction not made by the Model Penal Code. The act required for assisting suicide may be anything from aid to "solicitation," under which the code includes commanding, encouraging, or requesting, each with the purpose of promoting or facilitating.[12] Thus the code does not distinguish between someone who procures the instrument of suicide and someone who very persuasively convinces another to die but does not actually use duress. No state statutes distinguish aid and solicitation, either. But from the point of view of liberty, the distinction is an important one. Prohibiting solicitation may deter people from talking others into committing suicide; prohibiting aid may make it difficult or impossible for someone like Mrs. Roberts to act on the settled desire to end her life. Of course, in prohibiting assistance, the law does not coerce the potential suicide directly, but its impact on the ability to choose to commit suicide may nonetheless be very real. If the liberty to commit suicide ought ever to be legally protected, it might well be argued that such indirect interference is an unwarranted interference with the very freedom the law ought to protect.[13]

The general prohibition of assisting suicide proposed by the Model Penal Code thus does not rule out inflicting punishment even in very sympathetic cases. It also may deter and thereby interfere with the liberty of someone who needs help in order to commit suicide. These consequences are serious and demand an adequate rationale which the Model Penal Code does not give.

2. JUSTIFICATIONS FOR THE CRIMINAL STATUS OF ASSISTING SUICIDE

Why punish assisting suicide? The retributivist answer is that suicide is a grave wrong, primarily because it involves the unjustifiable taking of a human life, and intentionally assisting suicide is wrong because it intentionally furthers a wrong.[14] Completed suicide, of course, cannot be punished. Some retributivists are prepared to grant that the decriminalization of attempted suicide represents simply the recognition that the person who attempts suicide is an exceptional kind of wrongdoer, both psychologically and in terms of the theory of punishment. On traditional retributivist theory, death is the appropriate penalty for taking or attempting to take a life, but it would be ironic to greet the wrong of attempted suicide with the death penalty.[15] However, those who assist suicide are not exceptional in the ways suicides are and so ought to be punished like others who aid unjustifiable homicide.

Critical to this argument is the assumption that all suicides are grave wrongs. But suppose we assume instead, as Brandt argues, that it is morally permissible to die by one's own hand when it would be in one's own long-term, carefully considered, rational self-interest to do so.[16] In such a case assisting suicide would be assisting another to do what it is morally permissible for him or her to do—these are the "sympathetic" cases—and could not be wrong on the ground that it is assisting a wrongful action. If it is to be morally wrong, it must be so on some other ground. The Model Penal Code suggests selfish motivation on the part of the assister as such a ground, but even if we are prepared to grant that wrongly motivated actions are thereby wrong, it has already been pointed out that not all suicide assistance is selfish.

Another rationale might be that since suicide is such a final act, we want to insure that it is the settled desire of the suicidal individual, which we cannot do unless she or he takes all steps alone. While it is certainly true that suicide may occur more readily if the means are easily available—and this will be important further on—it does not follow that the only way to insure that a suicide is genuinely desired is to see that the individual must do it all independently. Other barriers, such as requiring the passage of time before the means are provided, might serve as well; and in view of the fact that some of the people who may have settled desires to commit suicide are those who are physically unable to perform the suicidal act, the use of such barriers might be morally preferable. The finality of suicide is reason for thinking that it is morally impermissible to make even what might be permissible suicides too easy, but it is not reason to think that it is always impermissible to aid suicide. Similarly, if we can ever know that another's suicide is morally permissible—and I think we can sometimes know that it is in the long-term, carefully considered, rational self-interest of another to die—the amount and kind of knowledge in principle available to the suicide aider does not provide grounds for thinking it is always impermissible to aid even permissible suicides. Unless other grounds are forthcoming, it appears that dropping the assumption that suicide is always wrong undercuts the retributivist case for making assisting suicide illegal on the ground that it, too, is always wrong.

Assuming that suicide is sometimes morally permissible also

helps bolster the freedom argument against a general prohibition of suicide assistance. If we assume that life-and-death choices are among the most important for the individual who makes them, and that important choices ought to be protected, at least when they are exercised in a morally permissible manner, it would follow that we ought to protect the choice to commit morally permissible suicide. I have argued earlier that prohibiting aid may be inconsistent with what such protection requires.

The traditional argument for punishing conduct which is otherwise morally permissible, or for interfering with otherwise protected liberty, is that we need to do so in order to prevent or deter other conduct which is impermissible. Here there are two central candidates for conduct we might want to try to reduce by means of the criminal law—selfish suicide assistance and morally impermissible suicide—but there are strong reasons for thinking that our central concern should be the latter. Impermissible suicide is wrong and involves severe and irreversible harm; and preventing it does not interfere with the freedom to do what is morally permissible. On the other hand, while it may be argued that selfish suicide assistance is always morally wrong because it is wrongly motivated, prohibiting it may compromise the freedom of those for whom suicide is permissible but who can get aid only from tainted sources. Furthermore, preventing selfishly motivated aid is not a very good way of preventing impermissible suicide, since people may often injudiciously, but unselfishly, aid suicide; this is the major flaw of the Swiss statute which punishes only selfishly motivated suicide assistance. Yet it seems to me that our major worry about selfishly proffered assistance is not that it is selfish but that it will push people into committing suicide when they really do not want to do so or when it would not be rational for them to do so—that is, that it may cause impermissible suicides. But if we have available other effective means for preventing impermissible suicides, we do not need to focus on preventing *selfish* assistance.

3. RESTRUCTURING THE CRIME OF ASSISTING SUICIDE

Suppose, then, that in redesigning the crime of assisting suicide, we work from the premise that the criminal law ought to try to prevent morally impermissible suicides and to permit those which are not morally wrong. The deterrence challenge would then be that we cannot effectively prevent impermissible suicides unless we prohibit all suicide aid. The challenge might be defended by arguing that we cannot distinguish conceptually among different kinds of suicide aid; by arguing that we cannot apply the conceptual distinctions, we draw to the facts of particular cases; or by arguing that the distinctions make it easier to believe that suicide assistance will go unpunished and thus weaken the incentives against both desirable and undesirable suicide aid. While I am prepared to grant that prohibiting suicide aid makes suicide of all kinds considerably more difficult, and that preventing impermissible suicide is highly desirable, it must also be recognized that a general prohibition of aiding suicide has serious costs for permissible suicides and those who would aid them: Frank Roberts and his wife are a case in point. It therefore seems important to try to respond to the deterrence challenge by some stronger method than simply suggesting that we rely on discretionary mitigation in the most sympathetic cases. In what follows I do so by considering two principal statutory lines which might be drawn.[17]

As I have already pointed out, the chief distinction drawn by the Model Penal Code is between suicide assistance which results in an attempted suicide, and assistance which does not. If our concern is preventing suicide *simpliciter*, this distinction makes some sense, since we might speculate that when no attempt results, the aid itself was less dangerous. However, if our concern is only preventing impermissible suicides, the distinction is less plausible, unless (as seems unlikely) there is some correlation between impermissibility and the attempts which actually occur. On the other hand, the distinction which the Model Penal Code ignores between solicitation and aid seems extremely important, for solicitation interferes with the decision-making processes of the suicidal individual while aid does not. Solicited suicides are thus more likely to be impermissible—because not freely chosen—than merely aided ones.

At the outset, therefore, I suggest separating the offenses of soliciting and aiding suicide. The distinction between solicitation (in the sense of commanding, requesting, or encouraging) and aid is well established legally, although there may be some troublesome borderline cases where comfort is what is provided. The portion of the deterrence challenge which is thus of most serious concern here is that making aiding suicide a separate offense will weaken the constraints on aid. One way to avoid weakening the constraints is to prescribe comparable punishments for both offenses, and to use the distinction only when considering whether defenses should be available to either offense. If suicide aid really is less problematic than solicitation from the point of view of preventing suicides which are not products of the carefully considered, settled desires of rational individuals, however, a case can be made for accepting lesser penalties, and somewhat less effective deterrence, for merely aiding suicide.

A second major legal innovation may also serve to prevent impermissible suicide without restricting permissible suicide. This involves an attempt to specify certain kinds of cases in which the clear moral permissibility of the suicide is a defense to the crime of suicide assistance. It must be granted that such a defense would be quite difficult to make legally precise; suppose, however, we consider further the kinds of morally impermissible suicides which we might especially want to prevent. First, in order to insure that the suicide is rationally chosen, we would want to insure that the individual choosing suicide is fully rational—that is, does not lack crucial information about his situation or alternatives, is not under emotional stress which prevents him from reflecting carefully on what he is about to do, or is not suffering from a mental disease or defect which prevents him from reasoning about his future. Second, we would want to prevent suicide in cases in which it is not clear that the potential suicide has formulated the settled desire to die; we might be especially concerned about the ready availability of aid in such cases because it is easier to act on a whim if the tools are immediately at hand. Third, although this rests on a more controversial theory of rationality, we might want to prevent suicide in cases in which while the suicidal individual is rational and has the settled desire to die, it is not clear that death is in his or her long-term self-interest. One approach to the problem of formulating the defense is simply to stipulate that it is a defense to the crime of assisting suicide that the suicidal individual was rational, had expressed the desire to die over a relatively long period of time, and that death was in his or her interests. However, standards for all of these, particularly the latter, might prove highly subjective, and it would seem preferable to stipulate kinds of cases in which suicide might well be rational: cases of terminal illness; cases of irreversible and severely crippling, debilitating, or painful illness or injury; and cases of severe and prolonged or untreatable depression.[18] What would then be allowed as a defense to aiding suicide is a showing that the suicidal individual was rational, had the settled desire to die, and suffered from one of the conditions just listed. While they are admittedly administratively cumbersome and perhaps emotionally difficult for those who must come before them, review boards suggested in voluntary euthanasia proposals might be used to insure that the suicidal individual meets these conditions before aid is proffered.

The chief objection to allowing this defense is once again that it may make suicide assistance too readily available and therefore fail to prevent some suicides which really ought not to occur. This objection is the reason I suggest making the permissibility of the suicide a defense: the burden of proof is on the aider to show that the suicide really met the conditions she or he claims. Making this a defense may mean that some potential assistants will be deterred and that some will suffer courtroom proceedings or even convictions if evidence is unavailable. In short, what I propose is not a very large step, because it seems to me that it is important to try to draw legal lines to prevent impermissible suicides. Nonetheless, it may be a very large step indeed for those for whom suicide is rational and very much wanted, but impossible without aid. One might also reflect that if statutory innovations such as the ones suggested seem intolerably vague, the current criminal law of assisting suicide is hardly better, and may be considerably more painful.

N O T E S

1. *People v. Roberts*, 211 Mich.187, 178 N.W. 690, 13 ALR 1256 (1920).
2. For a description of the unsympathetic cases, see M. Pabst Battin, "Manipulated Suicide," p. 169; for sympathetic cases, see Mary Rose Barrington, "Apologia for Suicide," p. 90.
3. See Section 2 for a discussion of when assisting suicide is arguably morally permissible.
4. See *Grace v. State*, 44 Tx. Cr. 193, 69 S.W. 529 (1902); *Sanders*

v. State, 54 Tx. Cf. 101, 112 S.W. 68 (1908). Texas has since made assisting suicide a separate statutory offense.

5. For a description of the Suicide Act of 1961 and its applications, see William L1. Parry-Jones, "Criminal Law and Complicity in Suicide and Attempted Suicide," 13 *Medicine, Science and the Law,* Vol. 13 (1973), p. 110. The approach of the Suicide Act is to make an exception to the rule that actively administering the instrument of death is murder, by stipulating that surviving parties to a genuine suicide pact can be at most guilty of manslaughter. In United States jurisdictions, active participants in a suicide pact would most likely be guilty of murder. See *Model Penal Code* § 201.5, Commentary (Tentative Draft no. 9, 1959), p. 59.

6. *Model Penal Code* § 210.5 (Proposed Official Draft, 1962). The Model Penal Code has been widely influential on recent revisions of state criminal codes. It was drafted by a number of legal scholars; reporters were Herbert Wechsler and Louis Schwartz.

7. *Model Penal* Code § 2.02(2)(a)(i) (Proposed Official Draft, 1962).

8. Thus in Frank Roberts's murder prosecution, it was important to the court that he had intended his wife to end her life as she wished. However, it is important to note that courts often treat "doing *y* with the knowledge that *x* will occur" as "intending *x*," especially if there is any reason to believe that the defendant stood to gain from the occurrence of *x*. Thus doctors who prescribe medication knowing that a suicide attempt is imminent might well risk prosecution.

9. Eight states have adopted by statute some version of this distinction between successful and unsuccessful aid.

10. *Model Penal Code* § 210.5, Commentary (Proposed Official Draft, 1962), p. 128.

11. *Model Penal Code* § 201.5, Commentary (Tentative Draft no. 9, 1959), p. 57.

12. *Model Penal Code,* § 5.02(1) (Proposed Official Draft, 1962).

13. An analogous argument which has gained legal acceptance is that punishing the sale of contraceptives interferes with a couple's freedom to make procreative decisions and is thus a constitutionally impermissible interference with privacy. *Griswold v. Connecticut,* 381 U.S. 479 (1965). For an argument

that there is a constitutional right to suicide, see Alan L. Sullivan, "A Constitutional Right to Suicide," p. 229.

14. If "suicide" is defined as the wrongful taking of one's own life, this view is true by definition.

15. This is not unknown; see the opening paragraphs of Alvarez's account of the history of suicide, p. 7.

16. R. B. Brandt, "The Rationality of Suicide," p. 000. This is a controversial claim which I think may be true but which I do not defend in this paper. My concern is limited to exploring the consequences of the view for the problem of suicide assistance.

17. The innovations I consider are by no means exhaustive. One might well also suggest incorporating a line between selfish and unselfish assistance. Or one might consider requiring that the suicide assistance be needed in order for the suicide to occur. This last suggestion is made by Jonathan Glover, *Causing Death and Saving Lives* (New York: Penguin Books, 1977), p. 183.

18. This last example is controversial, since those who suffer from such depression may not be able to choose suicide rationally. I have in mind the case of an individual who is capable of understanding the likely future course of his or her life and who is quite correct in thinking that she or he will be so irremediably unhappy that it is better not to continue living. Virginia Woolf is sometimes described in these terms.

SUICIDE: A FUNDAMENTAL HUMAN RIGHT?

M. Pabst Battin

Working from particular cases of suicide, Battin rejects traditional uniform notions that would insist that either everyone or no one has a right to suicide, and attempts to distinguish those individuals who do have a right to suicide from those who do not. She holds that one's right to suicide does not depend on one's obligations to other persons or to society as a whole, but rather on the capacity of suicide to promote human dignity. Aggressive, violent suicide of the self-hating or "get-even" type, which typically does not lead to human dignity, is not a matter of right; where the choice of death represents not self-annihilation but self-protection or protection of some important value, however, it may well be constitutive of human dignity, and so a matter of fundamental human right.

Do persons have the right to end their own lives, that is, the right to suicide? Of the philosophical issues concerning suicide, it is perhaps this which is most hotly disputed, and it is this upon which the most diverse claims have been made. Schopenhauer, for instance, says:

> . . . It is quite obvious that there is nothing in the world to

which every man has a more unassailable title than to his own life, and person.[1]

Wittgenstein, in contrast, holds:

> If suicide is allowed then everything is allowed. If anything is not allowed then suicide is not allowed. This throws a light on the nature of ethics, for suicide is, so to speak, the elementary sin.[2]

When we are confronted with actual cases, our own views may be equally diverse. Consider, for instance, the real-life case of a woman we shall call Elsie Somerset:

> . . . an 80-year-old woman who had for two years been living in a nursing home. She suffered from glaucoma, which had almost completely blinded her, and from cancer of the colon, for which she was receiving chemotherapy. Her husband was recently dead. To relieve her chronic pain, and perhaps to mitigate the side effects of chemotherapy, she was being given hydromorphone, a morphine-like drug. In order to save up a week's supply of hydromorphone tablets she suffered through 168 hours of uninterrupted pain. Then she swallowed her hoard and went into coma.
>
> She was rushed to a hospital emergency room and subjected to a variety of procedures to save her life, including the intravenous injection of naloxone, a powerful morphine antagonist. The naloxone worked and she was returned to the nursing home—still suffering from glaucoma and from cancer.[3]

We may be strongly inclined to say that Elsie Somerset had a right to take these pills, and a right to die undisturbed after she had done so. But our intuitions often swing the other way. In St. Paul recently, a fifteen-year-old boy jumped to his death from a bridge, saying that he was doing so because his favorite TV program, "Battlestar Galactica," had been canceled.[4] Here we are very much less inclined to say that such people—even if they were able to make a clear-headed choice—have a *right* to end their lives, and certainly not to assistance in so doing. How then, in the face of these two very different cases, do we resolve the issue of whether there can be said to be a right to suicide?[5]

I

There are two general strategies which have traditionally been used to attempt to resolve this issue. The first one attempts to show that although there is some general obligation or moral canon which prohibits suicide, certain sympathetic cases can be allowed as exceptions. For instance, Aristotle said that suicide violates one's obligation to the community; we might argue that exceptions can be made in cases where suicide benefits the community.[6] Plato and Augustine claimed that one has a prior obligation to obey the command of God; both acknowledge as exceptions, however, instances (like Socrates and Samson) in which God directs rather than forbids the ending of one's life.[7] Kant held that suicide is forbidden because one has an obligation to respect the humanity in one's own person; he, too, though otherwise strictly impermissive of suicide, recognized at least one exception: the case of Cato.[8] On this first strategy there is no right to suicide, though certain special cases may be permitted as exceptions to an otherwise general rule.

If, however, one finds the arguments for general obligations against suicide unpersuasive (as many contemporary thinkers have), a second strategy for taking account of our divergent intuitions concerning suicide may suggest itself: to grant that an individual may have a *prima facie* right to suicide, but point out that there are (frequent) circumstances in which this right is overridden. Under this second strategy, suicide is construed as a right in virtue of the individual's general liberty to do as he chooses, provided, of course, that his choices do not harm the interests or violate the rights of other persons. In other words, suicide, on this second strategy, is construed as a liberty-right (of the sort propounded by John Stuart Mill);[9] one then attempts to do justice to one's initial sense that suicide in some cases is not a matter of right by showing that the liberty-right to suicide is often overridden on the basis of considerations of its effects on others. The emphasis here is typically placed on the injury suicide causes to others, particularly in emotional and psychological ways, but often in financial and social respects as well. Since, it is argued, suicide can frequently be extremely damaging to the survivors of the individual who takes his own life—and clinical studies do show that it can severely distort the lives of spouses, parents, children, and intimate friends[10]—therefore the individual's *prima facie* liberty-right to suicide is often, or almost always, overridden. On this account, suicide ceases to be a right not because of what it does to oneself (since on Mill's notion of liberty-rights one may have a right to choose things which harm oneself), but because of what it does to others.

Like the first approach, I think this second strategy for taking account of our divergent intuitions concerning the issues of rights to suicide also fails. First, an account which restricts one's right to end one's life in cases in which doing so will have bad consequences for others may seem to oblige us to hold, in consistency, that one is obligated to end one's life in cases where the consequences would be good. Second, it leaves the hard work undone: it provides no settled account of what particular circumstances might override the right to suicide.[11] And third, it provides unequal treatment for individuals whose grounds for suicide may be the same but who differ in their surrounding circumstances or their relationships with others. Of two persons afflicted with an identical terminal illness, for instance, one might have a right to suicide and the other not, if one is free from family relationships and the other not, even though the pain and medical degradation—the reasons for the suicide—might be the same. And finally, although this is not fully distinct from the preceding objection, we see in appealing to cases that this way of construing rights to suicide really misses the mark: what is wrong with the suicide of the "Battlestar Galactica" youth is not just that his parents will be grieved; and what allows Elsie Somerset her right to end her life is not simply that no one around her cares.[12]

II

It may be tempting, at this point, to discard the notion that suicide is a matter of rights altogether, and to look for some alternative way of accounting for our sense that some suicide is permissible whereas other cases are not.[13] But I think this move is hasty. After all, persons have at least two sorts of rights:[14] not only liberty-rights of the sort we have described, but more basic, fundamental rights, to be accounted for in a wholly different way. I wish to claim, that the right to suicide is indeed a right, and a right of the fundamental sort.

These more basic rights, as distinct from the liberty-rights one has as a function of one's freedom to do as one chooses, we call natural rights, fundamental rights, or fundamental human rights. They are rights of the sort identified in the classical manifestos: the American Constitution and its Bill of Rights, the French Declaration of the Rights of Man, the Communist Manifesto, and the 1948 U.N. Declaration of Human Rights, among others. The rights listed, of course, vary from one manifesto to another, variously including rights to life, liberty, ownership of property; freedom of assembly, speech, and worship; rights to education, employment, political representation, and medical care. However, although the manifestos vary considerably in their contents, the conception underlying them is similar: they declare that certain universal, general, *fundamental* rights are held by individuals just in virtue of their being human.

I shall suggest, then, as a third strategy for achieving resolution of our conflicting intuitions regarding suicide, that it be construed as a *fundamental human right*. On this view, permissible suicide is not merely an exception to the general rules, nor is it mere exercise of one's liberty-right to harm oneself if one wishes. Rather, it is a fundamental human right, on a par with rights to life,[15] to liberty, to freedom of speech and worship, to education, political representation, and the pursuit of happiness. Although I do not have space here to give an account of the claims against others, both for noninterference and for assistance, which a fundamental right to suicide might generate, it is at least clear that if what had appeared to be a liberty-right to suicide turns out to be a *fundamental* right, the force of ordinary utilitarian arguments against it will collapse.

Of course, there will seem to be a good deal of evidence against this view. For one thing, the "Battlestar Galactica" case reminds us that we intuitively feel that there are cases in which persons have no right to kill themselves at all, let alone a fundamental right. Secondly, although listing in manifestos cannot be taken as a reliable index of whether something is a fundamental right, it is nevertheless a conspicuous fact that a "right to suicide" is listed in none, even among manifestos of the most politically diverse sorts.[16] And finally, the fact that we have starkly differing intuitions about rights to suicide in different sorts of cases suggests that if rights of any sort are involved, they surely are not fundamental ones: if suicide were a fundamental right, we should expect all persons to have it, not just some.

Let us consider, however, the way in which fundamental rights are to be accounted for. I do not of course have space here in which to develop a full theory of rights, but I would like to sketch what I think is a correct account, and one which I shall take in this argument as a basic premise. *Individuals have fundamental rights to do certain sorts of things just because doing those things tends to be constitutive of human dignity.*[17] ("Human dignity," though it is perhaps difficult to define, is a notion rooted in an ideal conception of human life, human community, and human excellence; I shall have more to say about the concept of human dignity in the course of this paper.) On this view, although we may take ourselves to have a variety of relatively superficial and easily overridden liberty-rights, we also understand ourselves to have more fundamental human rights because we conceive them to establish and promote human dignity. The right freely to associate with others we recognize as a fundamental right because we take free association with others to contribute to our dignity. Alcoholism, on the other hand, does not typically conduce to human dignity; hence, although it may still be a liberty-right, *viz.* when it does not harm other persons, it is not a fundamental right.

While this account of rights may at first seem to be an *ad hoc* device for resolving our conflicts about suicide, I think it may also help explain and resolve some of the more volatile disputes concerning other rights and show why there are no disputes concerning some. It is rarely disputed, for instance, that persons have a right to freedom, since it is very widely assumed that freedom contributes to human dignity. On the other hand, although Lockean liberals defend a fundamental right to private property, Marxists and others in the post-Rousseau tradition deny this right: what is really at issue, beneath this dispute about whether private property is a right, is whether the owning of property contributes to or detracts from human dignity, both for the owner and for others as well.

But although this account of rights succeeds not just for suicide but for fundamental rights in general, it is the particular case of the right to suicide that makes us notice the central way in which it differs from more conventional accounts. On this account, *because fundamental rights are rooted in human dignity, they are not equally distributed.* This claim may well seem initially counterintuitive and perhaps morally offensive as well; although we are of course accustomed to assume that liberty-rights are inequally distributed (since for different individuals different special obligations may override them), we insist that the distribution of fundamental rights is uniform: *all* persons have them, simply in virtue of their being human. But this notion that fundamental rights are equally distributed is an illusion (though I think a necessary and desirable one):[18] it reflects not the uniform nature of fundamental rights, but the fact that the things they guarantee tend to be constitutive of human dignity equally for all persons. Thus, it appears to be analytic of the notion of fundamental human rights that they are equally distributed; it is precisely the case of suicide that shows us they are not. Some persons in some situations, we shall see, have a fundamental right to suicide; others do not. Of course, the right to suicide, if it is one, is not alone among fundamental rights in being unequally distributed (we recognize this by saying that fundamental rights are abridged or overridden by such circumstances as incompetence or grave public need);[19] it is merely more unequally distributed than most. It is this matter of unequal distribution, I think, that has disguised from us the fact that suicide is a fundamental right.

In practice, of course, there are obstacles to this account of rights. To hold that fundamental rights are not equally distributed can very well invite abuse. And to claim that one has fundamental rights only when the things they guarantee are constitutive of human dignity brings with it problems, much like those in the calculi of utilitarian theory, of ascertaining the characteristics and outcome of the exercise of a given right. Nor is human dignity any easier to quantify than happiness or utility. Nevertheless, I think we must attend to this alternative account of rights if we are to resolve the issue of suicide. The traditional account of rights will not permit us to see *why* there might be a right to suicide; to claim that we do, or do not, have a right to suicide only adds, along with Schopenhauer and Wittgenstein, to the array of unfounded assertions in this regard. What we need to see is that we have a right to suicide (if and when we do) *because* it is constitutive of human dignity, and that this basis is the same as that on which we have all other fundamental human rights. Even though it may be very markedly unequally distributed, the right to suicide is not an "exception" or a "special" right, or a right which is to be accounted for in some different way; it is of a piece with the other fundamental human rights we enjoy.

III

Not all suicide is constitutive of human dignity. If we consider the "Battlestar Galactica" vs. Elsie Somerset cases, this may seem quite clear. Surely we can imagine other acts on the part of the youth which would grant more dignity than his furtive leap from the bridge: the futures open to him were varied and numerous, including no doubt love, purposeful occupation, social contribution, and the attainment of ideals. The boy's death lacks utility, of course, in that it does not promote happiness or well-being in the agent or in others, but it also lacks that dignity which might redeem this fault. Elsie Somerset's suicide, on the other hand, seems to be quite a different case. If we consider the futures open to her, at age eighty, we see that they are different indeed from those of the "Battlestar" youth, and a good deal less numerous. An unfortunately realistic picture of old age suggests that she can expect increasing debility, dependence, financial limitation, loss of communication and affection, increasingly poor self-image, increasing depression, isolation, and, due to her glaucoma and cancer, blindness and pain. There are alternative possible futures, of course: one of them is suicide. Another is that which she no doubt wants: a continuing, pain-free, socially involved, productive, affectionate life. But, given her physical condition and the social conditions of the society in which she lives, this is no longer possible, and so her options are reduced to only two: suicide, or the catalogue of horrors just described. Suicide, then, may be constitutive of human dignity in at least a negative sense; in Elsie Somerset's case it leaves one less example of human degradation in the world.[20]

This kind of observation invites us to establish a procedure for sorting suicide cases into those in which the act surely cannot be constitutive of human dignity (the "Battlestar Galactica" case), and those in which it is (Elsie Somerset)—the category of those who have no right to suicide (or only an overrideable liberty-right),[21] and the category of those whose right is fundamental; this would supply the basis for various practical social policies with respect to such activities as suicide prevention, psychiatric treatment, involuntary commitment, and the like. It may seem intuitively obvious that the first of these categories will include unhappy youths, star-crossed lovers, persons suffering from financial setbacks or bereavement or temporary depression; while the second category will include the so-called rational suicides: those who are painfully terminally ill or suffer from severe disabilities, incurable diseases, other intolerable medical conditions, or who have other good grounds for suicide. But it is just this sort of intuitive classification of suicides that is most dangerous and is the reason we need to be clear about the basis of any alleged right to suicide. To see this, we must examine the notion of dignity.

In one, originally Kantian, sense, all human beings have dignity, or what we might describe as intrinsic human worth. Dignity in this sense is an ideal, a construct which points to ends to be achieved; we might equate dignity with "worthiness of respect." But there is a second, empirical sense of dignity as well, which corrupt or abused persons may not have. In this second sense, we can distinguish observed characteristics of individuals as involving dignity from those which do not.[22] Just as we can observe whether a person is being treated with respect or "as a person"—that is, with dignity—in such situations as the classroom, in commercial relations, or in a bureaucracy, we can distinguish characteristics of the individual himself or herself which show that he or she achieves dignity as a human being. For instance, we can distinguish between the person who bears pain with dignity and the person who, in fright or panic, does not.[23] The ghastly lessons of the Nazi camps provide examples of human beings who suffered unbelievable mistreatment with dignity; and those—the so-called Muselmänner—who did not.

Working from a large range of observed phenomena, we can then begin to formulate the components of dignity;[24] they are probably jointly sufficient for the application of this term, though they do not all seem to be necessary. These characteristics include, to begin with, autonomy vis à vis external events, self-determination, and responsibility for one's acts.[25] Dignity also includes self-awareness and cognizance of one's condition and acts, together with their probable consequences. Dignity usually involves rationality, though this may not always be the case. It can also be said to involve expressiveness, or rather self-expressiveness, an assertion of oneself in the world. It surely also involves self-acceptance and self-respect: an affirmation of who and what one is. We can also suggest what tends to undermine dignity: anonymity, for instance, as in an impersonal institution; alienation of labor, crowding, meaningless and repetitive jobs, segregation, and torture.[26]

But dignity, for all its apparent initial similarity to happiness or other utilitarian desiderata, differs from these conditions of the individual in a crucially important way. Dignity is not simply a characteristic of the individual but a characteristic of the individual in relation to his world. This is what in part makes it so difficult to define. And yet I think we can isolate its most important characteristic: one cannot promote one's own *dignity* by destroying the dignity of someone else, though one can certainly promote one's own interests, happiness, or reputation at another's expense. My happiness may cost your happiness, and that may be a price I am nevertheless willing to force you to pay; despite this morally repugnant choice, I may still achieve happiness. But if I try to elevate my dignity by robbing you of yours, I lose my own as well—even though I may nevertheless gain happiness, satisfaction of my interests, and other utilitarian benefits. Thus the concept of dignity is not wholly empirical, but contains ideal features as well.

To destroy your dignity, of course, is not just to graze your ego or to hurt your feelings, and it is even possible, as the Nazi camps have shown, that I may seriously damage your interests or even kill you without destroying the dignity you have. But where an act of mine would tend to destroy your capacities for such things as autonomy, self-awareness, rationality, self-expressiveness, and self-respect, then we will begin to want to say that I lose my own dignity in doing such an act to you. Dignity, although it is a characteristic inhering primarily in the individual and is not simply a relational property, contains essential reference to the dignity of others where others are involved; no act which undermines the dignity of others can be an act constitutive of one's own human dignity, whatever utility it may produce, for it thus violates that ideal conception of human *community* in which the notion of dignity is in part rooted. Furthermore, although dignity contains essential reference to the dignity of others wherever others are involved, an act may also be an act of dignity even if it affects oneself alone—provided that it honors that ideal conception of human *excellence* in which the notion of dignity is also based.

Thus there can be no dignity tradeoffs, like the interests or happiness tradeoffs which plague utilitarian calculations; the problem of sacrificing the dignity of some for the dignity of others cannot arise. It is in this sense that dignity is both an empirical and an ideal notion, and it may be that the actual acts which contribute to dignity are in fact very few. Nevertheless, I do think it is a conception of dignity of this sort that lies at the basis of our ascriptions of fundamental rights.

But can *suicide* satisfy both the empirical and ideal criteria for dignity, and so be an act to which one has a fundamental right? And does the distinction between apparently irrational suicides and those for which one has good cause reflect that between dignity-constitutive suicides and those which are not?

IV

There are many different kinds of suicide, both in terms of the individual's interior states and the act's effects on others involved, yet they can be divided into two principal groups. On the one hand are the "violent" suicides: desperate, aggressive acts, which display both contempt and hatred for oneself and for others as well. Most common among these perhaps are the "get-even" suicides, which show a desire for revenge upon one's enemies or erstwhile loved ones and often a despising of the world as a whole. Animosity, ambivalence, and agitation are the symptoms here.

Others, in contrast, are "nonviolent": of these, some may be described as involving cessation or surcease rather than obliteration or annihilation, often anticipated and planned in a resigned but purposeful way; others, not always distinct from the surcease suicides, are sacrificial in character and focus centrally on the benefits to some other person or cause. The nonviolent suicides are nonviolent both toward oneself and toward others, at least in the clearest cases; they do not seek to punish oneself or to injure or retaliate against others. Very often these nonviolent suicides contain a component of what we might, paradoxically perhaps, call self-preservation, a kind of self respect: "I am what I have been," they sometimes seem to say, "but cannot be anymore."

They are based, as it were, on a self-ideal: a conception of one's own value and worth, beneath which one is not willing to slip. Whether the threat to one's self-ideal is from physical illness and pain, as in euthanatic suicide, or from the destruction of other persons or values upon which one's life is centrally focused, as in self-sacrificial suicide, the import is the same: one chooses death instead of further life, because further life would bring with it a compromise of that dignity without which one cannot consent to live.

This distinction between violent, self-aggressive and non-violent, self-respecting suicides is an intuitive distinction only; it is a distinction not much recognized in clinical practice, though perhaps only because psychiatric clinicians are very much less likely to confront cases of the self-respecting, nonviolent type.[27] It is important to be clear, in addition, that this distinction is not based on the means involved: some deaths by gunshot or jumping are of the nonviolent kind, whereas some deaths by tranquilizers or gas or even refusal to eat are of the violent sort, involving extreme self-aggression and aggression toward others. Nevertheless, it is possible to characterize generally the kinds of suicide that are common among certain groups and in certain kinds of situations. Violence toward oneself and others characterizes a good deal of youthful suicide, even that associated with depression; it is also found among the old. But nonviolent, surcease suicide is much more common in disability and terminal-illness cases, and particularly among the old. Self-death or self-directed death in these latter conditions, of course, we often term voluntary euthanasia or sometimes euthanatic suicide; we frequently attempt to distinguish them both morally and legally from "irrational" suicide in nonterminal conditions, that is, suicide for which one does not have good reason.

In distinguishing between irrational suicide and euthanatic suicide, we do recognize that there are important differences between suicide which precludes indefinitely continuing life and suicide in preference to inevitable death by another more painful or degrading means. But this distinction does *not* precisely coincide with the distinction between those kinds of suicide to which an individual has only liberty-rights or no right at all, and those kinds of suicide to which the individual has a fundamental human right, one which cannot be overridden by any particular obligations or claims. This is because some cases of noneuthanatic suicide may be constitutive of human dignity—Cato's death is a case in point—whereas some genuine euthanasia cases may not be acts of human dignity but acts of cowardice and fear—hasty, terrified measures which preclude any final human dignity rather than contribute to it. Some writers opposed to suicide in general would have us believe that all euthanatic suicides are of this latter sort—acts of cowardice and fear; I think this is false, but I think it is equally wrong to assume that all suicide in the face of terminal illness is a rational, composed, self-dignifying affirmation of one's own highest life-ideal.

It may be that as a practical matter the nearest workable policy is acceptance of the notion of rational suicide, and the devising of selective suicide-prevention and psychiatric-treatment measures to discourage suicide of the irrational sort. If this is the only really practical policy for selectively permitting suicides of fundamental right and prohibiting those which are not,[28] I think on moral grounds we ought to adopt it, in preference either to maintaining the traditional universal suicide prohibitions or adopting indiscriminately permissive policies. We should bear in mind, however, that the rational/irrational distinction does not quite mirror the difference we want.

Now we see why our temptation to classify suicides into dignity-constitutive and non-dignity-constitutive cases on the basis of external characteristics is such a dangerous one, particularly if such a classification is to become the basis for various practical policies: the circumstances under which it occurs do not determine the character of the act. There can be suicides of dignity in conditions of despair; there can be suicides without dignity when the circumstances are such that the individual might have every reason to die.

In his paper "Suicide as Instrument and Expression,"[29] David Wood invents a case: the suicide (by jumping) of an architect who pioneered high-rise apartment buildings and realizes too late what he has done. Is this a suicide of dignity, and so one to which he has a fundamental right, or is it a suicide of the violent, non-dignity-promoting sort, one to which he does not have such a right? We can imagine the case either way: as the final, desperate act of self-loathing and self-contempt, occurring as the confused climax of long years of self-reproach; but we can also imagine it as a considered, courageous statement of principle, a dignified final act transcending one's own defeat. If it is a violent suicide of loathing, we can imagine reminding the man that he has obligations to his family, his friends, his gods, and himself, that is, we can imagine treating it as a liberty-right, quickly to be overridden by the claims of others. But if it is a genuine suicide of dignity it is difficult to know what objection we could make, since we must only admire his attainment of a difficult human ideal. That the price of this attainment is high—very high—is perhaps lamentable, but it is not grounds for interfering with his exercise of the right.

V

What of Schopenhauer and Wittgenstein, and the disparate philosophical views with which we began? Perhaps now we can venture some explanation, which, though it is conjectural, may also explain the apparent inconsistency in our own precritical views. When Wittgenstein claims that suicide is "the elementary sin," he is perhaps conceiving (no doubt in an autobiographical way) of cases in which the act is an act of self-annihilation and the annihilation of one's social world; it is the ultimate act of disrespect and violence. When Schopenhauer, on the other hand, says that man has no "more unassailable title than to his own life and person," it may be that he is drawing upon a notion of suicide as the act of ultimate dignity: the final act of self-determination and self-affirmation in an immoral, unyielding world. In this way both views are correct, and not after all incompatible: individuals in the cases Wittgenstein has in mind have no right, or at most only an overrideable liberty-right, to kill themselves, while individuals in the cases Schopenhauer sees have a basic, nonoverrideable, fundamental human right to end their lives. The only real mistake Schopenhauer and Wittgenstein make is this: they assume that the "right to suicide" is a uniform right, which all individuals either have or do not.

NOTES

1. Arthur Schopenhauer, "On Suicide," from *Studies in Pessimism*, in *Complete Essays of Schopenhauer*, trans. T. Bailey Saunders (New York: Wiley Book Co., 1940). Although Schopenhauer

grants that man has a right to suicide, he holds that suicide is a moral and metaphysical error, since it results not from an ascetic cessation of the will, but from frustration of it.

2. Ludwig Wittgenstein, *Notebooks 1914–1916*, ed. G. H. von Wright and G. E. M. Anscombe (Oxford: Basil Blackwell, 1961), p. 91e. Wittgenstein continues, however, in this final entry of the notebooks:

> And when one investigates it [suicide], it is like investigating mercury vapour in order to comprehend the nature of vapours. Or is even suicide in itself neither good nor evil?

3. Adapted from Edward M. Brecher, "Opting for Suicide," *The New York Times Magazine*, March 18, 1979, quoting from the October 1978 issue of *Hospital Physician*.

4. *Minneapolis Star and Tribune*, Saturday, August 25, 1979, p. 1A.

5. One may be said to have a right to *x*, or a right to do *x;* that to which a person may have a right can be an object, a condition, a state of affairs, or an action. Construing suicide as an action, I shall speak throughout only of the right to (commit ["do"]) suicide, rather than, say the right to the object or condition (death) which suicide brings about.

6. Aristotle, *Nichomachean Ethics 1138a*.

7. Plato, *Phaedo* 61C–62E; Augustine, *City of God*, Book I, Chapters 17–27.

8. Kant, *Lectures on Ethics*, tr. Louis Infield (New York: Harper Torchbooks, 1963), "Suicide," pp. 148-54.

9. Mill, *On Liberty*. It is interesting that Mill does not discuss suicide directly, although it might seem the most crucial case for the application of his views. In *On Liberty* he argues that one may not sell oneself into slavery because this would fail to preserve one's liberty; one might infer from this that Mill would also repudiate suicide on the same grounds. However, one might argue that since after suicide the individual does not exist in an unfree state (but, rather, does not exist at all), Mill provides no basis for an objection to this practice.

10. There is a large sociological and psychological literature on the effects of suicide on those persons surrounding the individual. See e.g., Albert C. Cain, ed., *Survivors of Suicide* (Springfield, Ill.: Charles C. Thomas, 1972).

11. This is not of course a theoretical objection to the liberty-rights' account of suicide, but it does point out that without further elaboration the account is not a particularly helpful or informative one.

12. Paul-Louis Landsberg, in *The Moral Problem of Suicide*, trans. Cynthia Rowland (New York: Philosophical Library, 1953), p. 84, puts the point in this way:

> It is purely and simply antipersonalist to try to decide such an intimately personal question as to whether or not I have the right to kill myself by reference to society. Suppose I die a little sooner or a little later, what has that to do with society, to which, in any case, I belong for so short a space?

13. See e.g., James Bogen, "Suicide and Virtue," p. 286, who claims that an adequate treatment of the morality of suicide cannot be made in terms of obligations, rights, and duties.

14. In addition to liberty-rights and fundamental rights, we also recognize legal rights. Given, however, the very uneven situation of the law with regard to suicide (see in this connection the papers of Alan Sullivan and Leslie Francis, p. 229 and 254;), I have restricted the scope of this paper to moral rights alone.

15. Note that a fundamental right to suicide does not preclude an equally fundamental right to life, since both may be constitutive of human dignity. This is so even in euthanasia cases: there may be dignity in an individual's struggling against the inevitable oncoming of decay, medical degradation, and pain; there may equally well be dignity in his choosing to avoid these by ending his life. In general, one may have fundamental rights to various incompatible actions, as for instance one may have fundamental rights to own private property or to join a communal economic group, when either course of action is the kind which can be constitutive of human dignity. Thus, rights are not to be conflated with duties.

16. One might mention "the right to die" now being championed by various patients'-rights groups; this, however, is usually understood as the right to freedom from unwanted medical treatment, or a "right to passive euthanasia." The scope of a "right to suicide" would be considerably broader.

17. This account appears to resemble in some respects that put forward by William T. Blackstone in "Human Rights and Human Dignity," *The Philosophy Forum* 9, Nos. 1/2 (March 1971), and perhaps even the counterthesis in the same volume, Herbert Spiegelberg's "Human Dignity: A Challenge to Contemporary Philosophy." It also resembles one component of the account Arnold S. Kaufman defends in "A Sketch of a Liberal Theory of Fundamental Human Rights," *The Monist* 52 (No. 4), though for Kaufman fundamental human rights may be justified either on the basis of dignity or on the basis of maximum utility together with equality. Also relevant in connection with this issue is Michael S. Pritchard's "Human Dignity and Justice," *Ethics* 82 (No. 4, July 1972).

18. The fiction that fundamental rights are universally distributed is both necessary and desirable for the following reasons. The present account of rights (although I believe it to be correct) is hopelessly particularist, in that it holds that an individual has a fundamental right to do just that sort of act, or just that act, which is conducive to human dignity. But it is extremely difficult to predict whether an act of a given kind will in fact contribute to human dignity, and so be an act of the kind to which that individual has a fundamental right. This may vary from one individual to the next, or change for a given individual over a period of time. Furthermore, despite certain empirical earmarks of dignity, it is in principle impossible to diagnose with full reliability whether a given individual does or does not achieve complete human dignity. The best we can say is that *on the whole*, certain types of actions or things—e.g., free assembly, free speech, freedom from the quartering of soldiers in one's house, etc., tend to be constitutive of human dignity, whether or not we can in fact make a reliable, confirmable assessment in any given case. Thus we are forced to assume that fundamental rights are universally or at least very widely distributed; this is the "necessary" feature. But once we have made this assumption, we must then produce justification for any abridgment of those (alleged) fundamental rights; this is the "desirable" part. Because we allow ourselves to assume that the right to free assembly, for instance, is a fundamental right, shared by all human beings, we thus compel ourselves to justify any abridgment of that right. Hence protection of these rights is made much more

likely. If we were to recognize and honor an individual's fundamental right to, say, free assembly only in cases in which we could establish that the exercise of free assembly would conduce to the dignity of that individual, we would risk abridgments of this right in very, very many cases.

Whether such a fiction is either necessary or desirable in the case of suicide, however, is quite a different question. It is I think intuitively clear that not all persons in all circumstances have a right to suicide, though some persons in some circumstances may: we are not forced to assume that, *on the whole*, suicide is constitutive of human dignity, because we clearly see that it does not. Nor is it clearly desirable to adopt a fiction which, in practice, would place the burden of justification on those who would interfere with a suicide rather than on those who plan suicide for whatever reason.

19. Conventional theories of rights hold that fundamental rights are overridden in circumstances such as incompetence (e.g., the right of a severely retarded person to freedom of travel may be abridged) or requirements of community interest (the felon's right to freedom of travel may also be abridged); on the present account, fundamental rights are never overridden, but in cases such as these simply do not apply. It is silly to insist that the seriously retarded individual has a "fundamental right to freedom of travel" when travel (at least without assistance) can mean nothing but helpless wandering in an unfriendly world, or that the recidivist felon has a right to freedom of his person when exercise of that right conduces to anything but human dignity. Since this is so, nonvoluntary institutionalization of such persons does not genuinely represent an abridgment of their fundamental rights, though institutionalization in a cruel environment, or without facilities for special education, etc., might do so.

20. Human degradation in the empirical sense, of course. The dual concept of human dignity suggests that all human beings continue to have dignity in the ideal sense, that is, all human beings remain worthy of respect, regardless of how degrading the conditions and circumstances in which they are forced to live.

21. We cannot attempt here to resolve the issue of whether suicide, in cases in which it does not conduce to dignity and hence is not a fundamental right, is nevertheless a liberty-

right, or is, rather, no right at all. If it were a liberty-right, it would of course be subject to overriding on the basis of a variety of considerations. If it is a fundamental right, it is a liberty-right and should be a legal right as well.

22. This dual account of the concept of human dignity is developed in several of the papers mentioned in note 16.
23. See Abraham Edel, "Humanist Ethics and the Meaning of Human Dignity," *Moral Problems in Contemporary Society: Essays in Humanistic Ethics,* ed. Paul Kurtz (Englewood Cliffs, N.J.: Prentice-Hall, 1969), p. 234.
24. This is done here, of course, only in a somewhat a priori and very tentative way. But it is the sort of task we might wish philosophers will do.
25. This is the concept of dignity used by B. F. Skinner in *Beyond Freedom and Dignity,* especially in Chapter 3, and also the second sense of dignity for Marvin Kohl, "Voluntary Beneficent Euthanasia," in Kohl, ed., *Beneficent Euthanasia* (Buffalo: Prometheus Books, 1975), p. 133.
26. The list is Spiegelberg's, "Human Dignity," p. 60.
27. Surcease suicide in terminal illness is almost never reported as suicide, and is not recorded in that way by the coroner or by insurance companies. It is believed, however, that the practice of surcease suicide in terminal illness, often with the assistance of the physician in providing lethal drugs, is fairly common.
28. Criminal prohibitions, of course, would be most plausibly directed against suicides exhibiting violence against others.
29. This volume, p. 151.

SUICIDE AND
VIRTUE

James Bogen

Bogen argues that to understand moral questions about suicide in terms of rights, obligations, and duties is to miss the real question at hand: is suicide the kind of thing a good person would do? He points out the differences between this and the traditional ways of examining the morality of suicide.

After taking his Ph.D. at the University of California at Berkeley, James Bogen has taught at Oberlin College and is now at Pitzer College, a member of the Claremont Colleges. He is the author of Wittgenstein's Philosophy of Language *(Routledge & Kegan Paul) and of papers on theory of knowledge, skepticism, ancient philosophy, esthetics, and moral theory.*

Most contemporary philosophical discussion of the moral issues involved in suicide and suicide intervention presume that the crucial questions boil down to questions of rights and obligation: does one have the right to end one's own life, or does one have an obligation to refrain from doing so, and what ought third parties do to honor these rights and obligations? However, it is generally acknowledged among philosophers that no one has given a convincing argument to show that there is an obligation against suicide, at least when the suicide has no obligations to others whose fulfillment would be ruled out.

This makes it appear that if someone has a right to take his own life (because he has neither an obligation nor a duty not to), there should be no serious moral reasons not to do so, and this, I think, has been the prevalent view among philosophers at least since Kant.[1] I want to argue in this paper that this is incorrect, and that an adequate treatment of the morality of suicide must deal with questions which cannot be illuminated by a consideration of rights, obligations, and duties. I shall not attempt any answer to these questions, but if I am right to think they are both important and neglected, it should be worthwhile just to draw attention to them and show how they differ from the questions about obligations, duties, and responsibilities, which are (wrongly, I think) so heavily emphasized by philosophers.

I will assume in what follows that there are no such duties or obligations against suicide *per se,* and therefore that a man does have a right to commit suicide in cases where this would not lead to the violation of other duties and obligations (e.g., to friends and family) which he has no excuse for violating. Perhaps this assumption is more controversial than I take it to be, but that will not affect the argument of this paper. What I want to show is that *if* (as I take to be the case) a man does have a right to take his own life, grave moral questions which typically confront potential suicides and interventionists remain. Here are some hypothetical cases intended to show how little is settled by the view that a man has a right to, and no duty or obligation not to, take his own life.

Case 1: Jones suffers from Huntington's chorea and is convinced that in its progression the disease will become intolerable to him, that it is incurable, and that eventually it will make him a burden to everyone he knows, incapable of discharging any duties or obligations he might have. But he also believes that one ought not to be a coward and fears that his suicide would be a cowardly act.[2] To tell Jones he has a right (has no duty or obligation not) to commit suicide will do nothing to settle the moral issue of cowardice. That is because in cases in which a cowardly act does not violate a duty or obligation, we have a right to do what is cowardly even though cowardice is morally reprehensible. Thus a policeman has no right to refuse out of cowardice to pursue criminals, but that is because he has a duty to pursue criminals, not because he has no right to be a coward. Where a cowardly act does not involve the neglect of such duties, one has a right to do it, but all this means is that no one can justify moral criticism of the agent, punishment, or intervention intended to prevent or discourage the cowardly behavior *on the grounds that he has no right to it.* Nor can one justify the kind of coercive interference which may be appropriately directed against someone who is about to do what he has no right to do. It does not follow from a man's right to cowardice that there should be no intervention of any kind or that the coward's behavior is morally acceptable and not to be criticized, or that a man *should* do what is cowardly. The point is that what is wrong with cowardice is not that it violates duty or obligation, or that one has no right to it. Jones and those affected by his decision must decide whether his suicide would be inexcusably cowardly; but no amount of knowledge about his rights, duties, and obligations will shed any light on this question.

Case 2: Another Jones has good reason to think that taking his own life would harm no one and would be of great benefit to a number of people. If he believes he has a right to commit suicide, it would be perfectly consistent for him to ask if he (morally) *should* take his own life. He might so decide on the grounds that suicide would be a generous, charitable, or kindly act. But having a right to commit suicide (as Jones II believes he does) neither entails nor implies that he should do it. Jones II must ask whether in fact his suicide would be an act of sufficient kindness or charity to merit the sacrifice. It might be misguided (as when one donates money to an unworthy cause). In the long run the benefits to others might not merit the sacrifice. Alternatively, even if the act would be the sort of thing a genuinely charitable person would do, Jones II's real motive might not be the good his suicide would do for others, but, for example, an unworthy desire for posthumous gratitude. Such questions are by no means settled by the assumption that Jones II has a right to take his own life.

Case 3: A third Jones who is a friend of Jones I and Jones II must decide what to do about their contemplation of suicide. Should he try to talk them out of it? If so, how much can he do without becoming a meddler, and how little without falling short of being a true friend? Should he approach them or wait for them to come to him? Would any kind of restraint be justifiable? Should he help them in any way if he finds their decisions are irrevocable? And so on and so on. It seems to me that these are the sorts of questions which face people who find themselves in the role of potential suicide interventionists. And all of them can be asked by someone who believes Jones I and Jones II have a right to take their own lives. Once again, I think these are serious moral issues which are quite distinct from the question of rights, obligations, and the like.

Let us see, then, how the questions raised in the hypothetical cases differ from questions about rights, duties, and obligations.

The crucial distinction between them has to do with the fact that the various Joneses are concerned over whether certain conduct would be worthwhile and good, and whether alternative courses of action would be bad or unworthy. In contrast, rights, obligations, and duties tend in general to preclude such questions. If I violate a duty or obligation (e.g., I do not perform the services I am under contract to perform, I fail to do what I promised, I do not pay my debts, etc.) it is no excuse that what I did was good or for the good. This is seen clearly in the case of promises and the obligations they generate. In asking you to promise to do a certain thing, I want you to commit yourself to do it. A reason for extracting a promise is that I do *not* want you to decide later what to do on the basis of what is best or most worthwhile. It is to be expected that you will settle such questions before promising, and that once you have promised, all things being equal, you will not raise them in deciding whether to perform. This is one of the senses in which promises are said to be binding: they preclude certain considerations on the basis of which your decisions would otherwise be made.[3] But the same sort of point holds in general for obligations and duties. The performance of a duty or obligation is not morally required as a means toward some good end. If it were, nonperformance would be excusable on the grounds that it accomplishes more good than performance. Instead, it is simply required; *ceteris paribus,* considerations of what is best are not relevant to the question whether the obligation or duty should be performed. A related point holds for rights. If someone has a right to do something, it does not follow either that it is a good or worthwhile thing to do, or that its being good is a reason for honoring his right. Thus the right to free speech is, subject to certain very special limitations (e.g., the familiar limitation which precludes yelling "fire" in a crowded room), the right to say things even if they are so vicious and stupid that the saying of them will be bad for the speaker and those who hear him. Similarly, to say that Jones has a right to take his own life is to say nothing about whether he should (whether it would be good or bad for him to do so) or whether noncoercive intervention (e.g., trying to talk him out of it) would be morally commendable or not.

But now consider the questions faced by the potential suicide and the potential interventionist. Jones I's question is whether it is better to face (and whether he would be a better person if he faced) the dismal life that lies ahead for him as courageously as possible than to avoid it. Jones II asks whether it is better (and whether he would be a better person for doing it) to live on without making a sacrifice of great generosity than to make that sacrifice. Their friend asks whether a virtuous man would intervene (and if so, how) and, perhaps, whether it would be an act of friendship or kindness to help Jones take his life or settle his affairs if the intervention fails. These are not questions about what is obligatory or what is called for by duty.[4] They are questions about what is the best way to live and to end one's life, about what it is to be a good person, and about which sorts of circumstances and happenings should be welcomed, which should be tolerated and not avoided, and which should be feared as so genuinely bad that they should be avoided. And they are questions about what sorts of conduct are constitutive of or conducive to a good life and/or death. That is to say that they are precisely the kinds of questions which do not arise in connection with a theory of duty, rights, and obligations. They are the questions raised by Plato, Aristotle, the Stoics, and other ancient Greek philosophers, who had what is to us surprisingly little to say about obligations and rights.

Ronald Rubin has suggested to me in conversation that there is a good historical reason for this. In a society whose members agree pretty much about the good, little consideration need be given to the notion of rights. The concept develops into full use where the consensus is lost, and the members of a society find it intolerable to live according to each others' notions of what is good. To avoid this there develops the idea that certain conduct should not be interfered with by the state even though its ruling party, or other factions, believes it to be bad. This secures freedom of action without general agreement on what is good. If this is historically correct and the concept of rights developed to solve the problem of how to insure the freedom of those with whose conceptions of the good we disagree, it is not surprising that to decide what is within your or my rights is by no means to decide whether it is good or bad.

It will now be obvious why I cannot answer what I consider to be fundamental questions about the morality of suicide; their answer requires nothing less than a theory of the good and of the virtues (like courage and charity) which promote it and the vices (like cowardice and meanness) which oppose it. But I hope that the questions raised in the examples will strike the reader as genuine questions which do actually arise in real cases involving suicide, and that what I have said is enough to show that they are not questions of duty, obligation, and rights.

N O T E S

1. Kant is an excellent example of the view I oppose: that all moral issues concerning suicide (and everything else, as a matter of fact) are questions of duty. His famous attempt to show for a special and limited class of cases that suicide violates duty can be found in Immanuel Kant, *Groundwork of the Metaphysic of Morals*, ed. and trans. H. J. Paton (New York: Harper Torchbooks, 1956), p. 89.

2. At this point I face a serious vocabulary problem of a kind which is endemic and, for all I know, peculiar, to philosophy. In ordinary, nonphilosophical talk, we say we ought to do some things because they are required by duty and others because they would be good things to do, because they are means toward good ends, and for many other reasons. "Ought" is also used in nonmoral contexts, as in the advice, "Try this crowbar; it ought to be strong enough to move that rock." Part of the business of philosophers is to give accounts of ordinary concepts like these. Had I written this paper a long time ago, readers would have assumed (wrongly) that *all* moral "shoulds" and "oughts" have to do with what is good or conducive to the good. Today most moral and political philosophers assume (wrongly) that one ought to or should do something only if it is obligatory or required by duty. Thus many readers may object that I cannot say both that Jones (either one) ought (not) or should (not) take his life and also that this is not a question of duties and obligations. This objection begs the question. What I am trying to show in these

examples is that there are cases in which it is quite natural for nonphilosophers to ask what they should or ought to do, but where their questions are not questions about duty, obligation, or rights.

3. See John Rawls, "Two Concepts of Rules," *Philosophical Review* 64 (1955), pp. 3–32, and Robert Nozick, *Anarchy, State and Utopia* (New York: Basic Books, 1974), chapter 3, on this point. Very roughly speaking, the "all things being equal" clause amounts to the following. There are extraordinary circumstances in which it is excusable to rethink a promise on the basis of what harm its performance would do. Thus I may find out that although neither of us could know it at the time of the promise, its performance would bring about consequences neither of us could accept. But it is only in extraordinary circumstances that a reconsideration on the basis of what is best is admissible.

4. In support of this, consider the plausible and familiar claim that what is done *merely* out of duty or obligation, though it may be morally correct and praiseworthy, is not praiseworthy as an act of friendship, kindness, bravery, or charity.